The Geography of Hate

AF649204

The Geography of Hate

The Great Migration through Small-Town America

JENNIFER SDUNZIK

UNIVERSITY OF ILLINOIS PRESS
Urbana, Chicago, and Springfield

© 2023 by the Board of Trustees
of the University of Illinois
All rights reserved
1 2 3 4 5 C P 5 4 3 2 1
♾ This book is printed on acid-free paper.

Library of Congress Cataloging-in-Publication Data
Names: Sdunzik, Jennifer, 1986– author.
Title: The geography of hate : the great migration through small-town America / Jennifer Sdunzik.
Description: Urbana : University of Illinois Press, [2023] | Includes bibliographical references and index.
Identifiers: LCCN 2023005947 (print) | LCCN 2023005948 (ebook) | ISBN 9780252045424 (cloth) | ISBN 9780252087547 (paperback) | ISBN 9780252055027 (ebook)
Subjects: LCSH: Racism—Indiana—History. | White people—Race identity—Indiana—History. | Indiana—Race relations—History. |African Americans—Indiana—Social conditions. | African Americans—Indiana—History. | Great Migration, ca. 1914–ca. 1970.
Classification: LCC F535.A1 S48 2023 (print) | LCC F535.A1 (ebook) | DDC 305.8009772—dc23/eng/20230524
LC record available at https://lccn.loc.gov/2023005947
LC ebook record available at https://lccn.loc.gov/2023005948

To my parents,
Sabine Sdunzik and Ronald Kuß,
For instilling in me a desire to fight for my dreams.

And to my spouse and partner,
Daniel Kwadwo Bampoh,
With whom life is more colorful
Than I ever imagined.

Contents

Preface

This book is about whiteness. It starts off looking at the Great Migration in heretofore unexplored ways by considering small-town America as potential destinations for Black southern migrants. I anticipated telling this story of exclusion through the lens of Black migrant families. Yet a lack of records and detailed documentation about local Black families made this endeavor a daunting task. Though I start each chapter sharing the destiny and contributions of some local Black families, I was telling the story of how the Black presence in small-town white America dwindled and (almost) disappeared. I ended up tracing the deliberate efforts to preserve a cultural and racial small-town identity, which in many instances put in place mechanisms of erasure and exclusion that have been replicated in conscious and unconscious ways. I am taking us on a journey through Indiana to illustrate how these mechanisms protected whiteness in small-town America.

This book documents exclusion and erasure in small-town Indiana throughout time. To examine small-town Indiana community life, I conducted extensive archival, geospatial, and ethnographic research. Some excerpts from my interviews with community residents are included to corroborate the historical evidence and ground my argument about the legacy in the present day. I am currently working on my second book, which contextualizes contemporary (im-)migration to small-town Indiana in the conscious and unconscious structures erected to preserve white identity that is threatened by racial and cultural change. Both projects are a call to fight and dismantle white supremacy and everyday racism—by locating, naming, and documenting their legacies to better understand and fight contemporary exclusions and erasures.

I moved to Indiana to pursue hate crime–specific research for my doctorate. A year into my graduate career, I gave a talk in the local community on the experiences of the Iranian community in the Greater Lafayette area, deriving from an ethnographic project for a cultural anthropology class. My co-presenter, a U.S. American of color, and I addressed, inter alia, the prevalent local misperceptions that "all Iranians are terrorists" and resultant mistreatments of Iranians in the community. Post-presentation conversations with the elderly and exclusively white audience revealed that they were more comfortable with me—the white presenter—in sharing slightly insensitive and culturally inappropriate remarks about fellow international community members in the area. Although I was initially befuddled about the interactions, they taught me a critical lesson about my subject-position and standing among white small-town midwesterners.

I am perceived as white in this society. This comes with responsibilities and opportunities. Encounters like these made me realize that my whiteness trumped my citizenship status and language abilities. Whereas these are not my only identities, they are the most prominent ones in the discussion of belonging unfolding in this book. Historian Paul Spickard explains the "emotional preferences [of] many Americans" for "White immigrants" with "a deep-seated longing for a White republic," based on the assumption that "racial and cultural homogeneity are necessary to a successful country."[1] Being read as white first and immigrant second enabled me to conduct this research on racism in the Midwest. In other words, my racial identity provided the key to small-town America.

This key opened literal doors—to kitchen tables, living rooms, and attics—whenever my interlocutors chose their homes to speak with me about their lives in small-town Indiana. Figurately speaking, the key also opened gates to memory lane whenever people chose to share incidents and opinions on past and present changes in the community. The longer the conversation went, the more the residents opened up and shared the less glorious moments in the town, past and present. I attribute the increased level of comfort and trust to the color of my skin—particularly among my white interlocutors. My accent faded over time and my interlocutors did most of the talking, but my skin color was a constant and visible indicator that they were talking to *their* kind.

My whiteness also mattered in interactions with people of color in the field. Some folks I approached about my study simply brushed my inquiry off and walked the other way. In interview moments, my whiteness remained on their minds and was centered in questions about potential newcomers to the community and hypotheticals like "imagine if I were to move to town. . . ."

Independent of the initial response, I attempted to decenter and resituate my whiteness when adding other hypothetical scenarios, including individuals of different racial, national, sexual orientation, or religious backgrounds.

This book is an ethnographic public history of one Indiana community through a social justice lens. It is not intended to scapegoat the residents who openly shared their opinions with me. It is rather intended to uncover the ubiquitous legacies of systemic racism and endemic nativism—on a local, regional, and national level in U.S. society. Donald Trump's hyped rhetoric of the southern border wall with Mexico would have simply been the physical and thus visible reinforcement of long-standing exclusionary desires. The U.S. landscape has been dotted with many symbolic and invisible walls for decades if not centuries. These largely invisible walls are built around small-town communities meant to exclude the visible Other. My research helps uncover and unpack the socioeconomic, political, and cultural underpinnings in the societal climate that created and perpetuated the toxic climate we see and experience today.

This project encourages honest and active recognition of and reflection on personal and community roles in perpetuating legacies of injustice. My work prompts action toward disrupting present-day systemic racism, endemic nativism, and white supremacy, as they are outgrowths of exclusionary pasts. *The Geography of Hate* invites us to be uncomfortable and tell uncomfortable histories and uncomfortable truths. Though this book is geographically and socio-historically located in the racialized U.S. Midwest, I invite readers across the globe to reflect on how these mechanisms of exclusion manifest in their everyday encounters and local, regional, and national histories. I retrieved many locally forgotten and unheard stories from Clinton County's past, and it is up to all of us to value the lived experiences of all inhabitants in the nation to work toward a more harmonious coexistence for all of us who live here.

I would like to take this opportunity to thank the Clinton County community for welcoming my research endeavor, in particular the Frankfort Public Library, the Learning Network of Clinton County, and all the residents who took time out of their busy lives to share their experiences and perceptions with me. I will be forever grateful for these moments we spent together, and I hope you all embrace the scholarship for what it is worth.

I am deeply grateful to the staff members and colleagues at the libraries and archives I frequented over the years, especially the Indiana Historical Society, Purdue Archives and Special Collections, and the Inter-Library Loan office of the Purdue Libraries. Connie Richards, thank you for keeping up with my hundreds of microfilm requests and tracking down the most hidden sources with me over the years. Thank you to everyone at the Evaluation and Learning Research Center for supporting me and the research, and for celebrating each round of revisions and updates during my postdoctoral tenure at Purdue, especially Willie Burgess, Laura Warner, and Loran Parker.

To my scholarly family, thank you for giving me the opportunity to learn from you through the wisdom and knowledge you shared with me over the years. Thank you to Lee Bebout, Cornelius Bynum, Colleen Coulter, Susan Curtis, Liz Hall, Jennifer Johnson, James Loewen, Shannon McMullen, Bill Mullen, Hannah Noel, Jerald Podair, Marcela Poirier, David Roediger, Antonia Syson, Erik Wade, and Laura Zanotti. I am especially—and forever—indebted to Susan, Neil, Lee, and David, all of whom were instrumental in turning this project into the book it has become.

Finally, I would like to thank my family—Colleen and Cresta, Pat and Vanessa, Akua and Brent, Lauren and Paul, and Susan and Chuck, my fictive but forever kin who always gave me a home away from home. Thank you to my sisters, Jenny and Madlen, for ensuring that my physical absence from birthdays and vacations was not a deterrence. Thank you to my parents, Ronald Kuß and Sabine Sdunzik, for always supporting my adventures no matter how crazy. You stimulated my desires for books early in life, and now you have this one to add to the home library. And my emotional, spiritual, and intellectual rock, Daniel Kwadwo Bampoh. Your support, care, insight, perspective on life, faith, and love accompany all the pages that follow. This is our book.

The Geography of Hate

INTRODUCTION

How White Desires Determine the Fate of the Great Migration in America's Heartland

> But I know that there has been an increase of . . . African Americans into our community. I don't have a challenge with that, as long, you know, they behave themselves. I'd say that with the Caucasians, the white folk. You know? If you can't behave yourself, I don't want you to be here.
>
> —Doug, former business owner and Clinton County resident, April 2017

Doug is a white small-town midwesterner in his mid-sixties who never left his hometown. He is an active and visible member of the community through his employment, his involvement with his church, and his engagement in community activities. As a native of small-town Indiana, he matter-of-factly described his hometown as a small, close-knit farming and railroad community that experienced migrant workers in the past but remained "basically an all-white community"—until recently. Probed further about the lack of a Black presence in the past, he shrugged his shoulders and said, "There weren't any back then." Probed even further about why his community allegedly remained all-white for decades, he acknowledged Indiana's historical connection to the Ku Klux Klan. In the epigraph, he affirmed the recent growth in his community's Black population, to which he raised no objection—as long as "they behave themselves." Not only did Doug (maybe subconsciously) associate African Americans with trouble, but he also inserted what political sociologist Eduardo Bonilla-Silva calls "buffer" statements—camouflaging his reservations or opposition to the demographic shift—possibly to save face in our conversation and appear neutral on race.[1] Doug's nonchalant account and selective perception of his hometown as a homogeneously white community build the foundation of this book.

* * *

The Geography of Hate locates the Midwest as a critical site of inquiry and addresses how space, race, and culture intersect in ways that have historically reinforced civic and geographical borders for racial and ethnic minorities. First, it aims to explain this selective memory and simplified interpretation of history that undergird the culture of denial. A culture in denial accepts the coexistence of northern urban minority enclaves and white small-town America without ever assuming an intersection. Eager observers of these two socio-geographical phenomena tend to explain that the former resulted in the latter by way of white flight, when in the wake of the Great Migration (1915–1970), northern whites fled the urban areas, creating white suburbia and Black urban spaces. Furthermore, a culture in denial explains the absence of nonwhite communities in states along the migration corridor with the ephemeral existence of a white supremacist organization in its past, thereby simultaneously simplifying reality and absolving the white communities where the KKK once admittedly thrived. This study details how and why northern small-town America and Black America came to be understood as polar opposites. Second, it explores the lingering effects and detrimental consequences of this simplified and selective interpretation of history. It does so by locating the cultural amnesia in Indiana communities and identifying mechanisms, practices, and attitudes that actively generated and reproduced this culture of denial. This book will ultimately reveal the contours of a prevalent geography of hate in midwestern small towns. It will unmask the midwestern hospitality in these communities as *in*hospitable and unwelcoming, and unveil the midwestern normativity as normalized intolerance, white desires, and everyday racism.

The Geography of Hate invites us to challenge two grand narratives that have contributed to a mythical absence of Black people in the small-town Midwest, as the epigraph illustrates. It does so by first presenting a counternarrative to the Great Migration scholarship, which focuses on the points of departure, such as the traditional Jim Crow South, and the points of destination, the urban North. Indiana is an important state along the Great Migration corridor because many railroad lines originating in the South traversed it to midwestern metropolises like Chicago and Detroit. The expansion of the railroad lines allowed Black southerners spatial mobility beyond southern boundaries. They were able to relocate to spaces that offered opportunities for self-determination and socioeconomic improvement in defiance of their southern status quo of societal subordination. Indiana is also a prime agricultural state, offering plenty of fertile soil and opportunities for Black southerners and their kin who had become skilled farmers in bondage to freely build personal livelihoods from the vast arable lands of the rural Midwest. Black migrants, however, largely "chose to" avoid settling in Indiana towns. The book explains why.

Second, *The Geography of Hate* unpacks the contradiction between the cultural perception of traditional Indiana communities typical of the rural Midwest as welcoming and the nativist and racist ideologies that constrained the settlement of Black and other ethnoracial migrants. In this regard, the book provides a complementary narrative about the Ku Klux Klan and contextualizes the conducive environment that enabled the KKK to flourish in Indiana in the 1920s. Behind the veil of midwestern friendliness lies an abundance of mostly hidden mechanisms of white desires, which became visible ephemerally through the infamous reign of the second KKK. Lifting this veil illustrates how Hoosiers, or Indiana residents, created not a "Promised Land" for southern Black migrants, but rather a pervasive geography of hate, in which newcomers of darker hues have been struggling to reap the promises of American democracy—equal rights and pursuit of happiness.

In sum, *The Geography of Hate* disrupts these grand narratives. It disrupts the predefined destinations of southern Black migrants by illustrating that not all wanted to settle in big cities but intended to own businesses, raise families, or, in short, pursue life and happiness in the small-town Midwest. It disrupts midwestern whiteness by discussing racial minorities' experiences in the same landscape. Ultimately, it disrupts midwestern friendliness by uncovering the self-perceived understanding of Hoosier communities' midwestern hospitality that stands in stark contrast with the unwelcoming environment that outsiders experienced. While its approach is not all-encompassing, *The Geography of Hate* excavates the relationships between spatiality, identity, and citizenship in previously unconnected dimensions, unearthing whiteness as the denominator that connects these three in small-town Indiana.

As a phrase and a conceptual framework, the geography of hate encapsulates several meanings and phenomena. At the most basic level, it maps and thus makes visible white spaces. White inhabitants in those white spaces acted on their white desires and actively constructed their environment as all-white. Most of these actions were subtle; yet all of them demonstrate a possessive investment in whiteness[2], claiming entire towns and counties as their whites-only spaces. At times, white Hoosiers physically manifested their white desires in public, such as by demarcating certain sections in the town as neighborhoods of color through street names and designating city pools as white-only leisure spaces. In other instances, they used the mere power of their words, "encouraging" or rather threatening people of color to leave town. Capturing these instances, I spatialize hate in various shapes and forms. I follow Black Studies and Gender Studies scholar Katherine McKittrick's understanding of geography—"as space, place, and location in their physical materiality and imaginative configurations"—to illuminate how space is racialized and locate Black histories in white spaces.[3]

Though I include discussions of lynchings and KKK cross-burnings, most of the incidents described in this book are not the most visceral acts of physical violence one commonly associates with the concept of hate. Some might even challenge me that hate is too strong a word to describe the insidious acts of bigotry and discrimination that characterize everyday encounters between whites and people of color in small-town Indiana. Yet the ways white desires manifested and proliferated mostly surreptitiously and invisibly in these small-town communities demands a strong phrase—not only to unearth these attitudes and mechanisms but also to underline the detrimental and long-term effects these desires have on communities far beyond their small-town borders. Leaving violence unmarked and hate unnamed allows white racist history and incidents to keep being whitewashed, and it continues to exculpate the communities engaged in those acts and actions. The ensuing pages name them and make them visible. The ensuing maps invite readers to reposition their understanding of concepts like racism and hate—by associating hate not only with the overtly hateful and malicious racist acts, but also all instances of white dominance and white racism.

The geography of hate functions as a conduit between two seemingly disparate geo-socio-historical phenomena, enabling us to trace the Great Migration to the small-town Midwest. Though a complex, enduring, multilayered effort of human relocation, the Great Migration has been reduced to scholarly discussions around places of origin and destinations. This book, in contrast, turns the focus to the landscape traversed from the rural South to the urban North, namely the small-town Midwest. Anchoring the migration here allows for a comprehensive reexamination of race relations in Indiana, a state located in a region all too often—but falsely—perceived and imagined as white. Doing so, I write Black Hoosiers back into Indiana history while uncovering a preponderance of evidence of ways white supremacy created and perpetuated white desires for white spaces and white realities.

As an interdisciplinary endeavor at the intersection of Great Migration Studies and Midwestern Studies, *The Geography of Hate* unfolds a complex mosaic of institutional, communal, and personal histories of racial exclusion in a traditionally white racist midwestern state. Adopting a critical whiteness lens, I bring both scholarships into conversations while tracing gaps in and intersections between both scholarly fields. The next few pages will provide an overview of influential conceptual frameworks and situate this study spatio-temporally (the Great Migration time frame within the confines of the Midwest) and epistemologically (Critical Whiteness Studies).

Arching the Narrative: The Silence on Small Towns in the Great Migration Scholarship

The Great Migration, the massive relocation of southern Black people from the turn of the twentieth century until 1970, was a sociohistorical phenomenon that shifted American demographics and race relations forever.[4] The migration stream can be divided into two major waves—the first wave is generally framed from 1915 until 1930, triggered by and following World War I until the Great Depression; and the second wave was sparked by World War II, framed from around 1940 to 1970.[5] Although the first wave involved about 1.5 million southern African Americans relocating to the North, the second wave included up to 5 million.[6] This spatial and demographic reorganization of U.S. society has been investigated from various scholarly angles, including history, sociology, economics, and geography. Many twentieth-century studies focusing on the phenomenon explore reasons for leaving the South and/or analyze how the new Black arrivals were received in the urban centers of the North, such as Chicago and New York.[7] Twenty-first-century scholarship expands our understanding by examining the Great Migration of Black *and* white southerners, exploring internal migration patterns of Black migrants to southern urban centers, such as Houston, Louisville, and Atlanta, and investigating the extent to which Black migrants reconnected with nature in the North after settling in the cities.[8] Though each angle improved our understanding of who moved where and when (and often why), the subject seems not to have exhausted all perspectives.

This book provides yet another angle to our understanding of the Great Migration, adding an important caveat to this scholarly conversation. It invites us to challenge the myth that all southern Black migrants became urbanites—and to explore mechanisms in small-town America that actively and ultimately contributed to the formation of many Black enclaves in the urban North. "The urban America that emerged from the postwar era," historian Luther Adams writes in *Way Up North in Louisville*, "was a product of the aspirations and agency of African Americans as much as it was of the action of the state, the vision of urban planners, or *white resistance*."[9] It is the white resistance of small-town midwestern America that is the focus here.

The Geography of Hate challenges our historical and socio-geographical understanding of southern Black people's relocation. The Great Migration not only transformed the places of departure and arrival but also reshaped the sociopolitical geographies and legacies of towns along migration routes. For example, socioeconomic anxiety over an influx of southern Black people caused an increase in sundown policies across the nation, particularly in the Midwest.[10] Communities large and small engaged in white practices that signaled to nonwhite people that they were not welcome after dark, thereby manifesting their white desires in spatial realities. However, the scholarly silence on small-town America's role in shaping internal migration patterns implies that these areas have been relatively insignificant in shaping race relations or America's sociopolitical future at large. This study demonstrates the central role of small midwestern communities in that regard.

Small towns, if mentioned at all, have been discussed negligibly in Migration Studies. For example, James Gregory briefly refers to the appeal smaller midwestern and western cities, such as Indianapolis, Columbus, Kansas City, and Portland, had to Black migrants who came after World War II, and solely mentions as a side note that "in addition there was a certain amount of migration to the towns and rural areas of the North and West." He immediately readjusts his focus to the "the largest and most politically and culturally significant cities" as they absorbed "the main force of the African American diaspora."[11] It is not possible to know the exact number of Black migrants who left the South and settled in the rural North and the urban cities. Census data locates the most obvious increase and thus approximate numbers for southern Black migrants relocating to the North in urban areas, which explains the scholarly attention. But this is not the whole story. Although the number of southern Black migrants relocating to the small-town North may be comparatively modest, they should not simply be ignored and forgotten. By setting the minority of migrants to the side, we refuse to scrutinize the circumstances that curtailed their numbers in these areas in the first place.

In 1944, Gunnar Myrdal had already investigated the mobility and migration of southern African Americans, as the first wave of the Great Migration ended around the Great Depression. He tried to understand why more of them did not leave the South. He came to the following conclusion:

> The primary explanation seems to be that in rural areas of the West, white settlers *decided* that there were not to be any Negroes. That seems to have been true in most rural areas of the Northeast and in most smaller towns of the entire North. The closer neighborhood controls in smaller communities seem to have blocked the Negro from moving in when he was no longer protected as a slave.[12]

Assigning agency and decision-making powers to the "white settlers," Myrdal hints at the social pressures that northern whites might have imposed on a potential influx of Black people in their towns. These social pressures are worth investigating further, as they unveil how small-town northerners actively contributed to the rise of urban ghettos and creating an imaginary white Midwest. This study seeks to do just that, and it teases out how small-town America was affected by and affected the Great Migration.

Historian Jack S. Blocker's explorations of Black post–Civil War migration to midwestern small towns constitute one notable exception in the overall Great Migration canon. In *A Little More Freedom*, he compares Black motivations and experiences to settle in four non-metropolitan towns across Ohio, Illinois, and Indiana after the Civil War, ultimately concluding that the big city's lure and small-town white violence led African Americans to reject midwestern small towns. In an earlier publication, he explores the phenomenon of migration to Muncie, the Indiana small town best known as Robert and Helen Merrell Lynd's "Middletown." Blocker locates a shift in Black migration patterns to the bigger cities in the state around 1890 because of increasing land and machinery costs. But Muncie was an exception here, as its Black population constantly rose over the time frame examined, resulting in a Black population, as a proportion of the total, larger than major urban destinations such as Chicago. Blocker's findings align with the approach undertaken in this study, as he notes that many migrants arrived by train and that their decision to settle in Muncie was based on the small town being a desirable alternative to the big city, and he explores community attributes in determining the Black population's growth or decline in small-town America.[13]

Veiling a Region: The Challenge of Locating Race in Midwest Scholarship

Through its focus on Indiana, this book also deepens our understanding of midwestern history and culture. Whereas the U.S. Census Bureau incorporates thirteen states in its grouping of the region, I refer to the five states of Ohio, Indiana, Illinois, Michigan, and Wisconsin when referring to the Midwest. I base this classification on the Northwest Ordinance from 1787, which established a territorial government for the land north and west of the Ohio River, which incorporated these later-to-become states (in that sense, they were the first midwestern region before the label Midwest had been coined). Scholars have pursued various approaches to define the region. They have described the Midwest as amorphous and elusive, yet simultaneously, they have also identified it as the American Heartland, the most American part of America, and the quintessential America.[14]

I find myself agreeing with scholars who claim that the Midwest, or small-town America for that matter, is quintessentially American. Yet, unlike most scholars who claim that the region is the epitome of American exceptionalism, such as Jon Lauck and James Shortridge, attaching patriotic and nationalistic values to it, I contend that the region is quintessentially American because it is a microcosmic community that struggles over questions of belonging characteristic of larger U.S. society. Like the nation, these communities respond to these struggles along racial lines, upholding the color line by demarcating boundaries for racial and ethnic outsiders. This results in, among other things, actively and passively excluding, marginalizing, and forgetting the Other.

In their introduction to *The American Midwest: An Interpretive Encyclopedia*, historian Andrew Cayton and his co-editors note:

> Today, the American Midwest is a source of comfort and conformity, a place transformed from a nineteenth-century symbol of progress into a twenty-first century of stability, from the home of pioneers pointing the United States toward the future into the residents of guardians of the nation's traditions.[15]

I encountered all these midwestern values during my research and life in the Midwest, but I challenge these assumptions about the Midwest and ask: For whom does the Midwest provide "comfort" and "stability," and at what cost?

Several recent works have broken open the "white imaginary" of the Midwest, capturing long-negated and ignored but valuable ethnic and racial diversity in its midst. For example, Robert M. Taylor Jr. and Connie A. McBirney explore Indiana's ethnic and racial diversity, capturing in an expansive volume the ethnoracial histories and experiences in a state whose population was 95 percent native born (and 97 percent white) in 1920. Historian Debra Reid writes African Americans into the rural midwestern narrative, and American Studies scholar Hana Lee Moore writes Asian Americans into the white imaginary of the Midwest, identifying religious identity among Korean Americans as a key mechanism to cope with the racism they faced in the region.[16]

In the introduction to their essay collection *The American Midwest*, Andrew Cayton and Susan Gray make an important observation identifying the Great Migration as a catalyst for midwesterners to imagine themselves and their region as white. They write:

> Nothing was more critical to the flattening of white ethnicity in Midwestern regionality than the mass migration of tens of thousands of African Americans from the South, particularly in the decades after the two world wars. . . . African Americans posed a serious challenge to the self-image of white Midwesterners. Unlike other immigrants, they could neither be ignored nor assimilated. The color line made white ethnicity superfluous. For the first time in the history of the Midwest, racial prejudice made European Americans see themselves as one people. The sharing of color trumped all ethnic divisions. Blacks became to whites in the Midwest the epitome of people who failed to realize the potential of the Midwest because they failed to inculcate its central values of self-discipline and industry. This was a false reading of black life, but the power of this image is undeniable. Blaming blacks for their poverty and unemployment affirmed the legitimacy of white Midwesterners' collective self-image. As white ethnics fled the cities for the suburbs, the association of urban areas and blacks became a cliché.[17]

This study corroborates the potency of this self-image as the white Midwest; simultaneously, it shows that the self-perception as a white imaginary long preceded the Great Migration in places like Indiana. Throughout the nineteenth century, Hoosiers and neighboring midwesterners used laws and constitutions to curb African American civil rights and privileges, inscribing whiteness, exclusion, and negation into their white spatial imaginary and reality. Historian Anna-Lisa Cox delineates nineteenth-century African American migrations to the Midwest, unearthing "that odd Midwestern racism that was not based on numbers and could be touched off by the presence of only one black person, or none at all."[18] And the "odd Midwestern racism" held steadfast, as Debra Reid observes in her exploration of Black experiences in the rural Midwest post–World War II, "Rural race prejudice and white supremacy explain why few blacks considered the rural Midwest a destination."[19] Corroborating Cox's and Reid's observations, I will demonstrate that state policies and communal practices have defined and reinforced perceptions of their locales as white spaces throughout history. The subsequent cartography will lay bare how they became and remained white.

Beyond that, and maybe more important, I will unearth some of the detriments and consequences of this self-image that is largely based on decades-long exclusionary practices as well as the negligence and ignorance of diverse experiences in their midst. The lack of formal history and public debate left midwestern small-town America free to reimagine its past and commemorate moments of pride, such as being a stop on the Underground Railroad, without reflecting on the politics and attitudes that prevented Black southerners from staying and settling in their towns. Today's struggles in the region to adapt to demographic changes, in particular, are intricately linked to this white imaginary of the Midwest.

In recent years, scholars have paid much attention to the twenty-first-century demographic changes in small-town America, noting the cultural clashes and difficulties from uprooting their all-white reality. For example, journalist Stephen Bloom explores the clashes between white Christian Iowans and Hasidic Jews after a New York businessman purchased a defunct meatpacking plant in Postville, attracting Hasidic Jews and Latinx migrant workers to the small town, in *Postville: A Clash of Cultures in Heartland America*. In *A Midwestern Mosaic*, political scientist Celeste Lay investigates political socialization and rural attitudes in two midwestern towns that have experienced drastic racial and ethnic diversification through immigrant settlement. Similarly, in their ethnographic study *Apple Pie & Enchiladas*, Ann Millard and Jorge Chapa explore the social and economic realities of Latinx immigrants in the small-town Midwest, which are marked by negative community perceptions and widespread institutional racism. Along the same lines, Sujey Vega's *Latino Heartland* traces questions of belonging and everyday lived experiences of the Latinx population in small-town Indiana. My research aligns with and will enrich this scholarship, as I am paying attention to the origin of those prevalent attitudes and values perpetuated by the local white residents in small-town America. These values have a long history; the culture of exclusion has been in the making for decades if not centuries. This book will show how it came to life and how it matured, incessantly perpetuating an environment of *non*belonging and unwelcome to outsiders, particularly ethnoracial outsiders.

Hiding in Plain Sight: Theorizing White Desires in Small-Town America

Values and attitudes, based in experiences and perceptions, determine thought and action. To trace them, I will deploy sociologist Pierre Bourdieu's concept of habitus as it explains the social structure of the world according to people in it. Bourdieu defines habitus as "a system of *dispositions*, that is of permanent manners of being, seeing, acting and thinking, or a system of *long-lasting* (rather than permanent) schemes or schemata or structures of perception, conception and action."[20] Jean Hillier and Emma Rooksby summarize the Bourdieusian concept as "a sense of one's (and others') place and role in the world of one's lived environment . . . habitus is an embodied, as well as, cognitive, sense of place."[21] Capturing this sense of place, the book explores this set of values internalized by small-town Hoosiers. It delineates how Hoosiers think, feel, and act to identify "the deep cultural conditioning that reproduces and legitimizes social formations."[22] It uncovers the consequences of the "white habitus" of Indiana, a concept coined by political sociologist Eduardo Bonilla-Silva. Bonilla-Silva expands Bourdieu's concept to emphasize the racial aspects, defining it as "a racialized, uninterrupted socialization process that conditions and creates whites' racial tastes, perceptions, feelings, and emotions and their views on racial matters."[23] He identifies one of the key consequences of whites' segregated life as the promotion of "a sense of group belonging (a white culture of solidarity) and negative views about non-whites."[24] Bonilla-Silva's definition of the white habitus echoes critical race and education scholar Zeus Leonardo, who concedes that "Whites today did not participate in slavery but surely recreate white supremacy on a daily basis."[25] The small-town culture in the U.S. Midwest delineated in this project captures the white habitus and its consequences. Unfolding in this book are some of the strategies white Hoosiers deploy to perpetuate their racial supremacy, including erasure, selective memory, whitewashing, and ridicule.

The social construction of race, and whiteness in particular, is key to understanding the dynamics in midwestern small-town America. Scholars have connected whiteness to the construction of the American nation and national identity at large as well as noted the mutually constitutive relationship between race and space.[26] Political scientist Joel Olson contended that whiteness is bound to citizenship in the United States.[27] American Studies scholar Lee Bebout expanded this notion, weaving together racial logics, U.S. nationalism, and American exceptionalism. Whiteness Studies pioneer Ruth Frankenberg foregrounded whiteness as a social and spatial location, exploring how white people see race regarding racial Others but not themselves. She argued further that whiteness "generates norms, ways of understanding history, ways of thinking about self and other, and even ways of thinking about the notion of culture itself."[28] Geographer Helga Leitner found local white reactions toward immigrants of color to be informed by locals' understanding of the rural Midwest as a white place and of the United States as a white nation. American Studies scholar George Lipsitz uncovered the racial assumptions and imperatives of apparently race-neutral spaces in urban America, coining the term "white spatial imaginary."[29] I consolidate these different theoretical findings into a lens through which to view the white (spatial) desires in white small-town America.

Besides habitus, and more specifically white habitus, I found the concepts of normative whiteness and white racial frame useful for my analysis. Historian Paul Spickard coined the term "normative whiteness" to describe the unmarked assumption that "unless we are informed to the contrary, the people under discussion are White," introducing whiteness as the baseline for everything American.[30] Similarly, sociologist Joe Feagin coined the term "white racial frame" to analyze American society, demonstrating that such an analysis cannot be separated from the racial construction of reality. Noting the breadth and complexity of the frame, Feagin explains:

> Over time white Americans have combined in it a beliefs aspect (racial stereotypes and ideologies), integrating cognitive elements (racial interpretations and narratives), visual and auditory elements (racialized images and language accents), a "feelings" aspect (racialized emotions), and an inclination to action (to discriminate). Moreover, over centuries of operation this dominant white framing has encompassed both a strong positive orientation to whites and whiteness (a pro-white subframe) and a strong negative orientation to racial "others" who are exploited and oppressed (anti-others subframes).[31]

All these aspects unfold in this book. The normativity of everything white became particularly clear in comments on town events and town people. Negative stereotypes surface in discussions about racial Others as well as in local newspaper coverage, manifesting and reinforcing residents' white desires and white reality that they believe surrounds them. This project interrupts the invisibility of whiteness, through which it maintains much of its power, and explores it as a set of cultural practices that are not only unmarked but also exclusive.

These cultural practices of whiteness—reflected in statements like Doug's in the epigraph as well as in historical writings and state legislatures—are meant to uphold white dominance in the community, the county, and the state because, as Leonardo observes, "White domination is the responsibility of every white subject because her very being depends on it." Doug attempts to deflect in his comment any racial (let alone racist) connotation with the caveat that he would not like any "white folk" in his community if they can't behave either. But it is Doug's white habitus, his white racial frame, that made him associate African Americans with vice in the first place. Subconsciously or consciously, Doug expresses his emotions in a racialized fashion that exudes white dominance, corresponding with scholarly observations that "the feelings of white folks" are what "sustains both white supremacy as a system and white racism as individual and collective participation in that system."[32] This study will illustrate various examples of how white people cling to white dominance.

Though *The Geography of Hate* delineates the existence and potency of a white habitus in the Midwest and illustrates how the white racial frame works on a micro level, it simultaneously disrupts the traditional white imaginary of the Midwest. I complicate the conversation about the region and the "idea" of the Midwest by paying attention to lives of marginalized, silenced, and forgotten communities. Framing my argument within the Great Migration context, I contend that by glimpsing over the spaces in between origin and destination in migration streams, these small towns were free to imagine themselves as white communities, and they actively attempted to cement this reality as a fact of life. I lay bare how white desires went unchecked and how they produced and reproduced this "odd Midwestern racism."[33]

I also challenge the concepts of citizenship, belonging, and memory as they pertain to the "white" Midwest. All three concepts are socially constructed and abstract in nature, but with real-life implications. My discussions of belonging vs. *non*belonging accentuate both how citizenship operates and how cultural practices are reproduced on local levels in an attempt to provide community—a community that turns out to be exclusive and imagined. I illustrate the fluidity and flexibility of these concepts while noting context and limitations through structural and collective practices.

This book attempts to foreground how cultural practices and institutional processes intersect with embodied knowledge and behaviors to generate and perpetuate an unwelcoming environment to ethnoracial Others. Constructing their sense of belonging and their community through remembering their regional history, and sharing and reliving these collective practices, the white Hoosier voices in this book simultaneously reinforce their community boundaries—often through invisible yet impenetrable forms of exclusion, erasure, and forgetting of minority participation and contributions. People of color, in the white minds, do not belong in their community. The burden of this book lies in unearthing the racialized geographies of Indiana to illustrate the durability of inhospitable and exclusionary practices in small-town America. The racialized geographies of Indiana, as discussed in this book, will complicate notions of citizenship and show how it is negotiated, contested, and actively made—not only on a national level but also on a town, county, and state level. The subsequent chapters will reveal discourses and embodied practices of community, further advancing our understanding of community-making and a sense of belonging through focusing on history, memory, and active and passive forgetting.

Tracing White Desires: How to Capture the Actively Forgotten

A mix of sources and an interdisciplinary approach were needed to unearth and provide a detailed account of history that some (Hoosiers, midwesterners, and white Americans) chose to actively forget, or at least preferred to keep under wraps. I used multiple but complementary methods in this study, primarily archival, geospatial, and ethnographic research methodologies. I used census data from 1850 until 2010 to gain a general overview of the demographic make-up of Indiana communities.[34] I corroborated the census information with available decades of the manuscript census (1870–1940). Though at times inaccurate in the race category, the manuscript census was useful to identify southern Black migrants in the community through listed places of birth. It also recorded age, family status, profession/employment, and for some decades, home ownership and value of the home (worthwhile, especially if a family suddenly dropped out of the manuscript census, such as when they left town). As the census was recorded by the census taker going from door to door, it also provided an overview of the neighborhoods. Frankfort, Indiana, did not have enforced residential segregation, as individual African American families lived among white neighbors. In only a few instances did Black families live next door to other Black families. Thus, the census and the manuscript census helped to reconstruct the social geography of the communities under investigation. More important, the retrieved information addresses two central concerns of this book: on the one hand, it documents that northern small-town America provided opportunities for southern Black migrants, and on the other hand, it raises questions regarding white residents' erasure and neglect of their Black neighbors, which demands an explanation.

City directories and local newspapers proved instrumental in reconstructing events, town values, and official attitudes in the community. City directories documented individuals' home address and profession, as well as demarcated Black residents and social organizations with an asterisk or a "c"/"colored" next to the names, though inconsistently. These directories help fill in the gaps between the decennial censuses to trace when a particular person might have left town. Newspapers provide insights into what and who mattered in the community, but they also revealed local incidents of race-related friction in an attempt to preserve the town's (self-perceived) racial homogeneity.

Archival materials have proved pivotal in understanding direct legislative actions on a state level as well as personal attitudes from public county officials across the State of Indiana. This work presents the first interpretation of archival materials not yet studied by scholars. Specifically, I draw on the Black History Project files to challenge the claim that predominantly white small towns transpired coincidentally in the advent of southern Black migration through these spaces. With the help of this collection, I am able to delineate a pattern of sociopolitical exclusion and historical whitewashing of Black people's presence and achievements. The Black History Project complements my research findings and corroborates that this study could have taken place anywhere in Indiana and most likely the Midwest, as mechanisms of erasure and exclusion were not unique to Clinton County. Frankfort could have been "Anytown, Indiana" in these years.

To investigate the extent to which small towns mattered during the Great Migration, I mined the *Readers' Guide to Periodical Literature* from 1900 to 1970 to build a database of 1,213 Great Migration, Midwest, and small-town America articles published in twentieth-century print outlets with a wide, possibly national, readership. Indexes like the *Readers' Guide* frequently have been criticized for their large omission of African American newspapers and magazines, as they limit the distribution of "African American perspectives on civil rights issues that did not appear in the mainstream media before the 1960s and thus reinforced the perception of American life that dominant white Anglo-Saxon Protestant cultures defined."[35] Though a valid objection, it was less of a limitation for the scope of this research project, as I wanted to understand to what extent small-town America was discussed in the realm of the Great Migration on a national level—in "mainstream media."

Unearthing the erased and forgotten is a challenge—simply because people intended to erase and forget the incidents. White Hoosiers did not keep a good record of their strong antipathy and dislike of African Americans in their midst. They did not document how to keep communities white for decades. Consequently, I turned to cartography and used ArcGIS software to map the incidents of erasure and despatialization that I have been able to retrieve. "[B]lack lives are necessarily geographic, but also struggle with discourses that erase and despatialize their sense of place," Katherine McKittrick observes.[36] Visualizing these sociohistorical incidents spatiotemporally—across space and time—enables identification of trends and patterns of exclusion. As McKittrick poignantly remarks, "we produce space, we produce its meaning. . . . Concealment, marginalization, boundaries are important social processes. We make concealment happen; it is not natural but rather names and organizes where racial-sexual differentiation occurs."[37] For example, Map 1 in the next chapter clearly shows the spread of early Black settlements in the southern half of the state. One could assume that the southern half of the state is more open and welcoming toward African Americans. However, in Map 8 we see that the majority of Negro registers were kept in the southern half of the state, probably as a consequence of the numerous Black settlements. Map 12, in contrast, unveils an obvious pattern of exclusion as it juxtaposes the numerical increase of Black Hoosiers with the numerical increase of white counties over time.

In a project that investigates the experiences of southern Black migrants in northern small-town America, ethnographic research might be a little counterintuitive for some. But how do you research history that has not been recorded, documented, or remembered publicly? What are the implications and consequences of forgetting one's own history—for the individual, a community, and the nation at large? Ethnographic research methods enabled me to better understand Clinton County's contemporary identity and how the community celebrates and presents itself to the outside world, and this approach created a space for these populations to speak for themselves. Conducting semi-structured interviews with small-town residents allowed me to record their experiences in the area, their understanding of the local history, and their interpretations of changes that their town is undergoing. Residents described places and events, beliefs and values, and challenges and innovations. To fully flesh out how the individual maps onto the collective, I relied on history and memories of my residents, which, according to historian Susan Curtis, "bear an uneasy relationship to each other." She further explains:

> Memory is suspect; history is authoritative. Memory is deeply personal and subjective; it arises spontaneously and takes on different coloration, depending on what prompted it to burst forth from the recesses of the mind. History changes, too, as new perspectives are brought to bear on past events, as new bodies of evidence are examined and deciphered, and as the needs of one generation give way to those of another.[38]

Throughout this book, we will find analyses of historical documents, interpretation of antique collectibles, and reflections of interview moments. We will find some deeply personal and subjective memories at times prompted by the topic of conversation. We come to see that they were less reflective of the individuals who spoke and more reflective of the town mentality at large.

As this research project is more concerned with the town's identity (rather than individual players'), retrieving residents' memories regarding critical moments in their town history was an important methodological objective of mine. It allowed me to better trace how residents came to understand their surroundings as an all-white environment and perceive their lives as all-white reality. Memory is not only deeply subjective, as Curtis states, but also highly selective. However, as writer Diana Gittins notes, "the very process of selection in recollection provides *in itself* important historical data. In other words, *what* someone remembers can be a good indication of what has been most important to that person over time."[39] Generally, proud historical moments of the town community stood out in the interviews. Moments that mattered to the individual (and the town) were remembered. Less proud moments were erased, overlooked, forgotten—or simply withheld because, after all, I remained an outsider to the community.

Joe Feagin also highlights the central role of collective memory in the overarching worldview that defines the white racial frame and normative whiteness, noting:

> Most groups have important collective memories, but those with the greatest power, principally white Americans in the U.S. case, typically have the greatest control over society-wide institutional memories, including those recorded by the mainstream media and in most history books, organization histories, laws, textbooks, films, and public monuments.
>
> What the dominant racial framing ignores or suppresses is critical to the continuation of oppression. Collective *forgetting* is as important as collective remembering, especially in regard to the prevailing narratives of the country's developmental history.[40]

Not only have white residents in small-town Indiana been the dominant group to narrate their town histories in personal interviews, but they also publicly remember their version of history in county histories, public monuments, local papers, and Black History Project surveys. I paid as much attention to what was said as I did to was left unsaid in my analysis, retrieving instances of collective remembering as well as collective forgetting. Doing so, I unearthed many silences and made visible the powers that produce such historical narratives.[41]

The interviews were conducted between October 2015 and October 2017 and took place at locations of the interviewees' choice, including their homes, cafes, restaurants, libraries, and churches. Besides engaging one former southern Black migrant whose family relocated to Chicago during the Great Migration, I engaged twenty-eight individuals from the Clinton County community in semi-structured interviews—eleven women and seventeen men, ranging in age from their early thirties to their late nineties. Although I made a serious attempt to diversify my sample, given the demographics of the community under investigation, most of my interviewees were white (78.6 percent). Occupationally, participants were affiliated with the city, churches, and farms, as well as public institutions, including schools, banks, and community centers. Almost a third of my participants identified themselves as "retired," though "being retired" in a small-town setting does not mean a freely available schedule to participate in research endeavors like mine, as all of my "retired" participants were involved to various degrees in community activities and volunteering through their churches, club memberships, and local committees.

I identified individuals in the community through various strategies. First, I began interviewing residents I met during community events like town festivals, during which I engaged them in conversation about my research and inquired about their interest in participating in my study. One of my last questions during our interview session inquired about knowledge of other individuals in the community who might know about the history of the town, which resulted in various contacts. Because my aim was to gather a diverse sample from the community, I limited the number of names drawn from any one contact, selecting people based on their town "reputation," political leaning, or professional standing. This second set of interviewees was composed of individuals from snowball sampling. Finally, the third set of interviewees were residents that I had come to know quite well during my personal community engagement and other community-making activities. Because the goal of interviewing was to get a variety of residential opinions, not to have quantifiable data, this relaxed sampling method was sufficient.

In these interview sessions, I asked a few background questions such as place of birth and years they have lived in the community. The remaining questions focused on life in the community and the town history, encompassing topics such as neighborhoods and school environments, demographic diversity and relationships, community events and engagement, and community values and perspectives. When I met my participants for our conversations, I gave and explained to them the consent form, set up my notebook and tape recorder, offering to turn it off any time they asked. Confidentiality was assured; therefore, throughout the book, details about individuals have been altered to protect their identity. I have used pseudonyms for all interview participants to preserve their privacy, as their identity is not important. Rather, the content of what is said and how it is said reveal a more systematic approach to thinking about life in small-town midwestern America. Whereas the interviews were conducted with residents of Clinton County, I do not disclose names of the individual towns from which the respondents came, to further preserve anonymity.

Some might argue that I could have written this book without ethnographic components. My non-ethnographic data revealed enough evidence to make a strong argument about the detriments of the legacy of a racist society that never dealt with its racist past. Though my interviews complicated the narrative, they provided a more compelling and more accurate reflection of the subtle ways white supremacist ideologies have shaped people's worldviews and beliefs and continue to dominate the lived experiences of all residents in this country, Black and white, born in the United States and born elsewhere. The voices shared here teleport us to small-town Indiana, frequently into a white spatial imaginary world, and illustrate how their worldview came to be and came to stay. The memories undergird how the "whites only" attitudes from the past have persisted into the present and thus most poignantly exemplify the legacy of the geography of hate.

Mapping the Geography of Hate

Indiana's troubled race history far exceeds the reign of the Ku Klux Klan in the 1920s, though the KKK is probably the best (or only) known example. Although Indiana remained loyal to the Union during the Civil War, it is also a border state, and the influence of southern cultural traditions and ideologies through early white southern arrivals is noticeable. Indiana experienced a seven-fold increase in its African American population, from 45,668 Black Hoosiers in 1890 to 357,464 in 1970. However, despite the emergence of discernible Black communities in cities such as Indianapolis and Gary, migrants largely chose to avoid settling in Indiana towns. As discriminatory practices spread and hardened across the North throughout the twentieth century, de facto segregation also deepened in Indiana, most likely increasing proportionally with the number of Black Hoosiers.[42] It crossed all spheres of life—housing, education, public establishments, and social organizations.

The book is not an all-inclusive study of the extent of racism and discrimination in Indiana, but more a point of departure to name whiteness in small-town America for what it is—the legacy of a white supremacist system actively embraced and enforced by its residents. The juxtaposition of Indiana state laws and county-enforced initiatives illustrates the state's anti-Black nature. A close, in-depth analysis of Indiana's sociopolitical, legal, and cultural history regarding how its policies, laws, and attitudes affected people of color will unearth the ingredients of an unwelcoming small-town environment prevalent across the Midwest. Using primary sources from the Black History Project, an unprocessed collection at the Indiana Historical Society, the chapters in this book will share some of the collective memories that dominate white Hoosier minds regarding Black experiences in their midst. The Black History Project, though intended to map Black histories and experiences in Indiana, reveals the state's subscription to—and the durability of—whiteness. The subsequent pages will delineate a pattern of white Hoosier hostility and resentment toward Black residents in towns and counties across the state. Thus, Indiana serves as an example to illustrate how state and people surreptitiously work together, creating, fostering, and reproducing a racialized and culturally exclusive landscape over decades.

I aim to address explicitly how white desires and white policies are mutually constitutive and reinforced in everyday encounters in small-town America. I map white desires across time and space by weaving together legal, political, cultural, and social discourses and practices in Indiana since its inception as a state. I argue that only by spatializing and making visible the surreptitious and mainly hidden mechanisms of whiteness can we dismantle whiteness as a system and an ideology and advance the conversation toward a post-racial society. Only when we understand the historical institutionalization and operationalization of whiteness in time and space can we begin to counteract its detrimental legacies that continue to create divisions and manifest injustices.

I illustrate white complicity in historic-geographical patterns of exclusion. I complicate the notion of local county personnel as guardians, preservers, and documenters of local history by detailing how their white racial frame determines whose stories get told, whose experiences are commemorated, and whose identities are perceived as legitimate. I show how local histories were whitewashed not by obliviousness but by design. I trace the operationalization of various practices that deliberately preserved a utopian ideal of racial homogeneity in small-town communities, thereby producing and reproducing an unwelcoming environment for people of color.

As previously noted, the racial history of Indiana is too expansive to cover all incidents and conditions that enhanced or exacerbated race relations over time. Thus, I focus my attention in this book on disrupting the white Hoosier narrative as the representative Hoosier narrative. Instead of privileging white Hoosier voices, I am tracing Black Hoosier experiences in the state. I home in on Clinton County, a rural manufacturing county of 30,000 residents around forty miles north of Indianapolis. About half of the residents live in its county seat, Frankfort. The area's arable fields and spatial connectivity through train tracks and highways attracted but a small number of people of color, and their stories are not well known. Through the lenses of individual Black families in Clinton County, we come to celebrate the longevity of Black resilience spanning multiple generations and chastise the white actions that caused its erasure and denial across decades. Thus, the mechanisms that perpetuated white desires in the state across time resulted in a book about the Black experiences in Indiana through a white lens.

The book illustrates how the histories of towns, people, and migration pathways contribute to our contemporary understanding of race in the Midwest. With the exception of Chapter 2, the book applies a magnifying glass on Indiana counties. This in-depth focus on one state, and one county in particular, enables the dismantling of white spaces and white realities. Through exploring the power of whiteness since Indiana's inception as a state, the chapters trace the continuity of white desires while noting changes in their manifestations. Chapter 1 anchors white desires in Indiana and traces white complicity in rural patterns of exclusion across time. It lays out various ways that Indiana communities took the law into their own hands, lynching, driving out, or ostracizing its Black populations. Sometimes, ordinary white Hoosiers acted on their own accounts, and in other instances, they did so under the disguise of community-supported organizations such as the White Caps or the National Horse Thief Detectives Association. Regardless of the mechanism, white Hoosiers successfully blocked housing, education, and leisure opportunities for Black residents. I analyze Indiana laws, county histories, and newspapers, all of which demarcate the structural, institutional, and discursive marginalization of Black Hoosiers and affirm the geography of hate in the state.

Chapter 2 situates the small-town Midwest and Indiana within the context of the Great Migration. It challenges its urban-only narrative that proclaims that southern Black migrants did not stop in midwestern small-town communities. I analyze migrant letters for desires and motivations of Black southerners to complicate the master narrative of the city's lure. As the letters provide evidence for desires to improve economically and socially (regardless of geographic location), I explore national Black and white print media articles to discern living conditions and value systems in the small-town Midwest. I propose that race and geography cannot be dismissed in the context of the Great Migration, and we need to question the reasons and motivations behind giving up the dream of landownership, an aspect various scholars have identified as one of the key components for independence and self-sufficiency among southern Black migrants.[43] Population data over the course of the Great Migration clearly confirm that Indiana received its fair share of Black migrants, though the largest and most permanent settlements surrounded cities like Gary and Indianapolis. The juxtaposition of Indiana's Black population with identified *Green Book* locales as well as Indiana references in the print media already hint at the animosity that Black newcomers would find upon arrival in the Hoosier State.

White complicity and Black resilience, then, are central to the remainder of the book, to further illuminate the relationship between spatiality, ideology, and belonging. I set the scene for each chapter by sharing some Black family destinies in Clinton County and how the white community made their experience unbearable. Because historical evidence of a Black presence in the community exists, I explore the history of exclusion that rendered some parts of the population invisible and the extent to which they are still relevant today. Here I explore specific strategies of exclusion: erasure, silence, and selective memories. Chapter 3 is dedicated to the particular mechanisms of erasure that white Indiana communities operationalized. Some communities mastered erasure to the degree that many county residents and representatives seemed to have actively forgotten that they have a Black history. Chapter 4 investigates the silence surrounding white supremacist organizations in the state as well as other mechanisms that contributed to and secured all-white communities. Chapter 5 represents the various ways white Hoosiers remember and perceive Black people and Blackness. For the most part, the identified strategies of criminalizing, stereotyping, and objectifying African Americans in and beyond county borders lay bare the contaminated minds of white Hoosiers. I map all chapter discussions in the conclusion, visualizing the geography of hate in Indiana.

Despite its regional application to the Midwest, and particularly Indiana, the geography of hate pervades the nation. The narrower geographical focus simply enables tracing the breadth and depth of the devastating legacy of exclusion and hatred. I illustrate how white desires constantly strive to create, recreate, and perpetuate a white reality. Corroborating the ubiquity of community-enforced mechanisms of exclusion, we are seeing more and more projects like Mapping Prejudice, Segregated Seattle, and Mapping Inequality that unearth the legacies of racist policies and hostile attitudes. The Southern Poverty Law Center continues to track active hate groups in the United States on its Hate Map.[44] Projects like these convince me that Indiana is not the exception but rather the norm of (small-town) white America.

Journeying, mapping, and marking the racialized geographies of Indiana will illustrate the durability of this inhospitable and exclusionary small-town mentality to better understand the legacy of that unwelcoming environment. Ever since it became a state in 1816, Indiana displayed through its laws, policies, and attitudes that it is meant for white people. Consequently, it lends itself well to a discussion about the larger processes behind the geography of hate. I will uncover how belonging and citizenship function on a town, county, and state level, as local policies and exclusionary practices collectively signal *non*belonging and *non*citizenship to *non*white people.

CHAPTER 1

Manifesting White Indiana

> The only negro allowed to remain was an old barber, who was accorded this privilege on the demand of Henry Y. Morrison, and for a number of years he and his family were the only ones in the place.
>
> —Claybaugh, *History of Clinton County, Indiana,* 179

Joseph Parker could not read or write. He was born enslaved around 1840 in Raleigh, North Carolina. After gaining his freedom when slavery was abolished at the end of the Civil War, he relocated to Indianapolis and learned the trade of a barber. It is here that Joseph met Henry Y. Morrison, an influential attorney and citizen of Clinton County. Morrison would soon complete law school and return to Clinton County, but while still in Indianapolis, Joseph became his shoe shiner and carried wood to his room. When Morrison moved back to his home county, Joseph moved to Thorntown in the adjacent Boone County, where a small Black community had developed following the end of the Civil War. It is here where he met and married eighteen-year-old Rhoda Stewart in October 1867. Rhoda was born in Parke County, Indiana, but her parents were natives of North Carolina who had moved to Vigo County, Indiana, in pursuit of farming.

The young Parker couple soon had their first two children, Elnora and Howard. Following his former employer, Joseph moved his young family to Frankfort in the early 1870s and soon acquired a barber shop in the city. Within ten years, the family was able to purchase their house on 353 West Walnut Street. When the city erupted in a scandal involving racial mixing, the Parkers avoided the fate of other local Black families who were driven out of the community. The Parkers endured.

Remaining in Frankfort, Joseph and Rhoda grieved the losses of children in their infancies and rejoiced in the birth of others. Family members fell ill and recovered. Children grew up and made friends. They motored to nearby Lafayette and other Indiana locales. The Parkers built and fostered belonging in the slowly growing Black community by attending the local Bethel A. M. E. church, hosting social gatherings to celebrate their children's birthdays, high school graduations, and acceptance to state universities. Their sons and sons-in-law went to war, learned the trade of a barber, and took over the barber shop. Some of the children moved away—as far away as New York City and Birmingham, Alabama—and only returned to Frankfort for family visits—moments the Parkers rejoiced and celebrated.

When "Uncle Joe" died in August 1919, the local newspaper traced his life in the community, heralding the fact that he had been the "only colored man in the city for decades." Joseph was outlived by Rhoda and eight of their thirteen children, four of whom remained in Frankfort. The other four children had moved to bigger cities outside of Indiana. Howard went to Birmingham, Alabama, Marcus to New York City, Maurice to Detroit, and Myrtle, the first Black student to graduate from Frankfort High School in 1891, to Atlanta. Myrtle went to Indiana University in her twenties and moved to Atlanta via Birmingham.

Of the four children who remained in Frankfort at the time of Joseph's death, Homer and Lettie stayed with their mother in their house on 353 West Walnut Street. So did Lettie's husband, Fern Reed, a World War I veteran and native of Frankfort. He was also a barber, being employed by Joseph when the draft for "colored boys" reached Clinton County in 1918. Ivy (Iva) and Jennie (Jeanette) lived with their husbands nearby.

Rhoda passed away in September 1923 at the age of seventy-four. Soon thereafter, Lettie left Clinton County with her husband, Fern—not for the big city but for other counties in Indiana. They temporarily moved to Miami County, but ultimately settled in Kokomo, Howard County, where both of them passed away in 1943 and 1978, respectively. Jennie left Clinton County and relocated to a Black neighborhood in Indianapolis. Homer, Ivy, and her husband, Ross Brown, remained in the Parker house at 353 West Walnut Street, which by 1930 was worth $2,000.[1] Homer, who was known in town for "his jovial disposition and friendliness," died in July 1935. When Ivy died four years later, so did the legacy of the Parkers, one long-term Black family in Clinton County. The four remaining Parker siblings—Myrtle, Jennie, Lettie, and Maurice—resided in other midwestern and southern locales. The Parkers lived a regular small-town life in Frankfort for multiple generations. They are part of Frankfort's history. Why the Parker descendants left Frankfort for good, we may never know. But *The Geography of Hate* may explain why.

* * *

County histories provide a record of the local communities within the confines of any given county, capturing townships' formation, cities' growth, and biographical sketches of residents. Indiana county histories rarely capture Black experiences. If they do, they do not show the white residents in a favorable light. Joseph Claybaugh's excerpt explains why. In his historical tracing of Clinton County, he reveals profound insights into the attitudes of white residents. He first clarifies that "Clinton county's record in the Civil war [*sic*] was not due to any especial [*sic*] devotion to the negro." He elaborates on the Civil War, noting that it brought "quite a settlement" of "negro refugees" to Thorntown, Boone County, "from where they gradually spread out to neighboring territory, a number locating at Frankfort." He does not offer specific numbers, but they seem to have been sufficient to stir some fracas in town. Claybaugh writes:

> Towards the close of the war Frankfort became much excited over a scandal involving a negro and a white woman, and a crowd collected to "clean out the niggers." For a while there was danger of a riot, if not a lynching, but a few cooler heads prevailed, and as a compromise it was agreed to "pack them up, and take them back to Thorntown where they belonged." Wagons were secured, farmers from near the town giving assistance, and the colored colony was simply loaded up, hauled to Thorntown, and dumped there. The only negro allowed to remain was an old barber, who was accorded this privilege on the demand of Henry Y. Morrison, and for a number of years he and his family were the only ones in the place. But gradually the feeling abated, and others moved in, the negroes themselves exercising a supervision of the character of colored immigrants; and the colored population of Clinton county is now a very orderly and reputable factor of the community.[2]

Claybaugh describes a pivotal historical moment that reshaped the history of Clinton County and the Black experience within its borders. Clinton County rid itself of its Black population during the Civil War. The cause seems to have been a violation of Indiana's anti-miscegenation law. White residents uprooted Black residents from their homes and transported them not outside of Indiana but to the county south of Clinton County. The first part of the passage, in particular, clearly demarcates Black residents as not belonging to the community, robbing them of their humanity, agency, and citizenship.

Also, note the passive tone, in which Claybaugh describes the incident: "there was danger of a riot, if not a lynching . . . it was agreed to 'pack them up.' . . . Wagons were secured." White racist thoughts and actions are disembodied, but it was the white residents who contemplated "a riot, if not a lynching," and "agreed to 'pack them up.'" Zeus Leonardo observes, "when it concerns domination, whites suddenly disappear. . . . Their previous omnipresence becomes a position of nowhere, a certain politics of undetectability."[3] The passive voice absolves white residents from any culpability in manifesting their white desires as a spatial reality.

Claybaugh does not identify the "old barber" by name but rather his Samaritan. Judge Henry Y. Morrison, originally from Ohio, was one of the leading and "representative citizens" of the community. By naming the white individual while referring to the Black one as the "only negro," Claybaugh illustrates Paul Spickard's concept of "normative whiteness," the unmarked and unnamed characteristic of whiteness. Since we are not "informed to the contrary, the people under discussion are White."[4] By naming the white but not the Black individual in this passage, Claybaugh shows who mattered in the community and thus reaffirms that this is "white man's land." How Indiana was designed and came to be understood as a white state is this chapter's focus.

The "old barber" was "Uncle Joe" Parker, whose "snow-white head and aged, bent figure was a familiar sight" on Frankfort streets.[5] He was still alive at the time Claybaugh wrote the county history, yet his side of the expulsion that took place in Frankfort is missing. Parker's version might have revealed that Claybaugh's timeline of when Clinton County rid itself of its Black community was misremembered, as the Parker family moved into the community in the early 1870s. The forced expulsion thus would have occurred in the 1870s at the earliest rather than "Toward the close of the [Civil] war," as Claybaugh recalled. Claybaugh's historical sketches of "representative citizens" do not include Black residents, and neither do his genealogical records of the "old families"—even though the Black community allegedly constituted an "orderly and reputable" part of the county by the time of his writing.[6]

* * *

This chapter documents Indiana's legal and social history as it pertains to Black experiences. Though Indiana was founded as a white state, Black people existed here. Exploring state laws and their enactment on a county level illustrates that Indiana subscribed to racialized citizenship ideals that do not encompass African American citizens. I show how their citizenship was actively contested and undermined on a town, county, and state level.

By mapping the contours of Indiana's geography of hate, I reveal the institutionalization, adoption, and perpetuation of inhospitality, hostility, and exclusion. While white Hoosiers cemented and anchored whiteness as their way of life, I am cementing the traces, courage, and experiences of

Black Hoosiers and migrants in this unwelcoming environment. Doing so, I demonstrate the durability of whiteness as a system that's malleable in its applications. White Hoosiers found "creative" ways, such as racist policies, to manifest white Indiana—from "repatriation" efforts to banning entry of potential African American newcomers by law. Once these attempts failed, they deferred to other mechanisms, some physical and visible, others surreptitious and hidden—all of them more drastic and violent. Their inhospitable acts and exclusionary actions include enforced expulsions from communities across the state, lynching and riots, restrictive covenants, and white supremacist organizations.

Indiana: White by Law and Institutions

Indiana was founded as a white state. Residents and politicians alike perceived it that way, believed in it, and acted accordingly. "In the decades before the Civil War," Indiana historian and native Hoosier Emma Lou Thornbrough writes, "the assertion that the United States, especially the state of Indiana, was a 'white man's country' became a well-worn cliché in the mouths of a certain brand of politicians."[7] For example, in his 1857 speech, George Washington Julian, an Indiana abolitionist, proclaimed that "The sad truth is, that Indiana is the most pro-slavery of all our Northern States. . . . Our people hate the negro with a perfect, if not supreme hatred, and their anti-slavery, making an average estimate, is a superficial and sickly sentiment, rather than a deep-rooted robust conviction."[8] Uncompromisingly forthright, Julian colored what Claybaugh described as "no especial devotion to the negro" during the Civil War.

Many of Indiana's early white settlers came from the South, a fact that has shaped Indiana's culture, attitude, and politics, or in the words of Ruth Andersen, "Those who came to Indiana brought with them the strong feelings of superiority of the Caucasian race and the prejudices against the Negro people that had been predominant in their home states."[9] In 1950, William E. Wilson, an author native to Indiana, contributed a fifteen-page panoramic portrait about the Hoosier state to the journal *Holiday*. In it, he references the U.S. Highway 40, the Old National Road, as the dividing line between two settlement streams. He describes the northern part of the state as having been populated by "descendants of Yankees, New York Staters and immigrants from foreign lands," which made the region "more vigorous," "more progressive and aggressive, and the more prosperous half of the state." In contrast, he classifies the southern part of the state as having "been inhabited by descendants of Southerners, with a strong infusion of German and Irish in their blood" and "a more storied past and more varied scenery." Southern Indianans, according to Wilson, were "more leisurely and more gracious," and "more loquacious." In his article, Wilson fails to comment on Black Hoosiers or how his classification of northern and southern Indiana results in different attitudes toward Black Hoosiers.

While Claybaugh at least insinuated Black settlement in his county history, Wilson writes Black folk out of the state's history. He attributes the state's divided support during the Civil War to the fact that Abraham Lincoln left Indiana for Illinois. The author seems almost blind to the race question in his portrait, as he explains (white) Hoosier pride in its southern heritage as having "a strong sense of family loyalty as well as devotion to friends."[10] Wilson grew up in Evansville, which was one of the earliest towns in Indiana to attract a Black population. Evansville experienced its fair share of racial unrest from the late nineteenth to the mid-twentieth century, yet the author does not acknowledge the existence of Black folk in Indiana, mention race-related incidents, or connect the pride in its southern heritage to anti-Black ideologies.

Despite authors' white reflection of the state's history, Indiana was anti-Black from its earliest conception as a territory and later state. "While there was some difference of opinion among the residents as to the enormity of slavery," John W. Lyda writes in his 1953 study *The Negro in the History of Indiana*, "there was scarcely any as to the Negro and mulatto coming into the state under any circumstances; they simply were not wanted by a majority of citizens." Lyda was a Black Hoosier who taught in one of Terre Haute's segregated schools during the early- to mid-1900s, and his book was one of the first seminal histories of the Black experience in the state. According to Lyda, the reason white Hoosiers did not want African Americans in the state was they believed the common perceptions of the time, which included "lazy, shiftless, unable to support themselves . . . so criminally inclined that they committed an undue proportion of crimes, and that their coming tended to keep out the more to-be-desired white settlers that could be readily absorbed as part of the population while the Negro could not."[11]

Historians of the state agree with Lyda's interpretation. Thornbrough describes the prevailing attitude in Indiana "as neither proslavery nor antislavery but as anti-Negro," attributing it to the competition in the labor market and the overall antipathy toward Black people. In his most recent account on Indiana, James H. Madison notes, "Overshadowing the feeble antislavery sentiment was strong race prejudice." Darlene Clark Hine notes, "White Hoosiers resented the new Black arrivals. They steadfastly believed this to be a white man's country and fought to preserve Indiana as a white man's state."[12] A look at Indiana's laws and legislature illustrates this mission's severity. As part of the Northwest Ordinance of 1787, Indiana prohibited slavery and indentured servitude upon becoming a state.[13] Simultaneously, however, white Hoosiers made their racial antipathies known and cemented them in their first (and later second) constitution. Article VI and Article VII of the 1816 Constitution granted the right to vote and to serve in the militia exclusively to white male citizens.[14] Two years later, intermarriage between Black and white people was outlawed on Indiana soil.[15] The legislature also forbade African Americans from serving as jurors and offering testimony in cases involving whites.[16] In their zeal to make life for Black Hoosiers miserable and unbearable, "White Hoosiers continued to restrict rights and movement of blacks in the state and excluded them from white society over the next three decades." Using the law and institutions, their anti-Black actions include forming the Indiana Colonization Society in 1829, passing so-called Black Codes in 1831, and designating public schools to white children in 1843.[17]

At a time when the state's Black population constituted less than 1 percent of the total population, white Hoosiers were determined to preempt and quash any chances of an increasing Black population. Calls for the colonization of Black folk, for example, go back to the state's foundational days. In 1817, the Indiana General Assembly introduced a resolution "to colonize Blacks in the Far West." The same year, the American Colonization Society (ACS) was formed. Soon, calls for state auxiliaries followed. Indiana started organizing as early as 1820, and resolutions in favor of ACS were passed in the Indiana General Assembly throughout the 1820s. Officially formed as an auxiliary of the ACS in 1829, the Indiana Colonization Society hoped to "repatriate" Black Hoosiers to Africa, more specifically to Liberia.

Hoosiers supported these efforts for various reasons. As Ruth Andersen explains:

> The removal of the colored people was sought eagerly by some because they felt that complete separation of the races was the only answer to the controversial issue. Some Hoosiers felt that colonization would better the condition of the Negro since he could never hope to be the equal of the white citizen in the country. Religious groups looked upon colonization as a springboard toward the spreading of Christian civilization in Africa. Those who sympathized with the slave owners of the South favored colonization because they felt that free Negroes were a threat to the economic stability of the plantation system.[18]

Whatever the rationale, for many white Hoosiers, colonization became the solution to their "Negro problem."

Like other states in the Midwest, Indiana passed its own Black Codes in 1831. Black newcomers to the state had to register with a clerk in their county of residence and place surety bonds of $500 guaranteeing not to disturb the peace or become a public charge. By 1840, Indiana legislators toughened the anti-miscegenation law by increasing the fines and jail time for anyone in violation of the law and including punishment for anyone performing such marriage ceremonies.[19]

Indiana's white desires were not always hidden. On the contrary, with the passing of its second constitution in 1851, Indiana made it abundantly clear that Black people were not welcome, and for fifteen years, white supremacist desires governed the state without disguise. Article XIII, reinforcing the exclusion and colonization efforts from the last decades, *openly* banned African Americans from settling in Indiana and imposed fines on anyone employing or helping Black folk to settle in the state. Another section of the article guaranteed money for a state agent to encourage Black Hoosiers to emigrate to Africa. The so-called Negro Exclusion Article, being subject to an independent vote, was more popular than the rest of the constitution among white Hoosiers. One year later, Indiana legislators passed another law regarding Black people in the state, now requiring all Black residents to register in their county of residence.[20]

The impacts of the latest wave of stringent anti-Black laws were severe: for instance, the official ban on Black migration into the state resulted in a net increase of 166 people in Indiana's Black population between 1850 and 1860. It also caused almost 90 percent of the eighty-three identified Black emigrants from Indiana to Africa to leave between 1850 and 1854 in the immediate wake of the 1851 Constitution's passage.[21]

Efforts to keep Indiana white extended into the Civil War era. In a debate over emancipation in the District of Columbia in 1862, former governor and then-Senator Joseph A. Wright proclaimed:

> [A]s one of the central States, we do not intend to allow our region of [the] country to be overrun by the black race. Such is the prejudice, such is the settled conviction of our people, that the wall which we have erected is to stand. We intend to have in our State, as far as possible, a white population, and we do not intend to have our jails and penitentiaries filled with the free blacks.[22]

Wright admits the widespread and strong prejudice among white Hoosiers, as well as their firm belief in negative stereotypes about Black people, as he correlates "free blacks" with criminality. Considering that Indiana's Black population had never exceeded 1 percent of the total population before 1870,[23] the fact that Indiana enacted a plethora of laws that infringed on African Americans' civil and human rights is simply astonishing. Indiana was determined to maintain its whiteness.

On a legal plane, Indiana displayed anti-Blackness. Its constitutions declared whiteness as a prerequisite for citizenship rights and duties, and openly banned Black settlement within state borders. Additional laws annulled marriages, encouraged "repatriation" to Africa, imposed Black Codes and fines for violators, and introduced Negro registers. Yet Black folk continued to settle, intermarriages between Black and white people happened, and not all counties kept a Negro register. It is the people in the communities who respect, interpret, and enforce the law in their hometowns and counties.

Laws enact their power through the people they govern. And vice versa: people act and display their powers through the laws. Midwest scholar Richard C. Longworth classifies the Midwest outside the cities as "largely a social system based on everybody looking and acting like everybody else" and as a "social system based on respect for the law."[24] The very presence of Black southern migrants then and immigrants of color now mocks the social system and their laws, even though the newcomers might act "like everybody else" and respect the law. A closer look at Indiana's ninety-two counties illustrates how Hoosiers interpreted and enacted the state laws in their county communities, revealing a blanket of white hostility and animosity toward Black Hoosiers. On a county level, white Hoosiers sent the message that this is white territory and white property, where Black people simply are out of place. What becomes clear is that Indiana counties invoked whiteness in every sphere of life and that it is the people who (re)produce the geography of hate.

Navigating a Hostile and Exclusive Environment: Black Experiences in Nineteenth-Century White Indiana, 1816–1890

Many counties in Indiana have been home to Black residents, from the earliest days of non-Indigenous people settling the region. Many were brought as slaves. Complying with the Northwest Ordinance of 1787, Indiana prohibited slavery in its 1816 Constitution (Article XI). The article, however, did not concern owners of slaves before the state was founded. Those slaves remained in bondage. Of the 1,420 Black people listed in the 1820 census, 190 (13.4 percent) were listed as slaves. Almost two-thirds of them were located in Knox County, in the southwestern part of the state.[25] The 1850 census is the first census that no longer lists slaves in the northern state of Indiana, though indentured servitude might have continued beyond that point.[26]

Scholars focusing on early white settlements in the state frequently point to the prominence of Quaker settlements. Indiana had the fourth highest Quaker population in the nation by 1850, after Pennsylvania, New York, and Ohio, all states that had more than double the total population of Indiana. Due to the Quakers' well-known humanitarian and anti-slavery stance, many of the early Black arrivals settled in close proximity to Quaker locales, as they could expect help in the form of land rentals or purchase, work, or housing from their Quaker neighbors.[27] The 1860 census records registered a Black presence in all but six Indiana counties.[28]

Besides settling in or near Quaker communities, African Americans sometimes founded their own communities to escape hostile treatment from white Hoosiers, especially when no Quakers were in the area. Despite all legal and societal obstacles that restricted Black settlement during Indiana's pioneer period, Black Hoosiers had established at least sixty-one such rural farming settlements in the state by 1870 (Map 1).[29] These Black farming communities were spread across forty-three counties, half of the counties that registered Black residents among the county citizenry. One of the oldest and largest Black farming communities was Lyles Station in Gibson County, in southern Indiana.[30] Other well-known Black rural settlements include Pinkston Settlement in Dubois County and Roberts Settlement in Hamilton County.[31]

The 1851 Constitution's ratification opened yet another official and legal lane to discriminate against, shun, and exclude people of color from Hoosier life and society. While Black people continued to migrate to the state—despite Article XIII's legal ban on settlement, white Hoosiers anchored their white desires geographically—through countywide expulsions across the state. Maybe these counties felt emboldened by the new law of the land or interpreted the new constitution in a way that gave them the right to claim Hoosier territory as their own—white—land. Joseph Claybaugh attests to the fact that white residents in Clinton County took the law into their own hands and drove out the Black population—everyone but "Uncle Joe" and his family. Similarly, Xenia Cord notes in passing what she describes as a "curious" situation in Franklin County at that time. She observes that "only 28 of the more than 150 blacks living there in the early 1850s had registered by July 1853." She records a steep drop down to fourteen in the county's Black population by 1860, "the rest having scattered to communities farther north," and acknowledges that "what caused the exodus is not clear."[32] Elliot Jaspin studied this phenomenon with the aim of offering an explanation—namely,

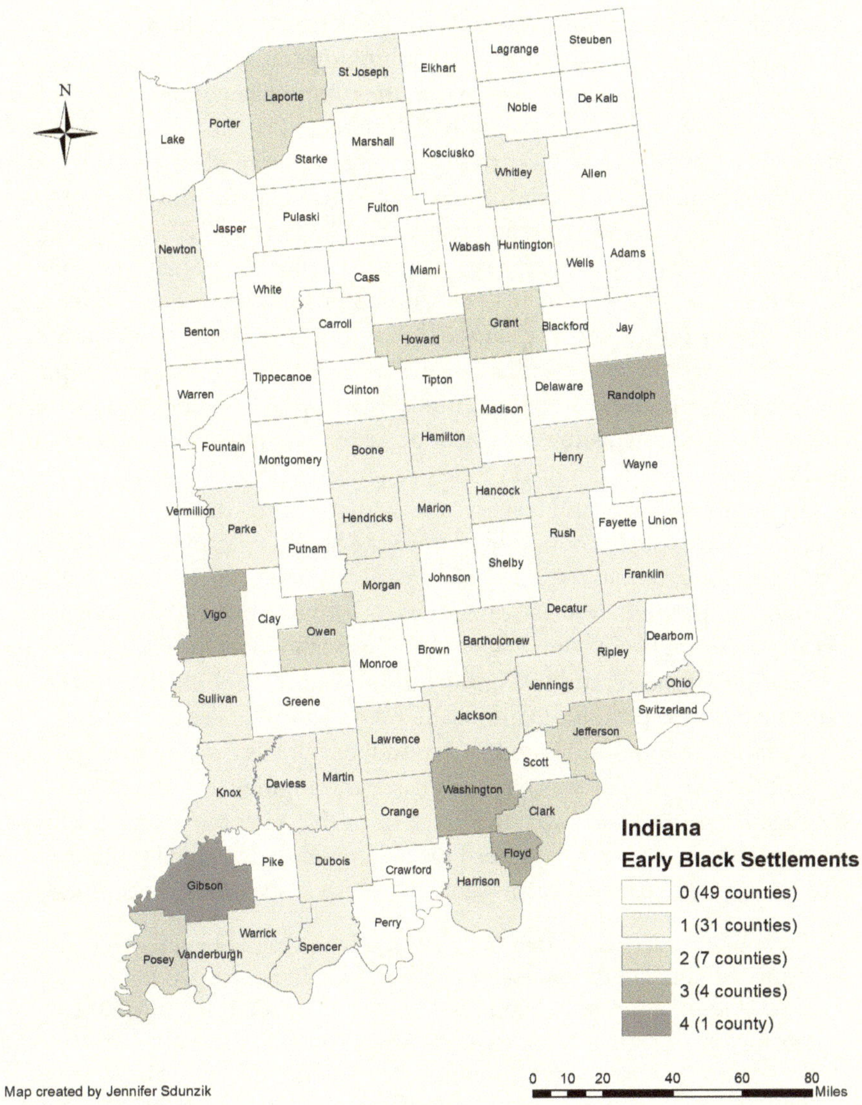

MAP 1. Indiana's early Black settlements

that the reason for the drastically plunging numbers of residents of color can be seen as "racial cleansing."

In *Buried in the Bitter Waters*, Jaspin analyzes in great detail twelve of the worst county-wide expulsions, or racial cleansings, across the nation, two of them in Indiana—in Vermillion and Washington counties.[33] Though each racial cleansing Jaspin unearthed is unique, the common denominators to define an incident as a racial cleansing include the intent of ridding the town/county of its Black population and a currently lower number of Black residents than before the cleansing. The racial cleansing in Washington County in 1864 took place amid the Civil War, seemingly just like Clinton County's incident. Unlike Clinton County, where white residents viscerally and violently responded to people violating Indiana's 1843 anti-miscegenation law, white residents in Washington County racially cleansed their county out of fear that "blacks one day might become voters and, by extension, members of the community."[34] Note in Map 1 that Washington County was one of four counties that had three Black settlements that we know of. Jaspin documents a drop from 187 Black residents in the county in 1860 to eighteen a decade later.[35]

In spite of the harsh and restrictive laws that marked the northern state of Indiana, Black people continued to leave the South, culminating in the first Black out-migration to the Midwest in 1879. Whereas Kansas was the prime destination for the Exodusters, Indiana constituted an attractive alternative because of promoters promising work as farm laborers. One such promoter advocating for the exodus to Kansas was Benjamin "Pap" Singleton, a separatist leader who promised land to the migrants in his personally founded colonies. In the Reverend John H. Clay, Indiana had its own "Pap" Singleton.

Like Singleton, Clay was a former slave and fugitive to Indiana who encouraged early southern migrants to settle in the state. More specifically, in a letter that Clay wrote to southern Black people, he described Indiana as "a rich State of fertile lands" ideally suited for Black workers. He elaborated:

> Those of our race who come from the South and locate here have greatly improved their condition, especially those who have engaged in farming. Thousands of good farm hands and house servants can readily find employment at remunerative wages, and when you have earned your money the law will compel payment, should it be refused, which is not likely to be the case. What we want is honest, industrious men, who know how and are willing to work on farms, and the same class of women to do housework. Loafers are not wanted.[36]

Clay reiterates Black folk's connection to the soil, urging farmers to come to Indiana and make a living. His letter also serves as a testament that as early as 1880, many southern Black people knew about the farmland prospects here. Clay affirms that Jim Crow does not rule Indiana by emphasizing that the law will guarantee adequate payment for labor, which was not always the case in the sharecropping South. He also specifically excludes "loafers," a term frequently used in the migrant letters thirty years later, corroborating the strength of negative stereotypes Black migrants had to overcome.[37] Unfortunately, not every community in Indiana and the larger Midwest had such outspoken community leaders like Clay and Singleton. And neither Clay nor Singleton anticipated that Jim Crow, though never the law of the (midwestern) land, would come to openly rule midwestern minds and actions a few years later.[38]

Regardless of active recruiting efforts, evidence shows that some counties witnessed an increase in their Black populations and shows how it was perceived in the state around the 1880s, as was the case in Owen County. The arrival of twenty-one Black newcomers sparked a big headline in the newspaper on January 8, 1880. The group came from Edgecombe County, North Carolina, and anticipated settling permanently. Within two days, each of the new arrivals had found employment, as local farmers in the area welcomed them with open arms. "But," cautioned the article, "while these men were being engaged to labor, something else was going on. The fact that a few of these people had arrived, had stunned the hot-headed portion of Democracy. Their contempt for these 'thriftless' men was boundless. Mob was talked."[39] While no extralegal violence was reported, local Democrats demanded a meeting immediately. In the meeting, residents determined that this was an "'importation of negroes,' not an immigration," and since they "were being over run [*sic*] with negroes[,] White men would lose their places, and bread could not be had for their children." The Democrats of Owen County lamented the arrival because it was on the eve of an important presidential election.

These hostile anti-Black sentiments were echoed in openly Democratic papers in these days, such as the *Indiana State Sentinel*, which also enjoyed a strong readership among farmers and stock-raisers across the state. In the paper's complete review of the migration, the writers blamed state Republicans for conspiring and importing "these pauper negroes" who "come to vote the Republican ticket, [and] to rob white laborers of the means of support." The article echoes common perceptions of the time, including perceiving Black people as "ragged, filthy, lazy, and improvident, they come to live upon public and private charities, or to die beggars and paupers," and repeatedly underlined that Indiana was a state "where they are not wanted."[40] The idea of white men losing "their places" and being robbed of their way to making a living also underscores the community's possessive investment in whiteness.[41]

In contrast, the article published in *The People*, an openly Republican newspaper, provides a more holistic picture of the situation in Owen County, featuring Democratic voices as well as the testimony of a Black preacher and fellow attendee of the meeting demanded by local Democrats. The preacher took it upon himself to correct some of the remarks: "He said the Negroes were not paupers. That all they wanted was a fair chance. That each of them had paid their way from the south, and had money when they arrived here. That all they wanted was work."[42] Clay, the *Indiana State Sentinel*, and the preacher all illustrate the omnipresence and power of negative stereotypes that Black newcomers had to overcome in their attempt to settle among white Hoosiers. Thirty years later, migrants during the Great Migration included the information about "not being a loafer" in their letters, underlining the longevity of such stereotypes.

In short, the second half of the nineteenth century for Black folk in Indiana demonstrates the resilience of people who were not welcomed in the state. In response to the white animosity and hostility in thought and deed, Black communities across the state of Indiana formed their own institutions to meet their social, economic, and spiritual needs. For white Indiana, this period demonstrates their continued efforts to send the "not welcome" message to their Black neighbors. The ratification of Indiana's second constitution in 1851 set the tone of hostility. But common white people reinforced it in their Hoosier communities in subsequent decades—revealed in disregard for and county-wide expulsions of Black Hoosiers.

Surviving Indiana's Most Vicious Years: Black Experiences in Indiana, 1890–1907

Indiana's white desires also manifested in actual physical violence. Indiana's lynching record, though not well recorded, provides another example of how white Hoosiers interpreted and enacted state laws. Indiana adopted an anti-lynching law in 1899 when race relations nationwide were at an all-time low.[43] Lynching as an extralegal measure was used against Black and white people in the state. American Studies scholar Erik Wade notes that the very fact that whites were lynched in the state resulted in the strong push for an anti-lynching legislation, explicating that "stricter laws against lynching was not about protecting black lives; it was a response to defend whites from lynch mobs."[44] Though the lack of record-keeping preempts me from providing a comprehensive overview of lynchings in the state, I traced seventeen incidents between 1845 and 1930 that resulted in the deaths of twenty-six Black people (Map 2).

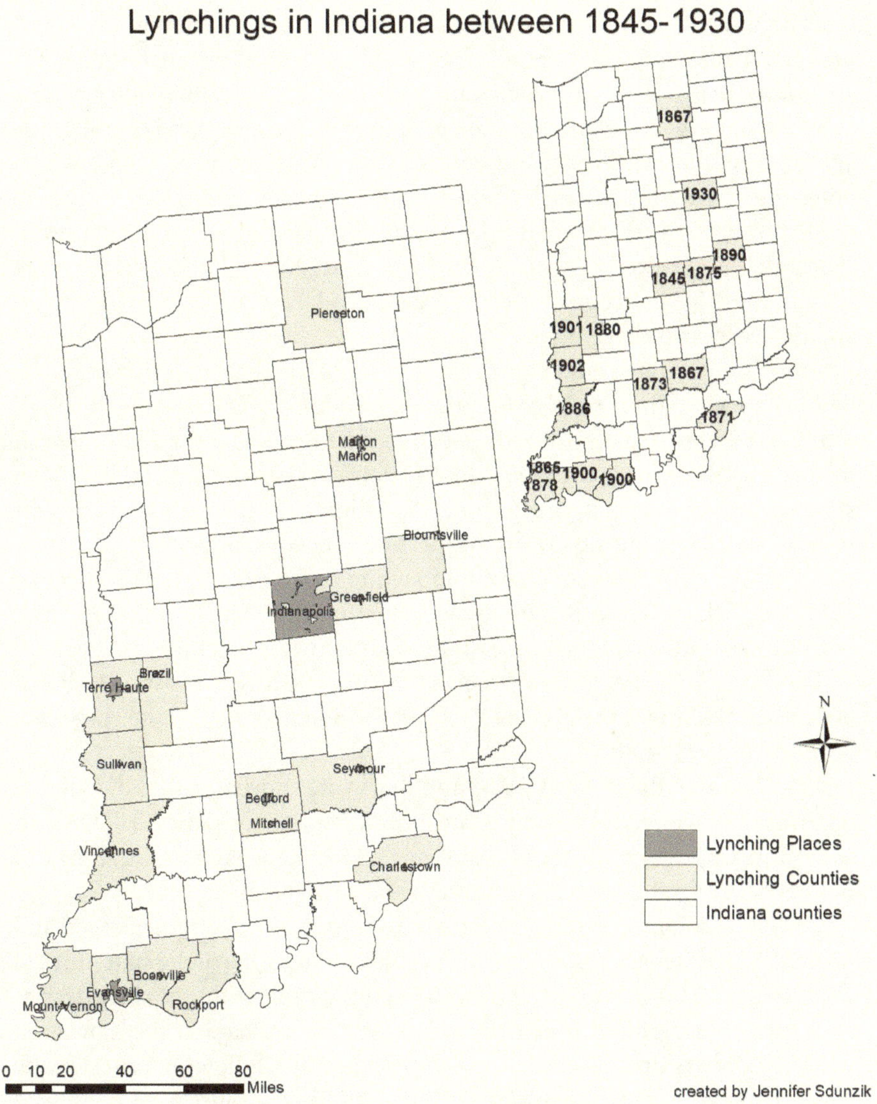

MAP 2. Locales and years in which Hoosiers lynched Black people. The sixteen counties in which lynchings took place are Clark, Clay, Grant, Hancock, Henry, Jackson, Kosciusko, Knox, Lawrence, Marion, Posey, Spencer, Sullivan, Vanderburgh, Vigo, and Warrick.

Two of those incidents, one in 1890 in Blountsville, Henry County, and another in 1893 in Bedford, Lawrence County, coincided with the heyday of the lynching era in the United States.[45] Before 1921, the first major attempt to pass anti-lynching legislation on a federal stage, many states, including Ohio (1896), Indiana (1899), and Michigan (1899), passed their statewide versions of anti-lynching law. Although the passing of such legislation is commendable, it is worth very little if not enforced and acted on.[46] On the contrary, one could argue that the turn of the century indicates the heyday of lynching for Indiana, as six Black men fell victim to such extralegal measures in four different incidents across the state between 1900 and 1902. In that short period, those six men constitute 23 percent of all the victims identified in an eighty-five-year period.

More broadly, one could argue that the turn of the century also reflects the nadir of race relations in Indiana. Indiana reinforced its whiteness through different means—legally and extralegally, violently and culturally. One such means was the National Horse Thief Detective Association (NHTDA), a state-sanctioned, legal vigilante body that illustrates the state's investment in whiteness by granting "white propertied men special powers to defend their belongings." Their subscription to white supremacy is most evident in the 1920s, "when they joined forces with the Ku Klux Klan," but the NHTDA began to spread throughout the state, mainly in central Indiana, decades earlier (Map 3). In 1897, one of their own became the governor of Indiana. James A. Mount was the NHTDA Grand President as well as the state governor from 1897 to 1901.[47]

Furthermore, the White Caps—another white supremacist and vigilante organization—spread across the state. Both organizations, the NHTDA and the White Caps, formed in Indiana years before the Civil War, but they did not become a "public nuisance" until the late nineteenth century.[48]

Besides condoning extralegal vigilante efforts, Indiana also embraced and normalized whiteness around the turn of the century. One of the state-funded university yearbooks provides a good example of how these white desires manifested culturally. Purdue University's 1902 *Debris* features the "Southern Club." Membership was exclusive and based on the following criteria: one "must be WHITE, must live south of the *Ohio River*, must have witnessed at least *one* Lynching, and must understand the various mechanisms of the so-called '*Blind Tiger.*'" That year, the club had at least twenty-one members. "Committee on Lynching," "Leader of the Whitecaps," and "Official Nigger Lyncher" were among the club's officer positions.[49] Although it appears to have been a prank club, it reflects attitudes held at the university and in Indiana society. Like the non-university vigilante groups, membership

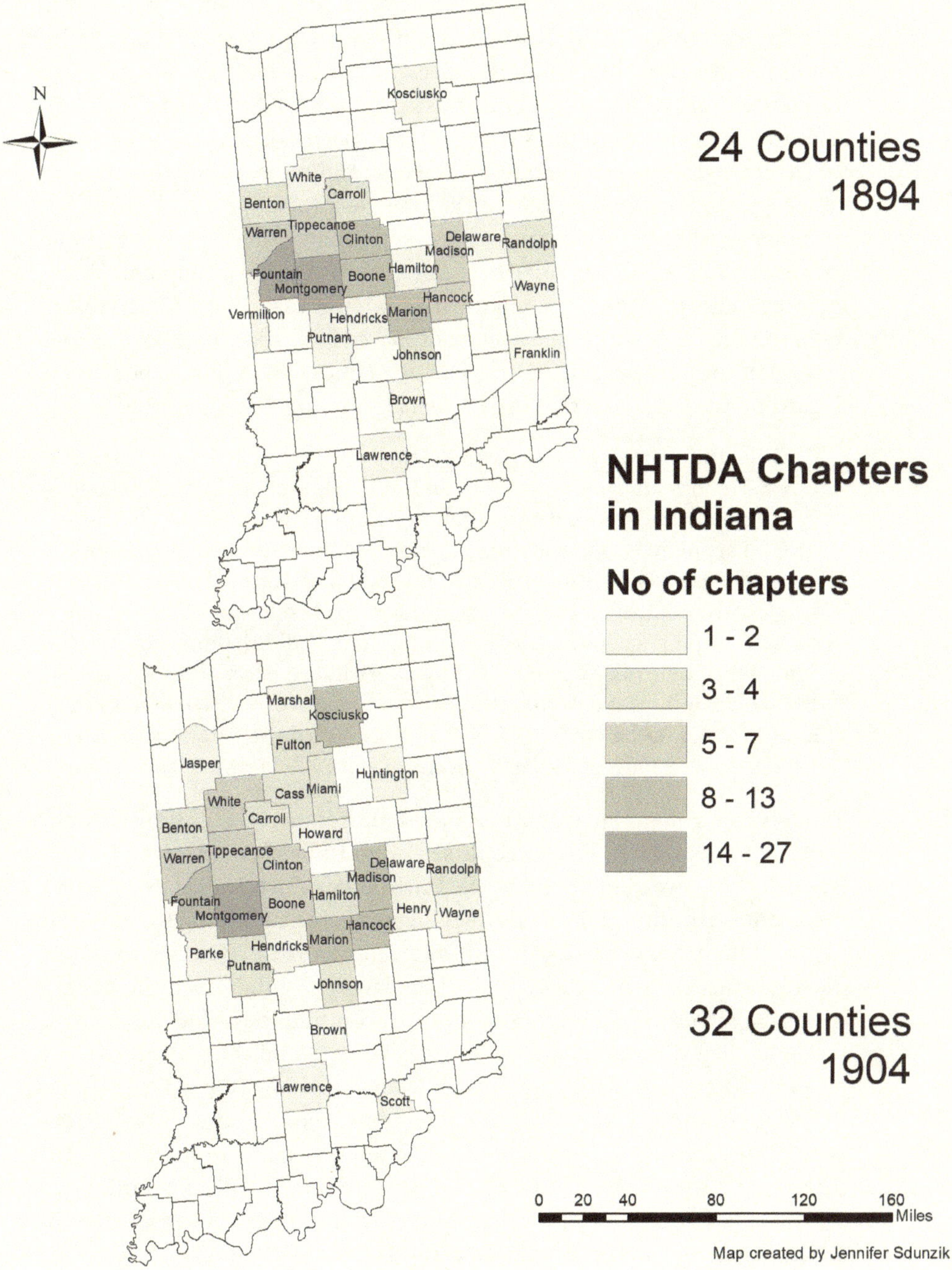

MAP 3. Maps showcasing growth of NHTDA chapters across the state between 1894 and 1904

was exclusively granted to whites. The club signals racism as a southern phenomenon by virtue of its name, but it existed at a northern university. Purdue University had a small number of Black students by that time, yet the sanctioning of a white supremacist club like the Southern Club indicates that educational settings were not safe spaces for Black Hoosiers, and well-educated white Hoosiers subscribed to and reinscribed white desires culturally, clearly signaling Indiana as white territory.

Indiana had multiple incidents of city- and county-wide expulsions around the turn of the century, similar to the ones recorded in Clinton and Washington counties. Carlisle, a small town with fewer than 1,000 inhabitants in Sullivan County, became "the Scene of a Fierce Race Riot" in 1904, only two years after the Sullivan community lynched James Dillard for alleged rape.[50] Regarding the local race riot, the *Frankfort Morning Times* reported:

> Carlisle, Ind. September 13—Jasper Hammond, colored, while resisting arrest Monday afternoon, was shot and seriously wounded by Constable T. E. Johnson. Hammond was trying to renew a quarrel with other negroes. Last night a mob gathered and drove all non-resident negroes out of town. Race feeling is intense and it is feared that negroes having homes here will be compelled to leave. Hammond was taken to the Sullivan jail for safe keeping when threats of lynching were made. The mob last night visited the home of every negro family. Every house, except one occupied by an old family, was deserted. These people were not molested, but doors and windows in the other houses were demolished. *No further trouble is expected unless the negro laborers make an effort to return to Carlisle.*[51]

Though disturbing, the article discloses four points relevant to this book's larger argument. First, Black people settled in Indiana small towns and villages. Second, even small towns like Carlisle, of which Indiana has plenty, drove out their minuscule minority population, reestablishing the all-white nature of their communities. Third, white Hoosiers displayed the same mob mentality that is often exclusively attributed to the South. Hence, these sentiments characterize midwestern small-town communities. And last, Carlisle residents allegedly spared one Black family while demolishing all other Black property. That particular family might have acquired the "token Black" status in the community, similar to the Parkers in Clinton County. Overall, the article attests to the "intense race feelings" in Indiana communities in the early twentieth century that resulted in the expulsion of Black families.

White Indiana communities had already fully embraced anti-Black sentiments by the summer of 1902. Decatur, in Adams County, was "suffering from a bad attack of 'Negrophobia,'" the *Freeman* reported, explaining that on "June 8th about fifty white men came together to drive all the Negroes out of the city," resulting in four of the six Black residents leaving immediately "and the remaining two, it is said, has [*sic*] since left." Who or what caused the violent outbreak is unclear, but the author speculated that "it is possible to act in such a way as to be offensive to the unwritten laws of communities as it concerns the races, and which constitute the race question of to-day." A week later, the same news outlet, one of the major Black presses in Indiana, recorded yet another expulsion: "Two weeks ago it was Decatur, now we have trouble at French Lick, [Orange County] Ind. The colored people have been warned to leave that place."[52] In the meantime, a Black person moved back to the recently declared "negro-free" city of Decatur, much to the white residents' displeasure. Insulted, mocked, and threatened with violence, he left within three weeks. This renewed display of anti-Black feelings made national and state headlines, with the *New York Times*, the *Indianapolis Recorder*, and the *Indianapolis News* reporting on the person leaving after being warned by Decatur's newly formed "anti-negro society." The *Indianapolis Recorder* concluded its Decatur coverage with the following remarks: "The anti-negroites in the city declare that, as the city is now cleared of negroes, they will keep it so, and the importation of any more will undoubtedly result in serious trouble." The *Indianapolis News* article, on the other hand, contextualized the incident in a larger statewide discussion on Black people. It preceded the coverage of the Decatur incident with: "From several sections of the State there have come stories of the maltreatment of negroes" and followed it with: "It is hard to believe that there could be such a condition of things in Indiana." About the Indiana experience, the paper further noted that although Indiana "had little to no persecution of men because of their race," there was "no doubt that the negro is thought less well of than he was a few years ago [as] Some of his best friends have turned against him and lost patience with him."[53] Articles like these help us understand how Indiana communities (re)established the all-white nature of their towns and how the residents avidly committed to maintaining their whiteness.

Other historical events around the turn of the century include urban outbreaks of violence, and the 1903 riot in Evansville probably ranks among the most infamous. Though these violent encounters in Evansville and Greensburg (1907) may have resulted in the (in)voluntary resettlement of Black residents, with both of these riot locations losing 15.4 percent and 33.1 percent of their Black population, respectively, between 1900 and 1910, Black people continued to migrate to and live in Indiana. Yet, historical county records such as county histories and survey requests from the Indiana Historical Society fail to reflect that reality. The incomplete knowledge about African

Americans in Indiana and the weak survey responses on the Black experience are of a piece. They represent two ways that whiteness has been silently instantiated in Indiana.

Despite the absence of official Jim Crow laws in Indiana, calls for segregated schooling became louder, especially after the turn of the twentieth century. Public schools were already designated for white children's education as early as 1843; no language on the education of Black children was included in the *Revised Laws of Indiana, 1843*. Yet this oversight was corrected in 1869. State legislators passed a law requiring communities to construct schools for Black children if there were enough, but if there were not enough Black children, the law clarified that they may attend the same public school as white children.[54] Some locales, such as Lafayette in Tippecanoe County, immediately seized the opportunity to segregate classrooms, and others educated children of both races together.

However, with the state's increasing Black population, white residents soon presented the many "advantages" of segregated schooling, as this Wayne County example illustrates. On July 3, 1907, a Richmond newspaper ran an article entitled "Segregation is Advocated," featuring the county's superintendent in favor of segregated schooling—all to the benefit of the "colored children," as there is evidence that "colored children who have had the public school and college education provided for them in institutions where the races do not intermingle are said to be superior in intelligence to those who have not had this training." Simultaneously, the article reaffirms the continued presence of white Hoosier hostility toward Black folk at the beginning of the twentieth century. The author asserted that a "colored school" would allow "colored teachers" to return to the county for employment because, after all, they had the mandatory qualifications to teach in the school system but tended to avoid Wayne County for teaching opportunities. The reason is simple: "They have shown the requisite ability but there is no township trustee who would consider favorably a proposition to place a colored teacher in charge of white children."[55] Myrtle Parker, who studied at Indiana University to become a teacher, ended up teaching not in Clinton County but in "colored schools" in Birmingham, Alabama, and Atlanta, Georgia. Thus, preventing qualified Black teachers from pursuing their career in Indiana became one strategy of maintaining white residents' schools and counties as white as possible.

The turn of the century in Indiana brought lynchings, race riots, Southern Club call-outs, and school segregation, showing that *non*belonging and marginalization remained a reality for Black Hoosiers in the twentieth century. Exploring Black experiences in Indiana throughout the twentieth century will reveal how white Hoosiers continued to exclude Black Hoosiers from life in Indiana, exposing overt collective practices as well as invisible forms of erasure, exclusion, and marginalization. Segregated spaces, lynchings, and the Klan represent some of the collective practices of exclusion and demarcate the geography of hate.

Navigating the White State: Black Experiences in Twentieth-Century Indiana

Though Jim Crow laws were not the law of the land, segregated life had become the norm of twentieth-century Indiana society. Forced by custom and convention and inspired by other Black people living in communities both large and small, African American Hoosiers took it on themselves to build parallel, albeit segregated, institutions to meet their needs. One such need would be a vacationing spot in nature. Because African Americans were banned from vacationing at white resorts, Black resorts formed. One such example is Fox Lake, where most of the "property owners, cottage renters, and visitors are Black." It was the only Black resort in Indiana and one of a few in the Midwest, located in northern Indiana's Steuben County. The resort developed during the 1930s, as "In those days, the surrounding lakes were populated entirely by whites, and there was an *unspoken rule* that 'coloreds'—as they were called then—weren't welcome."[56]

Unspoken and/or unwritten rules frequently appear in publications that describe Black experiences in twentieth-century Indiana. They applied to the housing and real estate market across the state: "In Indianapolis there was said to be an *unwritten* rule among members of the Real Estate Board that no member would sell a house to a Negro unless there were already two Negro families in the block involved."[57] It is this tacit understanding that allows a Century 21 broker to demonstrate blissful ignorance in 1982: "For some reason, blacks have really congregated at Fox Lake."[58] The silence, denial, and ignorance compel research into the ways white northerners achieved Jim Crow segregation while putting on an otherwise hospitable face to the world. The fact that they did not keep a written record of these rules allowed them to maintain this impression of hospitality throughout the century, all while smilingly excluding people of color from their communities.

The lack of diversity often served as a point of pride for white Hoosier communities as it enabled them to demonstrate who mattered in the community and why. For example, a Clinton County newspaper ran various advertisements in the summer of 1925, praising the fact that "Frankfort has the smallest foreign population of any town its size in the United States." This lack of foreigners, according to those ads, "prevents various social evils, such as extremes of poverty and wealth, labor troubles, and race riots." Similarly, a story run in an Adams County newspaper proclaimed that "Monroe Township has one Indian child of school age. Not a Negro in the county. No other county in the state can say as much."[59] Both presses underlined that African Americans did not belong—the former did so more surreptitiously through the "foreigner" label, and the latter did not mince words.

Indiana county histories further illuminate the marginalized, ostracized, and excluded position African Americans occupied in Indiana's racialized landscape. Every fifty years, so it seems, Indiana counties have captured their progress since the inception of the state and of their respective counties, painting a perfect picture of their county's history, its residents, and its cities as well as townships, often omitting the less pleasant events. The first batch of county history publications can be dated around 1880, the second one between the 1910s and 1920s, and the latest one between 1970 and 1980.[60] The county histories published in the twentieth century either expand on the first achievements of their county, captured in the 1880 volumes, or focus on the county's relevance in the twentieth century.

County histories from the early twentieth century rarely comment on Black experiences. If they do, they provide insight into the white minds in the county. Joseph Claybaugh's 1913 *History of Clinton County, Indiana* served as an example to open this chapter. Another example is Frank M. Gilbert's *History of the City of Evansville and Vanderburg County Indiana* [*sic*], published in 1910. Located in the most southern part of the state, Evansville experienced a rapid increase in its Black population ever since the Civil War, too fast for many white Hoosiers, as the community experienced its first race riot in 1865. The most recent violent racial outbreak took place in 1903. Gilbert was an established newspaper owner and editor in Evansville praised for his wit. In his county history, he reflects on the Black community in the city as follows:

> One of the greatest evils with which we are confronted at the present, is the horde of little negroes who are growing up. They seem to have reverted and are lazy, idle, expert thieves and natural born liars. I have seen hundreds and hundreds of cases where it seemed impossible for them to tell the truth about anything. They refuse to go to school, wear clothes that ought to put them back in the forests of Africa, prowl through alleys committing all sorts of evils and when they are caught, immediately proceed to shed tears and draw on their well-worn stock of ready lies. The average police man does not believe one story one of these little fellows tells and in this he is right. Just how to combat this evil I do not know, but this city would be a great deal better off if quite a number of these youthful savages were

set outside of its limits forever. They are not the children of respectful and self-respecting parents. They are the offspring of the worthless niggers.[61]

As a newspaper man, Gilbert was most likely well aware of the concerns and attitudes in the local white community, which makes the passage more representative of the town. The language is dehumanizing and invokes disturbing images and stereotypes of Black people prevalent in Indiana at the time. Gilbert used the same degrading tone that was used in the 1880s newspapers when the first wave of Black migrants reached Hoosier land. While we learn about his disregard for Black children, we actually do not know whether Evansville schools were segregated in those years. The passage affirms once more the inhospitable and racist environment that Black migrants to the state faced.

The Sesquicentennial Historical Record Commemorating the 150th Anniversary of Union County, Indiana (1971) and *The 1979 History of Adams County, Indiana* (1979) are two examples published in the latest wave of county histories that deserve further exploration here, as they indicate strongly diverging approaches toward Black history in their counties. The former contains the chapter entitled "Early 'Colored' Settlers of Union County," written by Elizabeth H. Rile Kelley. In the opening of her chapter, Rile Kelley acknowledges the difficulties of tracing early Black arrivals to the area and their acceptance, explicitly noting the missing history as: "The true and accurate facts of how they were accepted at first are either not recorded or they are lost." She continues, asserting without evidence: "But, suffice it to write, now, that many of them found helpful, trusting, encouraging and lasting friends among their Caucasian neighbors."[62] It remains unclear how she arrived at this conclusion if records were not kept. The "now" might also refer to the time of her writing, 1971; however, in that case it is a rather bold claim, as the 1970 census lists only thirty Black residents in the county out of a population of 6,582 (0.5 percent). Despite her acknowledged lack of available resources, Rile Kelley states that African Americans "soon adjusted to the tolerant environment and perhaps for the first time in their lives these 'coloreds' began to experience partial dignity and develop the self-respect of a human being, a whole person, and to enjoy the unity of an unbroken family." Rile Kelley continues her entry with a tone that resembles entries in the Negro registers that were once in place in Indiana, and maybe Union County, stating that "newcomers to Union County came in various shades and hues of tan and brown coloring. Rarely were they generally or truly pure black."[63] She uses this description to transition into accounts of two Black men in Union County who were among the early arrivals, one a free Black man and one a runaway slave. It is in this passage that she identifies herself as a descendant of the two men.

Written in the early 1970s, Rile Kelley's remarks raise some troubling questions for various reasons. First, as a reader, one questions why the author had to qualify the county as a "tolerant environment." What exactly sparked the qualifier, who questioned the level of minority acceptance, what kind of incidents occurred that would make people think otherwise, and does the author know more than she is sharing? These are some of the questions that could arise. Second, what led the author to describe Black living experiences in Union County as developing feelings of "dignity," self-worth, "a whole person" and "unbroken family"? These descriptors recall the imagery of slavery, no question, but should one infer that the same stigma of Black people held true outside of the South and more than a century after slavery was abolished? Her family has been native to Union County for more than a century, so how does this analogy position her family? And how true does it ring for the time of her writing? Third, what is the intent of whitening the newcomers by emphasizing that most of them actually were not "truly pure black"? Does the whitening help acceptance in the community? Reading Rile Kelley's entry closely, many things were unsaid. With much being unsaid, Rile Kelley's descriptions of early Black arrivals in Union County resemble Gilbert's reflection on Black people in Evansville in 1910 to some extent. Though sixty years apart, both authors degrade African Americans and imply white superiority. The fact that Rile Kelley herself is a person of color underlines the power of the white spatial imaginary and the white habitus even further. She might have simply adopted the tone and tenor of her environment.

Unlike the aforementioned county history examples, *The 1979 History of Adams County, Indiana* does not shy away from dark historical moments, covering various "taboo" topics, such as lynching, Black people in the county, the Ku Klux Klan, and the Horse Thief Detective Association. Unlike Rile Kelley, editor Dick Heller did not leave things unsaid about Adams County and Indiana. Heller was a native of the county and was the publisher of the *Decatur Daily Democrat* for almost three decades. Thus, like Gilbert, he might have had a good idea about the attitudes concerning race in the local community.

The entry about "Blacks in Adams County" establishes the cloak of white supremacy and illustrates the invisibility and normalcy of Indiana's white culture of exclusion and inhospitality that characterize the geography of hate. The opening paragraph reads as follows:

> Adams County's record toward blacks, Chicanos, Indians, and other "foreign" races has been generally that of rural, white America—terrible. While Mexican-Americans have been tolerated as laborers, first in the sugar beets and later in the tomato fields and factories, and even Jamaican blacks have been permitted to pick tomatoes, the race record here has been a bad one.[64]

In plain language, Heller sets the tone of the entry while stating an unpleasant yet real aspect of Indiana history. The simple, matter-of-fact tone continues when he describes the *white* residents of Adams County in the next paragraph: "The average resident believes there are no Negroes here, never have been, and probably never will be. This is not at all true, but it is the sentiment and feeling of the overwhelming majority of the people here."[65] Here, Heller teases out how Black folk are erased in residents' self-perceived, imagined white community. They did not exist in the white habitus of Adams County residents.

As an editor of one of the county's dailies, Heller took it on himself to berate past Adams County print media coverage, stating that "the Adams County newspapers that we have seen, without exception, were violently anti-Negro, from 1857 until the early 1900's—using language that is totally unacceptable today." To illustrate his point, Heller lets the newspapers speak for themselves, providing plenty of evidence that Adams County did not spare any efforts to paint Black people in a negative light and excluded them whenever possible. Descriptions like "black demon" and "burly nigger" accompany an 1891 controversy, in which a Black person allegedly performed an abortion on a white woman that resulted in her death. Consequently, "The people of Willshire are raising up in their might against the colored population which has infested the region for some time past, and it seems from the present indications that there will be a Negro exodus take [*sic*] place within a short time." Even speculations about potential lynchings were circulated in print around that time, resulting in absurd headlines like "A BIG SCARE one of the funniest 'lynch' stories ever read" and "Are they going to lynch tonight?"[66] Lynching is connected to amusement, and who is "they" referring to if not white folk? So wouldn't it have been more accurate to ask, "Are we going to lynch tonight?" The answer must be no if one intends to preserve the community's white innocence by distancing oneself from any potential lynch mob.

Another attempt to rid the town of Decatur of Black people was made in 1902 after a Black man allegedly made "insulting remarks to a young lady." This is the same incident mentioned above that caught the attention of the *Freeman,* the *Indianapolis Star*, and the *New York Times*. With this account, we get to know the reason. The absence of a racial identifier suggests that the young lady the Black man allegedly approached was white. The incident resulted in threats of violence to every Black person not leaving the town by a set deadline. Eventually "the disturbance had the desired effect, and not a member of the dark race may now be found within the limits of the city, and it seems they will never be able to have very comfortable headquarters here." Subsequent newspaper reports in 1903 and 1905 confirm the discouragement of Black settlement.[67]

As a county history, Heller's matter-of-fact descriptions of racial antipathy as an unpleasant reality stand out. Also unique is his unearthing of the county's sundown past, labeling these all-white communities as "sundown" towns, and his observation that in the early 1960s, "Indiana law still [forbade] miscegenation, or intermarriage of races" when describing an interracial couple's attempt to settle in Decatur.[68]

This brief survey of various county histories published in Indiana over time illustrates the consistent and continuous nature of white Hoosier hostility toward African Americans. At times, the writers explicitly conveyed the county people's attitudes and opinions. In other instances, they adopted the prevalent tone to reflect on Black experiences, leaving many things unsaid. Regardless of the extent of bluntness, the tone and demeanor of the writing, and whether the shared opinions reflect the writers' personal attitudes, we learn from the county histories how preconceived notions and degrading stereotypes were nourished in Indiana, perpetuated over time, and contributed greatly to creating an unwelcoming environment for people of color.

The firm stance in anti-Blackness and belief in white supremacy build the foundation for the geography of hate. This chapter documented Indiana's legal and social history as it pertains to Black experiences. It is not a pretty race record. From its nascent stage, white Hoosiers perceived, designated, and maintained Indiana as a white space. State laws and their enactment on a county level reminiscent of the Jim Crow South attest to it. Though geographically located in the North, Indiana subscribed to racialized citizenship ideals that did not encompass African American citizens. I showed how their citizenship was actively contested and undermined on a town, county, and state level.

The Parkers lived in Clinton County, Indiana, through many of these citizen-infringing law changes until they no longer could. The community's accompanying hostile attitudes most likely resulted in their final departures—pursuing life and happiness in other communities, large and small, but with a larger Black community at their side.

The prevalent geography of hate marginalized Black Hoosiers in structural, discursive, and institutional ways. The various exclusionary and inhospitable histories of different counties in Indiana, taken together, reveal the larger processes at work, namely exclusionary practices that made counties inhospitable to Black migrants, selective memories that actively and passively forgot inglorious moments of the past, and ultimately the continuation of these racist and inhospitable practices over time. In short, the geography of hate in Indiana is an intricate quilt of laws, acts and actions, threats, landmarks, newspaper headlines, documents, and memories, all of which produce an unwelcoming environment for people of color.

Before interrogating white desires in Indiana further, we must revisit one of the most pivotal moments in the twentieth century to impact American life. We must advance the conversation on the Great Migration to include small-town America and small-town Indiana. Here we turn to a new understanding of how the Great Migration affected every American in every hamlet—regardless of whether migrants settled there.

CHAPTER 2

Crossroads of Desires

> Frankfort one of the most beautiful and home-like cities is situated in the northwestern part of the state and it has five steam railroads and two interurban lines coming and going every hour. There are about twenty colored families who own their homes. Some are in business and others are holding good positions. There is one church, mixed schools, and a K. of P. Lodge of about thirty members.
>
> J. D. Kersey and Jos. Parker own the leading barber shops and have all the modern conveniences known to the art. Nat Powell represents the race in the way of federal appointments as mail carrier, he is also chairman of the Endowment Board of the Grand Lodge K. of P. In the graded schools there are about twenty pupils. Misses Esther and Ruth Harper attend High School.
>
> —*Indianapolis Recorder*, Feb. 25, 1911, p. 3

> Pretty much the African American population moved, migrated to the cities rather than the country.
>
> —Rick, retired farmer and Clinton County resident, October 2016

This "portrait" of Frankfort, Clinton County, heralding opportunities for Black folk in small-town Indiana, was featured in the *Indianapolis Recorder*, Indiana's most prominent Black newspaper. The beginning of the twentieth century marks a time when many southern Black people started to contemplate alternatives to sharecropping by moving out of the South. The first paragraph, with its emphasis on home ownership, mixed schools, and transportation, reads like an invitation to potential migrants who would like to relocate to northern small-town America. The message is reinforced in the second paragraph, highlighting the different professions available for Black residents in Frankfort. The K. of P. (Knights of Pythias, a fraternal organization) is mentioned twice, underlining the importance of community-oriented social organizations so people could interact with each other and offer mutual support. These two paragraphs speak to the dreams southern Black migrants later expressed explicitly in their letters to northern Black newspapers like the *Chicago Defender*. That these aspirations were not far-fetched can be seen in the portrait above about Frankfort.

Yet, many people in Indiana believe that the Great Migration did not affect small-town Indiana, as the second epigraph illustrates. Rick's statement reflects what we all seem to know about this historical phenomenon, framing it as a mass movement from the rural South to the urban North. But the narrative about the Great Migration as we know it does not fit Black migrants' experiences in small-town Indiana. And southern Black migrants did land in Indiana towns like Frankfort during that time. For example, Albert William Idle, native of North Carolina, and his wife, Jeanette, rented a house in 1910 and owned one in 1920. However, by 1930, the couple had relocated to a Black neighborhood in Indianapolis. Samuel Culpepper, a native of Kentucky, worked as a porter in Frankfort in 1920 but does not appear in any local records thereafter. Similarly, Mattie Williams, another Kentucky native, worked as a servant in a local hotel in 1920 but was no longer in Frankfort during the next census. John Green, a native of Nashville, Tennessee, chose Frankfort "as a resting place and is employed at a local barber shop" in early 1929, but he was not registered in the manuscript census only a year later.[1] Alexander and Mollie Andrews made their way up from Kentucky sometime between 1910 and 1920 and rented a house in town. By 1930, their work as farm laborer, cook, and janitor paid off, as they were homeowners. However, Alex died in Indianapolis in 1936, indicating that he had left Clinton County despite home ownership. Frankfort, Indiana, was indeed a destination for southern Black migrants, but the foregoing examples attest to the transitory nature of their stays in the small-town Midwest. Thus, despite amicable small-town portraits like the one shared in the epigraph, the question remains: why didn't Black residents stay permanently in small-town Indiana? This chapter and the book overall answer this question.

* * *

The geography of hate serves as a conduit to explain what we know about both the Great Migration and the small-town Midwest. African Americans lived in small-town Indiana, yet we barely know anything about their destinies in these locales. Against the backdrop of the Great Migration, we learn how Black Americans—though present in small-town America—were made invisible in the midwestern landscape and the stories about the Great Migration.

Scholars describe the Great Migration as a gateway to freedom and liberty for southern Black Americans. This chapter rejects the conventional wisdom of the Great Migration as a relocation effort by Black migrants exclusively from the rural South to the urban North and the Midwest as this big white region. It demonstrates instead the interplay among these notions and how they shaped and overshadowed—and thus made invisible—Black experiences in the small-town Midwest.

In general, Great Migration narratives focus on leaving the oppressive sharecropping South to achieve full citizenship rights in the North. In their zeal to frame the migration phenomenon in the urban context of the North, scholars seemingly overlooked the fact the North is more than metropolises like Chicago, Philadelphia, and New York City.[2] Equating the Great Migration with the urban North[3] clouds the answer to a seemingly logical question if one expresses the wish to leave one's home: Where to? I embarked on this research journey because I struggled to accept "the lure of the big city" as the only answer. The switch from the plight on the southern farm to the anticipated better life in the urban industrial North seemed incomplete, if not unlikely. While leaving a place that denies basic human and civil rights, including obtaining an education and casting a vote, makes sense, the change in career choice does not. Black southerners were deprived of educational and job opportunities in the South, and farming guaranteed survival for them and their families since emancipation. Reaping the benefits of American citizenship and opportunity in arable environments therefore constitutes a suitable alternative to the rural citizenship-depriving South. Assuming that the emancipatory desires for northern liberalism excluded rural environments overlooks how labor and work practices, as well as imagined quality of life in the North, equally shaped interests to go North. With its focus on the interstitial spaces between the rural South and the urban North, the geography of hate becomes a tool and a lens to trace the Great Migration to small-town America and beyond.

However, the scholarly predilection for the urban environment makes sense. Many migrants ended up in cities and transformed many urban neighborhoods, work sites, and community institutions by their presence, even though they didn't anticipate settling in cities. For example, Chicago was a major destination for southern migrants. While Chicago grew in size, it simultaneously became a pioneer in and major research hub for ethnographic research, with the University of Chicago as the front-runner in the field of sociology. St. Clair Drake and Horace R. Cayton offered a panoramic account of Black life in Chicago in the first half of the twentieth century in *Black Metropolis*. Within the broader context of U.S. racism and exclusion, the authors detailed life, thoughts, attitudes, and customs on the South Side of Chicago. Studying the clusters of migrant groups in the areas that surrounded the university certainly facilitated establishing ethnographic research as a major component in sociological scholarship. However, the problem with this approach is the underlying assumption or generalization that *all* migrants went to the cities and that the study subjects represent *all* migrant experiences. And the same strategy of emphasizing the urban migrant experience was applied in writings during the era of the Great Migration, be they academic or journalistic. The cities seemingly were the exclusive destinations for southern Black migrants. Consequently, their experiences and interactions in the small-town Midwest became invisible and remained hidden, manifesting whiteness as a way of life in a region already imagined as white.

However, investigating whether and how people migrated to rural spaces is not unusual or atypical. Anyone familiar with the history of the Exodusters will ask not so much why southern Black people decided to leave the South, but rather where to. In *Exodusters*, Nell Irvin Painter explores the "rural-to-rural migration" of southern African Americans to Kansas.[4] This exodus to the Promised Land preceded the Great Migration by three decades, culminating between 1879 and 1881. Before the exodus to Kansas and ever since emancipation, Black people had frequently moved westward to the frontier South, which already indicated their desire to continue farming. The "Kansas Exodus," as it came to be known, was the first major attempt for Black people to relocate outside of the South. Painter's study explicates Black southerners' desperate and disenfranchising conditions that also became push factors during the Great Migration. Painter notes about the letters written by Black southerners around the time of the Kansas Exodus, "Almost without fail, the first question concerned terms under which land could be acquired. . . . Unequivocally, Black farmers in the South desired above all else to own their own land and to be independent farmers."[5] When it became clear that desires for land ownership and independence were, for the most part, unattainable in the South, southern Black farmers looked to the North to pursue these desires. But the focus of the Great Migration scholarship implies that these rural desires must have changed entirely within one generation, as migrants in the twentieth century allegedly flocked into the cities exclusively.

This chapter revisits the desires for land ownership, enriching the urban-only narrative of the Great Migration in the twentieth century. I will demonstrate that southern Black migrants did have a desire to settle in the Promised *Land* of the North—*land* meaning literally owning land, farming, and living a small-town life. These voices stand in stark contrast to the print media articles of the time, which presented the relocation of southern Black migrants overwhelmingly in urban terms and thus explains the scholarly focus on the urban destinations. While most migrants landed in big cities, this is not the whole story. A close examination of the in-between spaces along the migration corridor is warranted, as most of these communities that surrounded the big cities were or became overwhelmingly (if not exclusively) white during the same time. This juxtaposition of African Americans' desire for land and small-town life with white attitudes and policies that undermined and prevented Black settlement in the same space will help us understand why most Black southerners ended up in the big northern cities *despite* rural desires. Following the path of rural desires to the small-town Midwest begins to unveil the geography of hate, unmasking previously hidden mechanisms and invisible practices that caused such unwelcoming environments.

Excavating Black Migrants' Rural Desires

Because the Great Northern Drive[6] happened a century ago, finding migrants who participated in the first wave of the Great Migration is nearly impossible. I interviewed one participant, William,[7] who was less than a year old at the time of the family's departure from Birmingham, Alabama, to Chicago in the summer of 1919. Though he did not have any personal memories of the family's motives for leaving the South and deciding where to settle, he grew up fostering the narrative that he already knew at this young age that the South was not a good place for Black folk. In his own words, "The humorous story goes like this: Things were so bad and having the attitude of my father, when I was eight months old, I looked around in Birmingham and saw what was going on, and I said to my mother 'shit, I'm leaving here.' So, I brought my family to Chicago." He provides this caveat, explaining his sarcasm: "Now I tell it that way to humorize it, but also to give the reader and the listeners an idea of how bad the South is."[8]

Knowingly or unknowingly, Emmett J. Scott captured Black migrants' rural desires in two collections of migrant letters, published in the summer and fall of 1919.[9] As Special Assistant for Negro Affairs to the Secretary of War in the Woodrow Wilson administration, he looked into all matters affecting life and interests of Black soldiers and citizens during World War I. The Great Migration was one major ongoing event that affected the Black population during his tenure in the Department of War. His compilations of migrant letters capture how. These written memories of Great Migration migrants elucidate expressed (yet unfulfilled) hopes for the North, the Promised Land. Although most Black migrants ended up in big cities, the letters demonstrate that many of them did not necessarily anticipate that to be their destiny.

The letters indicate the major city and state from which they were sent, but none of the authors signed their letters. On the contrary, some writers specifically asked for their letter not to be published, fearing potential repercussions once their desires to leave the South came to be known. Scott honored their requests and compiled letters anonymously. Scott understood the purpose of his compilations to be providing "information concerning the Negroes in the North . . . where the Negroes settled, what they engaged in, and how they have readjusted themselves in the new situation."[10] The statement appears slightly exaggerated, as only the last fourteen letters in "Additional Letters" were written by migrants who had relocated in the North by the time they sent the letter. Although the letters do not reveal where the prospective southern migrants settled or whether they left the South at all, we can retrieve from the letters where they *anticipated* or *desired* to settle. With that in mind, I am reading these letters with the specific purpose of demonstrating that Black southerners had the desire to and eventually left their southern homeland, but not exclusively to relocate to the urban industrial centers, as the dominant Great Migration narrative wants us to believe. Instead, migrants expressed specific desires to settle in smaller towns and more rural areas that resembled the environment they would leave behind.

The letters document how migrants approached leaving the South. They identified economic, political, and cultural factors that shaped their decisions while emphasizing their aspirations for a better life elsewhere. Two in five migrants did not include any references to desired locations. The writers instead described their work experiences and skills for various jobs in which they could envision themselves. At times, they included their physical descriptions, their family status, and requests for transportation for themselves and others. In other instances, the letters simply expressed the utmost desire to leave the southern soil behind. The letters exude the migrants' agency, confirming that "They were choosers, makers, and doers," as historian Florette Henri has aptly noted.[11]

Regarding geographical references, 121 letters, or 40.9 percent of all letters, express the desire to simply go "North."[12] This is important because it voices the desire to leave the South behind—at least the oppressive structures of the South that also come with uncertain and insecure economic incomes and unsatisfactory civic, social, and educational conditions. Yet the fact that the "North" is always synonymous with "urban" seems to be an academic interpretation of the Great Migration. Early works on the Great Migration actually agreed that most migrants were sharecroppers with little experience in urban life, yet scholars rarely inquired why the city was the only destination.[13] Instead, scholars shifted their stance on "prior" urban experiences in the South before coming North. For example, environmental historian Brian McCammack writes, "it seems that . . . many if not most migrants had significant urban experience before moving North, undertaking a step migration from the rural South to the urban South before making the leap to cities in the North."[14] Whereas I agree with McCammack's view on the step migration process, I am proposing yet another step before the leap to the city that might have taken place, instead of or in addition to the urban South experience, adding the rural North experience. Here are two potential alternative scenarios:

Rural South → Urban South → Rural North → Urban North
Rural South → Rural North → Urban North

The data are too sparse to know for sure, but both scenarios seem possible when we return our attention to the migrant letters. Slightly more than one-fifth of the letters (20.9 percent) contain explicit city references: sixty-two letter writers openly expressed the desire to relocate to a northern urban environment. Meanwhile, a little less than one-fifth (17.9 percent) of the letters contain small-town references: fifty-three letter writers indicated preferences for a small town, a more rural environment. Of all the letters that contain a reference to the North (n = 121 letters), almost one-fourth also include a reference to small towns (twenty-nine letters = 24.0 percent). The combination of North and city is less common, as only eighteen letters (14.9 percent) include city references when talking about desires to "go North." Six of all 296 letters contain references to all three categories—"It does not matter where, that is; as to city, country, town or state since you secure the positions."[15] Thus, geographical preferences expressed in the migrant letters do not support the Great Migration's all-too-familiar urban-only narrative. To illustrate their rural and small-town desires further, I let the migrants speak for themselves.

"Anywhere Up North"

One prospective migrant from Pensacola, Florida, writes, "*Dear Sir*: I seen in the Chicago Defender where men was wanted in small towns near Chicago at fair wages." A fellow Pensacolan would like to be put "in touch with a firm in a small size town, where it would send [him] a transportation." Another Floridian from St. Petersburg is "coming north and [wants] to know of a good town to stop in." Yet another Floridian, this time from Sanford, wants even more specific information "about conditions in some small town near Chicago."[16] These four letters from Florida illustrate an important point. Regardless of their location of origin and its size (if we assume that the writers resided in or close to the post offices from which they mailed the letters), they all inquired about relocating to a small town in the North. Although the St. Petersburg and Sanford letter writers' desires for a small-town environment make sense, with both of these locales being small towns themselves (the 1910 populations, according to the U.S. Census Bureau, were 4,127 and 3,570, respectively), Pensacola residents were more accustomed to a somewhat urban environment, as it already had 22,982 residents in 1910. One could hypothesize that an adjustment to at least a medium-sized city environment for the Pensacola residents was easier, yet all these prospective migrants expressed interest in relocating to a northern small town.

Frequently, migrants express their small-town desires through metonymy. Some letters do not specify their desired locations or the type of locale they prefer, but they simply express the desire to leave the South and go "up there."[17] However, their small-town desires at times shine through indirectly when a migrant describes himself as a "good farmer" and a "Curch member" with a "niCe famely" or "a christians," maybe in an attempt to appeal to northern small-town residents.[18] In a similar vein, a carpenter from Anniston, Alabama, plans to come "north" and inquires if "you mite no of som good town in that secson."[19] Here, instead of describing himself as a "good" person, the migrant is in search of a "good" town, another preferred metonymy for a "typical small town."

Often, migrants are more outspoken in their letters and map out their anticipated new life in the North. This Alabamian, for example, does not shy away from expressing his explicit desire to relocate to and pursue business opportunities in a small town in the North:

> *Gentlemen*: Gentlemens desious of Settling in some Small Northern Town With a modrate Population & also Where a Colored man may open a business Also where one may receive fairly good wedges for a While ontill well enough azainted with Place to do a buiseness in other words Wonts to locate in Some Coming town Were agoodly no, of colard People is.[20]

Not everyone is explicit in describing their anticipated business plans, but many migrants are explicit in their desire for a small-town environment when relocating to the North: one Memphian desires a "job in a small town some where in the north," while one New Orleanian requests advice on "a good place where I can get a good job out in some of the small places from Chicago about 50 or 60 miles." Indicating the distance from Chicago, he makes clear that he would like to relocate in the North but is not attracted to the metropolis. Neither is this preacher from Starkville, Mississippi: "I dont care for the large city life I rather live in a town of 15 or 20 thousand."

These letters express socioeconomic uplift, as well as explicit desires for a small-town lifestyle.[21]

As the migrants sent their letters to the *Chicago Defender*, the most prominent Black weekly of the time with national readership, Chicago frequently serves as point of reference for the prospective migrants. Chicago is most likely the only place they could name, as the reputation of many small towns usually does not cross state borders. Thus, migrants hook themselves onto the familiar and express their small-town desires in relation to Chicago, like the New Orleanian above inquiring about "small places from Chicago about 50 or 60 miles." Likewise, a fellow New Orleanian writes, "I beg to state to you that if your could secure me a position in or around Chicago or any northern section with fairly good wages & good living conditions for myself and family." He repeats the same sentiment a little later.[22] Similarly flexible in his destination—in relation to (not in) the metropolis—is another fellow from Cedar Grove, Louisiana, asking about firms "of your city & your near by surrounding towns of Chicago." The inquiries frequently include phrases like "in or around Chicago" and "factory work in or out of the city will do," but also mention employment "with living wages, on tobacco farm or factory." Others indicate that they "are making preparation to come north and are not particular about coming to Chicago." Some letter writers include their conversations with recent returnees to the South to express their desire to go North, but "would rather be in some place. other then Chicago. or near Chicago."[23] Though Chicago is referenced in most of the examples, the desire for socioeconomic uplift is palpable. Thus, the letters also show livelihood and occupational desires, reflecting different practices of citizenship.[24]

"Why should they not seek homes in the rural parts of the North?" asked G. S. Dickerman in his 1917 editorial published in the *Crisis*, the national organ of the National Association for the Advancement of Colored People (NAACP). Dickerman wrote his editorial in response to a recent survey that identified most migrants stemming from the rural South. He answered his own question, stating:

> They are needed there. All good tillers of the soil are needed on northern farm lands as they never have been needed before in the history of the country. They are needed to help raise food crops, not only for this country, but for half a dozen other great countries on the brink of starvation.[25]

Dickerman used World War I to emphasize and explain the "need," a word he chose four times in the passage to illustrate the northern rural vacancies and underline his point that Black migrants should consider the rural North when leaving the South behind.

Dickerman's plea was heard if one considers other migrant letters. The idea of "Some of us like farm work" is expressed throughout the letters, underlining the fact that not all southern Black migrants were attracted to the big city and planning to sacrifice their occupational livelihoods.[26] The fact that they wrote the letters demonstrates their interest in leaving the South behind—regionally/geographically but not environmentally/occupationally—as the references to farming indicate. After all, "this are farming people they were raised on the farm and are good farm hands." Writing on behalf of "15 or 20 familys," an Alabamian explains that "the greater part are farmers & good worker & honest people" in his letter that details Black folk's plight in the South. He reinforces the desire for farm labor later in his letter again: "We want to imigrate to the farmers who *need* our labor."[27] Though written five months earlier, the letter reads like a response to Dickerman's plea. Another one writes, "I am expecting to come with my family to your town, or some smaller town near you, in the near future. Would like to farm near Chicago or some small town near Chicago where my children can have good educational advantages."[28] Again, Chicago serves only as a reference point for the general desire to relocate north of the Mason-Dixon line; the emphasis is on the small-town farm lifestyle.

Some writers even explain that they are waiting to finish the harvesting season in the South before wanting to go up North—another way to stress their close ties to farming that they would like to continue outside of the geographical South:

> *Sir:* I am looking for a place to locate this fall as a farmer. Do you think you could place me on a farm to work on shares. I am a poor farmer and have not the money to buy but would be glad to work a mans farm for him. . . . I will be ready to leave here this fall after the harvest is layed by. I am planting cotton.[29]

The letter attests to the fact that, regardless of work, Black migrants desired to leave the South—and some indeed preferred maintaining their connection to the land. This humble request does not even anticipate land ownership in the North, but it strongly identifies the man's desire to stay in the farming occupation.

Dickerman also entertained the idea of land ownership in his editorial. After indicating that "Here on the farms, too, are the finest prospects for accumulating property and becoming independent landowners," he recognizes that, "Of course, it will be the best way to begin as a hired farm hand, for this is the path to acquaintance with the methods of northern farming and the friendly relations with the neighborhood where one is at work." Circling back to his argument for landownership opportunities, he continues, "But one should not rest satisfied with being a mere farm hand. He should make up his mind at the start to buy some land as soon as he has the money to pay for it, and this should be kept steadily in view, till he has a farm and a home of his own."[30] And one can find evidence of a similar thought process in the migrant letters. A prospective migrant from Pascagoula, Mississippi, implies the desire to buy land when writing: "We will work in any small town in Illinois. All of these men are property owners and have large families. We'll *leave* families 'till later on."[31] The information snippets of "property owner," "large families," and "'till later on" express these men's desire to achieve the same status as property owners in the North to provide for their "large families" once they reunite in the Promised Land.

Whereas most of the letters in Scott's compilations were sent from the geographical South, one letter was sent from the Midwest. A gentleman from Topeka, Kansas, is in search of bettering his position himself, noting the difficulties for Black folk in acquiring factory jobs in the Midwest. Recent *Chicago Defender* coverage of "some appearantly well organized league" that "found openings for negro workmen in some parts of Wis. and Ill. that could not be filled" may have encouraged him to consider relocation within the Midwest, though that is speculation. However, Wisconsin and Illinois are the only specific geographical references in his letter.[32] The letter was sent from Topeka, which already had a population of 43,684 by 1910, with 4,538 (or 10.4 percent) of them Black residents.[33] If Kansas was the Promised Land three decades prior, the situation for Black Kansans certainly deteriorated over time. Calls for school segregation became louder and more frequent since the beginning of the twentieth century, and discrimination became more prominent and widespread, including denial of services in restaurants and hotels. The expansion of discrimination in industry then undermined Black economic uplift and security even more drastically.[34] The deteriorated race relations that the letter writer lamented in 1917 might have been based on his inability to acquire a position in industry as a Black man, which was common in many midwestern cities at that time.

Kansas was not unique in implementing segregation and discrimination in many areas of public life. Particularly before World War I, jobs in northern industry were difficult to obtain for Black workers, as employers and unions openly discriminated. Black people at this point were mainly hired as strikebreakers, which fueled northern white hostility further.[35] With the rise of the Black population in the North, housing and school segregation became a widespread strategy to relocate Black folk to the margins of society. The stop to immigration and the World War I deployment, however, opened the industrial gates widely for Black workers—including in midwestern states. The Kansas letter is also important because it exemplifies that migrants who ended up in the industrial centers did not exclusively come from the South, and it speaks to one of the alternative step migration scenarios discussed above that included the rural North.[36]

Weighing their options, migrants still might have considered the Midwest the better alternative, despite discrimination. This notion, as well as desperation to leave the South, seems to be the only constant in the letters. For example: "too glad to come north east or west, any where but the south," "Anywhere north will do us and I suppose the worst place there is better than the best place here," and "it makes little or no difference as to what state they can go to just so they cross the Mason and Dixie line."[37] In his second compilation, Scott sorted the letters according to the main themes expressed in them: employment and educational opportunities, as well as the terror experienced in the South, dominated the canon. No matter the reasons the migrants listed, the desperation is palpable across the letters.

Whereas Scott's compilations of letters are by far the most famous reflection of migrant voices, other journalists also cited their experiences at that time. George Edmund Haynes, for example, quoted migrant letters to underline the hope for the Promised Land that the migrants expressed. None of the letters he used expressed explicit desires for a life in the city, but all emphasized the image of the liberating North.[38]

Another important journalistic voice in fleshing out post–World War I migrant experiences was Lester Walton, who dedicated various articles to the exodus from the South in 1922 and 1923. By 1922, Walton had established himself as a special writer for the *New York World*, a liberal vanguard newspaper of its time. Through his articles, he was able to share with the paper's readership why and how Black migrants left the South. What makes Walton's migration series stand out is that he gave a voice to the migrants from the second peak within the first wave of the Great Migration. Through his portrayal, we come to see many similarities between the migrants from 1922–23 and the migrants from 1879–80 participating in the exodus to Kansas. For example, Walton writes in 1923:

> These artless travelers possess an imagination elastic as that of a child of six indulging in fanciful reveries about the visit of Santa Claus. Crossing the Mason and Dixon Line to them is akin to entering another world. With sparkling eyes and faces wreathed in smiles they tell you with a display of animation what is nearest to their minds and hearts—*of a longing to live in a land where lynching is not a favorite pastime and where race discrimination in its various forms is not so pronounced.*[39]

Walton couches his main point—why the migrants leave—in lighthearted language of how a child sees the world to starkly contrast the violence southern Black folk were escaping. Walton's articles already echo the plight of Kansas Exodusters when looking at his headlines in 1923: "Negroes in Terror Fleeing the South; Whites Alarmed," "Cotton Fields Lie Weed Choked as Negro Stampedes," and "Negro Migrants Say Southerners Force Them Out."[40] Phrases like "in terror," "stampedes," and "force them out" illustrate the ad hoc and desperate departure of southern Black people because of unbearable living conditions while simultaneously causing a sigh of relief and understanding among the readership. Generally, the threat of violence and lynching was proportionately more emphasized in Walton's migrant testimonies than in Scott's compilations of migrant letters from 1916 to 1918. The aura of internal refugees that late-nineteenth-century Black migrants carried with them to Kansas resurfaced among the migrants leaving the South in the early 1920s. While Walton successfully conveyed the desperation and fear that led to escaping southern white violence, he could not anticipate and thus warn of the white violence these migrants would find upon arriving in the North. This book unmasks the northern white hostility, inhospitality, and exclusion Black migrants experienced once they acted on their rural desires and relocated to midwestern small towns.

The Topeka letter writer—like many others—notes recent *Chicago Defender* coverage pertaining to the southern outmigration to the North. Some letters specifically mention job advertisements outside of the big city that they encountered in the *Defender*:

> Concerning of labor as I was reading and advertisement of yours in the Chicago Defender stateing that those who wish to locate in smaller towns with fairly good wages to bring their children up with the best of education will kindly get in touch with you.
>
> *Sirs:* I was reading in the defender that theare was good openings for Men in Smalle towns near Chicago would like to know if they are seeking loborers or mechanics I am going to come north in a few days. . . . I am not particular about locateing in the city all I desire is a good position.[41]

The references about small-town life with the focus on educational and employment opportunities echo the Frankfort portrait from the *Indianapolis Recorder* in the epigraph. These examples attest to the fact that the *Chicago Defender* did not feature employment opportunities and job advertisements only in northern cities but also in northern small towns—a fact generally overlooked by migration scholars.

While an in-depth discussion of *Chicago Defender* small-town coverage is beyond the scope of this chapter, two examples will illustrate the paper's non-letter coverage of the rural North.[42] In 1924, for example, the *Chicago Defender* explicitly celebrates farmers, farming, and land ownership. The article reports on prospective migrants from the South "seeking to buy small tracts of land in Illinois, Indiana, Wisconsin and Iowa, states where diversified farming is the regular routine." It notes that "these migrators will not all be headed for the large Northern cities, but a goodly portion will settle on farms as owners, share-workers or help," speculating that this would "pave the way for land owning on a large and profitable scale by our people." It also appears as if the article directly speaks to the prospective southern migrants, noting, "We also realize that we have within our group a large percentage of men and women better fitted for this line of work than for any other" and concluding that "It is a hopeful sign when our farmers of the South, weighted down with unbearable living conditions, do not abandon their calling for the bright lights of the city, but seek more congenial environments where they may continue to till the soil and live in every sense of the world [*sic*]."[43] The article clearly spells out and supports Black rural desires, going as far as referring to farming as "their calling."

Similarly, the second example, entitled "Small Towns in Illinois Are Growing Fast," advocates life in midwestern small towns by contrasting the advantages of small-town life with the "congested centers of population." It notes the demographically diversifying impact of the Great Migration as follows:

> Recent conditions have brought about a considerable change in the homogenous character of the population of the Prairie state and these conditions of migration and settlement of thousands of our people from the southern country have largely affected the present status of the state of Illinois, it is reported. The experience of these migrants in farm labor and other work of the small cities and town districts has wielded considerable influence in stabilizing the present high standard of living conditions in the smaller towns of Illinois.[44]

The article then notes the recent unrest that had taken place in southern Illinois due to the migration but ends on the positive note that "conditions have improved and though still far from ideal, they present a more favorable impact than before the great influx. All these factors have entered into the plan of making Illinois the industrial opportunity of the immediate future and in converting its formerly small drowsy towns to live, thriving communities." This article resonates with the Topeka letter discussed above, as it acknowledges the hurdles Black newcomers might have faced in the Midwest by mentioning the difficulties small-town residents in Illinois had in adjusting to the newcomers.

The *Defender* also regularly published columns with news from various midwestern states. In these columns, state correspondents summarized happenings, visits, and achievements by Black residents of featured towns. They reported on recent travels or returns of their local Black residents. This way, they created a record of southern migrants settling in Indiana small towns, who previously called Henderson, Kentucky, or Memphis, Tennessee, home.[45]

These columns also confirm that Indiana towns were not oblivious to the ongoing Great Migration. On the contrary, some communities proactively pondered how to best cater to the southern newcomers. For example, the Civic League of Terre Haute announced an upcoming roundtable "discussion on the recent exodus of the Negro from the South" and plans to make the organization "a local branch of the National Urban League" in early 1917. The Civic League was a local nonpartisan political Black organization concerned with civic pride and community involvement that entertained the Terre Haute community with Emancipation celebrations, as well as lectures on city and neighborhood improvement.[46] The roundtable announcement from February 17, 1917, is important because it shows that this part of Indiana had either already witnessed an increase in its Black population or at least anticipated such an increase. A week later, the *Defender* reported on the event's outcome. Black Methodist church leader Rev. L. M. Hagood gave a speech on "The Migration of the Negroes from the South," which resulted in creating a local committee to "look into the best means of helping those who arrive."[47]

The migrant letters and *Chicago Defender* coverage demonstrate clearly that the urban-only narrative of the Great Migration is incomplete. Most letters simply expressed desires for a geographical relocation outside of the South. The difference between explicit city and small-town references is 3 percent (20.9 percent vs. 17.9 percent), or nine letters. The *Chicago Defender*, the organ for past and prospective migrants as well as employers across the North, included happenings in and ads for smaller locales. Let's return our attention to Indiana and see whether Black folk considered this primarily rural state a viable option to fulfill their desires for land and small-town prosperity.

Crossroads of Desires: Black and White Indiana during the Great Migration

The Great Migration recorded previously unseen population shifts in the United States—and Indiana was no exception. Black migrants did not only pass through the state, the self-designated crossroads of America, but also acted on their desires for land ownership, better education, and adequate pay

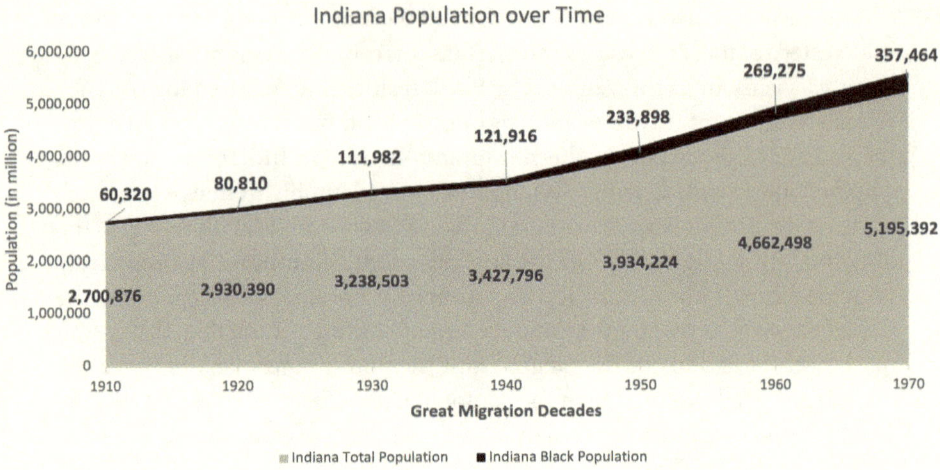

FIGURE 1. Population change in Indiana from 1910 to 1970

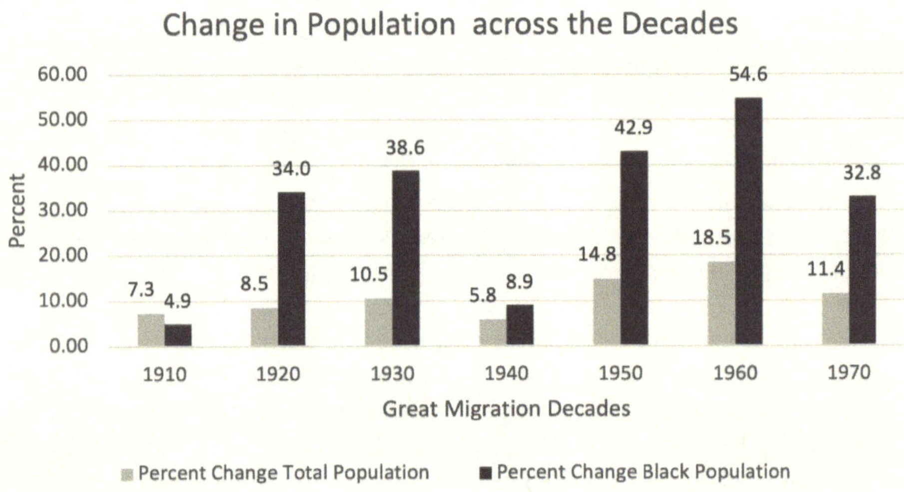

FIGURE 2. Percent change in Indiana population from 1910 to 1970

and settled in the state. Over the Great Migration decades alone, the state's Black population more than quintupled while the total population almost doubled (Figures 1 and 2). Figure 1 illustrates that Indiana's Black population, though overall a small percentage of the state's total population, was rising, particularly during the second wave of the Great Migration (1940–1970).

The second wave of the Great Migration also coincided with the publication of the *Negro Motorist Green Book*, commonly known as the *Green Book*.[48] Starting in 1936 and continuing for the next three decades, the *Green Book* listed establishments, including restaurants, hotels, and gas stations, that catered to Black customers, to facilitate road travel for Black travelers in the continental United States. With the rising Black population in Indiana during that time, we could expect more safe spaces for Black travelers in 1966–67, the last edition of the *Green Book*, compared to when Indiana establishments first appeared in the guide in 1939 (Map 4). Surprisingly, a closer look at the two publications disappoints, as the total number of individual locations and counties remains steady (thirty-four locations across fifteen counties), though we can see a slight shift in where the spots are located. Housing the largest Black population in the state, Marion County, with Indianapolis as its county seat, listed the highest number of safe spaces in the state, with seven in 1939 and nine in 1966–67. Despite the threefold increase in Indiana's Black population from 1940 to 1970, safe spaces in Indiana remained few and far between.

Map 5 maps the identified *Green Book* counties onto the change in Black population from 1940 to 1970 to discern whether there is a correlation between the number of Black residents and safe spaces listed in the *Green Book*. At the first glimpse, both maps in Map 5 look quite similar, despite three decades of continued Black migration into and across Indiana. When we look closer, however, we might notice a few interesting details—despite the unchanged number of *Green Book* locales. For example, despite an almost threefold increase in its Black population between 1940 and 1970, Indiana has the exact same number of counties with a nonexistent (or almost nonexistent) Black population—twenty-seven counties, or 29.3 percent. Also, there seems to be no obvious correlation between *Green Book* listings and Black population. Vigo County, in the western part of the state, has a similar percentage of Black residents in both years (4.06 percent in 1940 and 4.7 percent in 1970), yet it no longer has a safe space in 1970. In contrast, Knox County, in the southwestern part of the state, has a similar percentage in both years but added a safe location in 1966–67 (0.59 percent in 1940 and 0.84 percent in 1970). Madison County, in central Indiana, witnessed an increase in its Black population of close to 4 percent and had a Black population of 5.8 percent of the total county population in 1970, yet unlike in 1939, it no longer included a safe space in 1966–67.

In an attempt to locate, restore, and celebrate Black midwestern small-town achievements, I unearthed what Anna-Lisa Cox coined the "odd" mid-

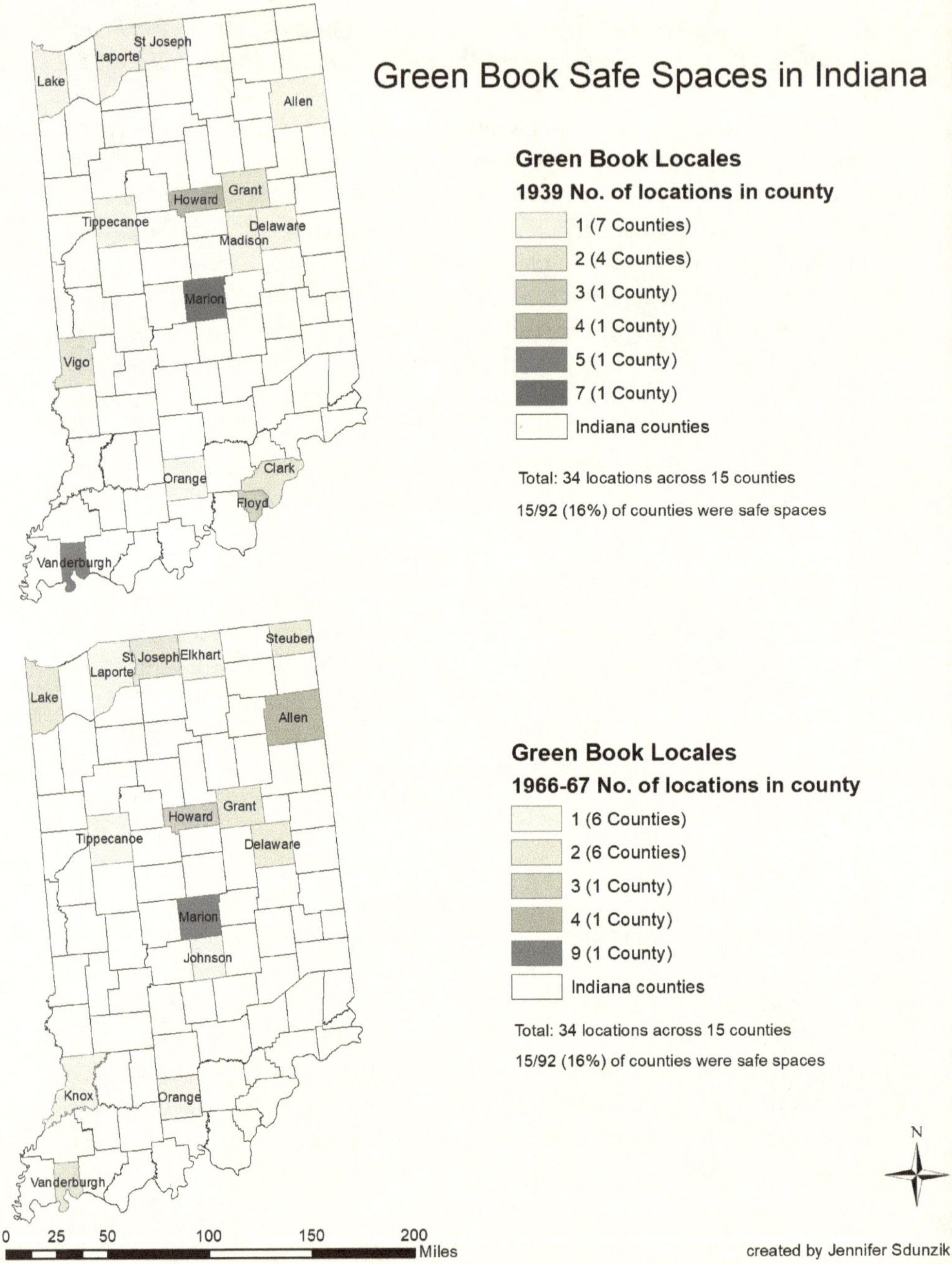

MAP 4. *Green Book* locales in Indiana, 1939 and 1966–67

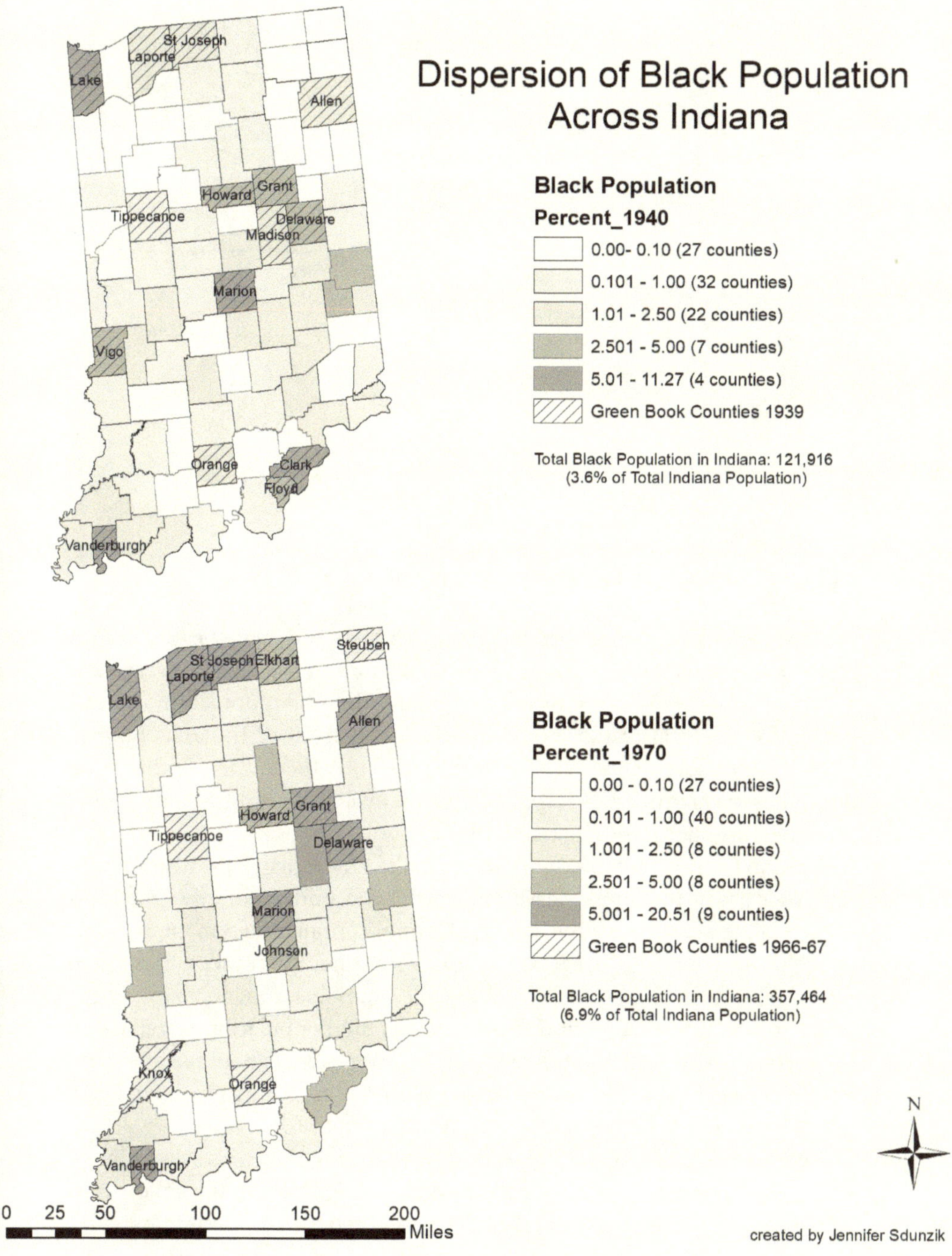

MAP 5. Indiana Black population in 1940 and 1970 with identified *Green Book* counties

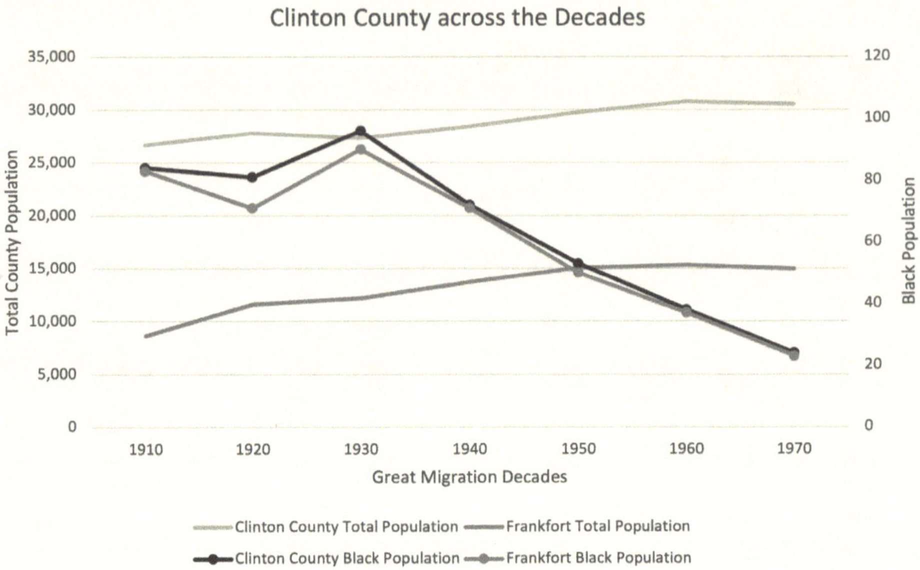

FIGURE 3. Clinton County population from 1910 to 1970

western racism, which "was not based on numbers and could be touched off by the presence of only one black person, or none at all."[49] Her observation seems accurate when considering the minuscule Black population (up to 1 percent of the total county population) of two-thirds of Indiana counties in 1970 (sixty-seven counties; see Map 5). Overall, the burden of this book lies in answering the question of why so many counties in the state visibly remained untouched by the rising Black population.

Clinton County and its county seat, Frankfort, the prime locations under investigation in this book, serve as a gateway to understand the phenomenon. Unlike the state at large, Clinton County's population remained steady over the course of the Great Migration, with a net difference of less than 4,000 inhabitants from 1910 to 1970. While Frankfort grew in size over the course of the Great Migration's first wave, its total population plateaued in the second wave, with a net difference of 1,250 residents between 1940 and 1970. However, the same cannot be stated for the county's minuscule Black population, where we observe a stark decline (Figure 3).

Indiana became the crossroads of desires during the Great Migration—where Black Hoosier desires for the pursuit of happiness in the small-town Midwest clashed with white Hoosier desires to keep their communities white. Figure 3 insinuates that African Americans started to abandon the small-town Midwest for other places, though we may not know their final destinations.

We do know, however, that Clinton County, like many other Indiana counties, became whiter as the state at large became blacker.

Black southern migrants wanted to settle in the small-town Midwest, and white midwesterners wanted to keep their communities white. How did this dynamic unfold in the national press? A brief discussion of how the national press covered the migration phenomenon while it was going on will elucidate the extent to which small-town America embraced Black or white desires.

White Supremacy by Home Address: Black Newcomers Meet White Midwestern Hostility

The Great Migration mattered in the national press.[50] The articles overwhelmingly discussed the migration's causes and consequences. Identified causes for the relocation included economic freedom and educational opportunities. Violence through the KKK and lynching, as well as voting and the boll weevil infestation of the cotton crops, were also listed as reasons for leaving the South. As the national press primarily derives from urban areas, it mainly discussed the consequences of the migration as city problems, ranging from job and housing discrimination to health and sanitation issues in the segregated, depleted areas, as well as an increase in violence (including riots) and crime. World War I was frequently identified as the catalyst of the migration stream, as it halted European immigration and increased demand for labor across the country.

The attempt to gauge small-town mentions produced the most obvious difference from the migration letters compiled by Emmett J. Scott, as small towns and rural areas in this canon were barely touched upon. Only 23.7 percent of articles that discuss the migration include small-town references (28 of 118 articles), in contrast to three times as many articles mentioning cities (85 of 118 articles). In Scott's compilation of migrant letters, city references slightly outweighed small-town references, with a 3-percent difference. The national media coverage, on the other hand, weighs heavily in favor of city references, which to some extent can explain how the urban-only narrative became the grand narrative of the Great Migration.

In the context of the Great Migration coverage, small towns are, in most instances, a side note or point of reference in the national press. A closer look at the twenty-eight articles that mention small towns disappoints, as my generous coding of small-town references reveals a mainly superficial treatment of small towns by the writers. The rural and small-town nature was mainly attributed to the South, and northern small towns are rarely discussed as a viable option for southern Black migrants' relocation. Notwithstanding, the articles attest how white Americans displayed a blatant animosity toward the Black newcomers in northern small towns, hinting at why these locales may not have been considered worthwhile among Black migrants. Such maltreatment is generally associated with the traditional South, but these attitudes were present in white minds across the nation and across time. Inadvertently or otherwise, the national press elucidated some of the reasons for the maldistribution of African Americans across the North, namely difficulties traveling, northern white people's love of the race but hatred of individual Black people, Black Codes and sundown laws, and expulsions (I will further elaborate on these reasons below).

The documented hostile encounters of Black newcomers in northern small towns across the twentieth century demonstrate persistent white prejudicial attitudes and supremacist ideologies. This small-town mentality and culture produced an unwelcoming environment for any community outsider—particularly Black newcomers on their quest for the Promised Land. Apparent race-neutral spaces like the small-town Midwest were not race neutral, but they conceptualized and operated under George Lipsitz's "white spatial imaginary," revealing that a landscape considered congenial and hospitable by white Americans is no longer friendly and welcoming once breached by nonwhite Americans. It is then that these white locales became marked and visible.[51]

For example, Faith Adams describes the hostility and troubles a Black intellectual middle-class family encountered when moving into a small suburban northern community. White neighbors hurled expletives at the African American family, viewing them as an "intruder" to the "white community" where they sought to settle.[52] Adams was a graduate student who had settled in a northern New England small town at the time of the writing in 1920. The author poignantly explains the paradox of the Black family having sacrificed their son in World War I and fighting a lawsuit to reside in the northern white community. Practicing citizenship by joining the country's military (civic duty) did not extend to practicing citizenship through property ownership (civic rights). In short, African American citizenship continued to be contested, if not denied, even above the Mason-Dixon line.

Once the Great Migration was under way, coverage of Black folk struggling to exercise their citizenship rights and practices in the North was also a recurring concern in the *Chicago Defender*. In its column "And This Is Civilization," the paper notes the paradoxes of American society. Black people risk their own lives to save white people in precarious situations but are left to die when the situation is reversed, and first responders are white.[53] In 1929, the same column stands out as it reflects midwestern discrimination at its worst. "[T]hree respectable ladies, not white, of Chicago were refused the use of the comfort station" at a gas station between the Michigan state line and Michigan City, Indiana.[54] As the ladies relieved themselves in the nearby bushes, "the man keeper was objecting to even the car standing there for the very few urgent moments and threatened to charge for parking." The risk of traveling while Black becomes more obvious in the third paragraph, which reads: "This station and succeeding ones in Indiana read, 'We cater to white trade only.' This will spread into Michigan and Illinois." The article ends with a thought-provoking question: "Can the U.S. commerce body or other proper authority act to force equal safety and comfort service to travelers by highway traders?"[55] Although the development of the automobile and expansion of highways improved Black people's spatial mobility, racist attitudes and violent threats curbed it. For decades throughout the twentieth century, transit through and settlement in midwestern small towns came with a great risk for Black migrants.

At times, the national press captured racial animosity in its coverage of outbreaks of racial violence that took place in big cities and small towns alike.[56] And in both scenarios, white desires were at the forefront. For example, in the wake of the East St. Louis riot, local white residents organized various anti-Black meetings in 1917, during which agitated white people circulated the idea that the city "must remain a white man's town."[57] By 1917, East St. Louis had a population of more than 60,000. In smaller locales, these outbreaks frequently resulted in "requests" by white residents for Black residents to leave town. Liberal congregational minister Rollin Lynde Hartt discusses four such incidents in "When the Negro Comes North," a three-part series of articles on the migration mainly dedicated to the causes and impact of the Great Migration. The incident in South Bend, Indiana, resulted in letters being "sent to Negroes ordering them to leave town," and in an Ohio township, "'vigilantes' tried to drive out the Negroes." In Johnstown, Pennsylvania, the mayor himself expelled 1,200 Black residents.[58] Those expulsions actually became newsworthy on the national stage at times. For example, in 1923, the *New York Times* reported "All Negroes Driven from Indiana Town" with the subheading "White Miners at Blanford Act after an Assault on a Young Girl."[59] Besides revealing that white midwesterners actively contributed to making their communities all white, articles reporting on these expulsions are also a testament to the existence of Black residents in small-town midwestern America.

Segregation was a reality for Black folk in the North as much as it was in the South. Despite assumptions that the longer the Great Migration went on, the more northern whites would get used to the idea of a Black neighbor, the situation did not improve much for Black newcomers in the Midwest over time, as George S. Schuyler documented in "Jim Crow in the North" in 1949, for example. Schuyler was a self-proclaimed Black conservative, who ventured politically from the socialist to the extreme conservative side throughout his life. But his politics aside, he remained a keen observer of Black life in the North. The article was published in the aftermath of World War II and the Double V campaign, which inspired more and more African Americans to push for recognition and an end to racism at home. "Sett[ing] the record straight," Schuyler accorded that Black folk were still second-class citizens across the nation and encountered discrimination across the North, "more subtle, not sanctified by state law, but nevertheless almost inescapable."[60] He acknowledged that discrimination was a reality in urban and rural areas, affecting work, housing, and leisure. He condemned the schooling situation in the North as "appalling," correcting the popular misconception by mentioning that "there are plenty of racially segregated public schools."[61] He echoed reasons that underline the necessity of the *Green Book* when he discussed the obstacles Black travelers needed to overcome to find a hotel or a restaurant in the North, observing, "In about half the cities of the North, Negroes are never accepted. In the others they are accepted but made to feel that they are unwelcome." He drove his point home by noting that sixteen of the twenty-nine states with anti-miscegenation laws are located outside of the South, uncovering that the "most savage penalties, as a matter of fact, are in the North."[62] Hospital and cemetery segregation (including dog cemeteries) built the culmination of his argument that Jim Crow ruled the North just like it did the South.

The geography of hate excavates the hidden and invisible Jim Crow mechanisms of the North, revealing that space is more than bricks and mortar but instead divulges people's lives and (in)humanity. Housing and the consequent breach into white neighborhoods dominated the news in the 1950s and thus constitute an ideal lens into the minds of white northerners. Southern migrants soon realized that people "talk integration [but] act segregation" in the North, and restrictive covenants became the "great weapon of the segregator" in 1954.[63] "Race Trouble in the North: When a Negro Family Moved into a White Community" describes the race troubles in Levittown, Pennsylvania, in 1957, the year when the first Black family moved into town. The article abstract describes Levittown as a "normally peaceful Northern community"—a common description for many midwestern small towns (then and now). Peaceful—until their livelihoods seemingly have been threatened by Black newcomers. But it was not the Black newcomers who threw stones and assaulted police, but those very "peaceful" residents of the town.

White resident voices quoted in the article reflect their entitlement to claim the neighborhood as theirs, reflecting the hypocrisy of northern whites who claim they did not mind equal rights for Black folk *until* they move next door. The article uncovers another interesting conundrum surrounding this hypocritical situation in Levittown. Even though the Myers family was the first Black family moving into town in 1957, all five swimming pools in the town already barred Black folk from using them.[64] One wonders how such policy could have been in place already, even before African Americans' first attempt to settle there. Unless they were not the first.

Contemporary observers of the Great Migration frequently captured northern white attitudes and opposition to Black people attempting to settle in their white towns, as experienced in Levittown. They described the paradox as the fact that the North loves the race but hates the individual Black person, whereas the South hates the race but loves the individual Black person. It is this paradox that explains that the South is seemingly more integrated than the North. The article "South in the North" juxtaposes the level of prejudice in the North and South via two small-town communities in Illinois and Tennessee, respectively:

> There are several ironies in this tale of two cities—one being that Clinton, in the South, with most of its citizens admitting they do not believe in or want integration, is nevertheless partially integrated, while Deerfield, in the North, with the majority of its citizens assuring the world they believe in integration, is nevertheless totally segregated.[65]

Rooting the basis for discrimination and prejudice in the belief that white people are superior to Black people, the author identifies housing discrimination as a "key to northern segregation" and as one of the crucial mechanisms to prove white superiority, elaborating: "Symbols of that superiority differ. In the South they include separate school and lunch counters. In the North, the symbols of status are houses, the pecking order of suburban communities. Superiority here may be established by a man's address."[66] Invisible to the eye but far from race-neutral, white supremacy is embedded in these spaces—through attitudes and policies that represent white values and predetermine white wealth.

Similarly, Stewart Alsop and Oliver Quayle published "What Northerners Really Think of Negroes" in 1963. The authors conducted more than 500 interviews across the East, West, and Midwest, which led them to conclude that the "white North is no more ready to accept genuine integration and real racial equality than the deep South."[67] The issue of housing, once again, builds one of the key points in which northern white people's real attitude shines through, as "more than three out of four, believed that a white man should have the right to refuse to sell his house to a Negro on the basis of race." Providing examples of white northern attitudes on a wide array of social and cultural equality issues, the authors concluded their study with an important observation: "The danger lies less in violent Negro action than in violent white reaction."[68] Here, Alsop and Quayle challenge conventional wisdom by debunking the stereotype of Black people stirring up fracas that lead to violent outbreaks and hint at the fact that the violence in such city riots was often spurred by white anger, fear, and resentment.

This book calls out these white reactions for what they are to interrupt the durability of normalized white inhospitality and exclusionary practices. For example, let's focus on the strict enforcement of vagrancy and trespassing ordinances, which became a popular means in Frankfort, Indiana, to control access to the city and mark Blackness the longer the Great Migration went on. As we shall see, Frankfort was, in fact, a destination for southern Black migrants. Whereas the early-twentieth-century arrivals of Samuel Culpepper, Mattie Williams, and others were not noted in the *Frankfort Morning Times*, the local newspaper captured the arrivals of Black migrants mid-century, as they were arrested on trumped-up charges. Such coverage not only marked Blackness but also reinforced the stereotype of Black criminality: why else would they break the law and get arrested? Note the consistency in referring to the Black newcomers as "transient"—one of the discourse strategies the *Morning Times* deployed to "despatialize their sense of place."[69] For example, in early 1942, "Negro Transient" Bennie Rogers was taken into custody because he "had violated a federal code by leaving his home in Gretna, Louisiana, without notifying his local draft board."[70] Three weeks later, Virgil C. Hamilton, another Black migrant—this time from Lexington, Kentucky—was detained for "trespassing on railroad property."[71] Hamilton was arrested on Nickel Plate property by "special agents of the Nickel Plate," which may or may not indicate that he arrived in Frankfort by train. He likely did, as Frankfort had four major railroad lines for freight and passengers. "Negro Transient" Essec Ree Walker, from Magnolia, Arkansas, definitely arrived via train in Frankfort in 1949, as he was hurt "stepp[ing] off a moving boxcar and crash[ing] into a signal standard." Two other migrants, treated in the local hospital, were facing "charges of riding unlawfully in a moving freight train." If the word spread, the number of arrests might have been a deterring factor for Black migrants not to get off the train in Frankfort any longer. The word was definitely spread as a strategy to discourage Black people from settling in Frankfort, as the *Morning Times* reported three days after their arrest that "The fine and costs were suspended *on condition the two leave town immediately.*"[72] Many migrants did not have a penny upon arriving in the North. Since the two were arrested before securing employment, it was probably easiest to comply with the request to leave town.

Despite the fair share of "negro transients" who "disrupted" Frankfort tranquility, the *Frankfort Morning Times* never contextualized them within the larger ongoing Great Migration. When it started covering the Great Migration's effects on northern communities, it couched its coverage in general national terms, again conveying the impression that the Great Migration does not concern the local small-town community. After all, the few migrants who did arrive had been taken care of by the laws designed and enforced to protect their ideal white world. However, we can draw a few parallels and inferences from said coverage. For example, in May 1956, the *Morning Times* printed "Problem of Race Relations Not Confined to South; Discrimination in North, Too." Besides identifying housing as the major issue of contention and racial tension, Associated Press reporter Bem Price acknowledges the existence of sundown towns in the Midwest, noting that "There are cities such as Cicero, Ill., adjacent to Chicago, and Dearborn, Mich., next to Detroit, which exclude Negro residents *through community pressures*" and adding that "you can find instances in the North of mob action when a Negro family moves into an all-white neighborhood."[73] "Community pressures" served as an extralegal, unofficial tool to preserve all-white communities without admitting racist intentions. As Chapter 4 will reveal, Indiana communities resorted to this strategy frequently regarding Black residents.

Black migrants did arrive in the small-town Midwest. In their chosen new environments, they were met with white hostility—open and outward as well as subtle and hidden. While such white hostility did not prevent them from migrating, it might explain the less dispersed settlement of Black folk across the Midwest. Small-town attitudes and policies might have simply overridden their desires for land ownership. How many Black migrants attempted initial settlements in the smaller towns of the Midwest during the seven decades of the Great Migration, we might never know. Regardless, it is important to note the overwhelming obstacles and animosity they faced when doing so. The sole narrative that the Great Migration involved Black migrants settling exclusively in the urban North obscured Black experiences in the small-town Midwest. For far too long, these formerly all-white communities across the Midwest have been excused and exculpated for their active contribution to creating urban "ghettos." For far too long, white small-town midwesterners have been acquitted of playing any role in the below-standard accommodations in the segregated areas and the violent unrest erupting in urban spaces for equal rights and equal treatment of Black people.

This chapter attempted to correct the conventional wisdom that the Great Migration and the small-town Midwest are polar opposites. Instead, it demonstrates the intricate interplay of how one was circumnavigated in the other. Doing so, we learned that many migrants expressed interest in small-town America in the North. We know from Scott's compilations of migrant letters that many migrants were eager to relocate in the North and envisioned the small-town North as a viable relocation option. It was in these small towns where the migrants saw themselves easily adjusting and practicing different aspects of citizenship, including access to a living wage, quality education, and the ballot box. It was in these small towns where the migrants envisioned themselves making a living with the trades they have known all their lives—farming and agricultural labor. Yet bringing small-town America and the Great Migration into conversation with one another also unearths the hidden legacy of exclusionary policies and attitudes of the American Midwest that kept the region overwhelmingly white for decades during a time when the nation experienced a major demographic shift. In this regard, it contributes greatly to our understanding of the Great Migration as a socially engineered urban phenomenon.

Introducing some white hidden mechanisms and practices operationalized and perpetuated in the region, this chapter leaves us with a desire to dive deeper. In particular, the last section of this chapter leaves us wondering about this inhospitable culture that characterized the small-town environment that migrants had idealized in their letters. The next three chapters will delineate the white and Black experiences in Indiana, teasing out these small-town elements that made African American migrants feel unwelcome. Survey respondents in the Black History Project files provided a wealth of explanations for the absence of Black folk in their communities, displaying a range of attitudes toward Blackness in their county. A closer look at the apologies and justifications will lay bare an intentional manipulation of Indiana history—from erasing and criminalizing Black experiences to whitewashing white supremacist desires. No matter the strategy, consciously or unconsciously, Indiana's white residents perpetuate the systems that made the state a white state.

CHAPTER 3

Erasing Histories

A Black Church and a White Pool

> This survey about Blacks does not apply to this County as there has been only about one dozen Black Families that have lived in this County from the start of the County.[1]
>
> —Carroll County Historian, March 1988

Frankfort's Black past has mainly been forgotten. One resident—let's call him Bob—recalled that Frankfort "had a Black church at one time." And indeed, built in 1885, it soon became the anchor and beacon for the Black community in Clinton County, organizing field trips, choir concerts, and local fundraisers, and hosting picnics, barbeques, and church suppers. The local papers didn't bother covering any of these events.

Joseph Claybaugh succinctly acknowledges the church in his 1913 county history. In four lines, he notes the existence of the "African M. E. Church" as the "only church organization of colored people" and lists G. F. Crossland as the pastor and a membership of fifty-five.[2] Claybaugh's second brief reference to Black people in the county concerned the county-wide expulsion of all African Americans that allowed only Joseph Parker and his family to stay in Frankfort, as discussed in Chapter 1. Let's remember, Claybaugh noted that the white animosity "gradually" subsided, resulting in more Black residents who had, by the time of Claybaugh's writing at the early twentieth century, become "a very orderly and reputable factor of the community."[3] Here, the author explicitly notes a small Black community in town, which means there is more to uncover. And indeed, the Black population increased. From merely four Black people in the county in 1870, the number increased to forty in 1880 and fifty-eight in 1910.[4] Yet again, none of the Black community members were "reputable" enough to be included among Claybaugh's "representative citizens," and the local papers did not acknowledge them, either.

The *Frankfort Morning Times* first acknowledged the local Black community in 1918. Clinton County had received a draft call for Black men during World War I. Resulting coverage illustrates the local paper's negligence and indifference regarding its Black residents. Two weeks after announcing the draft call for "colored men," the four eligible men—John Williams, Robert L. Kersey, Fern Leon Reed, and Lela Edward Roberts—had volunteered for military service. The paper reported on the joyous sendoff for the "Colored Boys," during which Rev. Washington, the minister of the local A. M. E. church, "presented the comfort kits to the boys."[5] All men except Williams were natives of Frankfort. The paper did not indicate the ages of the four men, leading me to initially assume that the men were indeed teenagers. Further research revealed the ages of the three Frankfort natives, who all were between twenty-four and twenty-seven years old. All three returned to Frankfort after the war,[6] though the local paper did not consider it noteworthy to report on its Black hometown heroes (unlike their white counterparts, who were frequently celebrated and their war-related activities widely circulated). It never printed any of their letters from abroad, and neither did it cover when they were injured, maybe died, nor when they returned home. Honoring Clinton County service members in word and picture never encompassed Black service members.

The Bethel African Methodist Episcopal Church had been in place for more than four decades when it was first included in the *Frankfort Morning Times*'s church directory on February 5, 1927. The "Methodist A. M. E." was one of nineteen churches in the city back then. Church, one of the small-town community pillars that fosters a sense of belonging, became a means through which the Black community temporarily put an end to its invisibility in the paper. The *Morning Times* started to cover church-based events henceforth, though sporadically, such as a "Concert of Negro Spirituals" with a choir comprising "local talent" in 1931 and a church-sponsored barbeque at the local fairgrounds in 1932. Ephemerally, the paper even listed "Colored Notes" in February 1935 to list Bethel A. M. E. Church activities. Yet the column only appeared this one time.[7] Membership in the church was dwindling by the 1950s, and within two decades, the church ceased to exist. But the local papers remained silent.

* * *

The geography of hate can best be understood by illustrating how it is operationalized, manifested, perpetuated, and reproduced. This chapter is about erasure. In white Hoosier minds, there were no Black people in Indiana small-town communities. County historians accordingly echo these perceptions and make us believe there is no Black history in these areas. “One could say then,” critical race philosopher Charles Mills puts forth in *The Racial Contract*, “that *white misunderstanding, misrepresentation, evasion, and self-deception on matters related to race* are among the most pervasive mental phenomena of the past few hundred years, a cognitive and moral economy psychically required for conquest, colonization, and enslavement.”[8] Centering the conversation in this chapter around erasure, I am revealing various strategies employed to *un*remember local Black communities and talk Black Hoosiers into nonexistence. Frankfort has a Black history, though one wouldn't know when strolling through town, reading county histories, or talking with locals. In my conversations with community members who have lived in Frankfort for the majority of, if not all, their lives, “There weren't any back then” became a common refrain in response to inquiries about Black residents. Though such remarks stand in stark contrast to the openings of each chapter in this book, they indicate the white town mentality. Some talked the Black presence away, and others revealed prevalent stereotypes about African Americans in the community. Both ways demonstrate how Frankfort created “passive” barriers to an inclusive environment. Both strategies send a clear message of who belongs (and has always belonged) and who never did (or still doesn't). Both attitudes convey a layered system of indifference from the white majority. Unpacking these layers of indifference will be the focus of the next three chapters. They will illuminate why more African Americans did not settle in Clinton County or Indiana at large and explain why the few who did left. Doing so, these chapters will illustrate how whiteness (re) produces the geography of hate in small-town America and vice versa: how the geography of hate anchors whiteness in the small-town Midwest.

I could use historical documents exclusively to demonstrate the instantiated absence of Black folk in local Indiana communities. Newspaper snippets like the ones from the *Frankfort Morning Times* above contradict reality but clearly display white residents' negligence toward their Black neighbors. Instead, I am focusing on how white Hoosiers talk about Black people in their communities to underline the power of those narratives, those beliefs—which, once created, never left but have frequently been perpetuated publicly and in conversations. This emphasis makes palpable mechanisms that sustained white supremacy and Black subordination in the state across time, unearthing the persistence of exclusionary practices and inhospitable acts—or, in short, the durability of white desires in small-town Indiana.

Erased from memories and historical records are not only Black histories but also the violent white acts and actions that precipitated white residents' opportunity to erase Black experiences. Thus, erasure constitutes a powerful tool in the geography of hate, as it obscures history as it happens and allows people to whitewash it. This is the collective memory of white Hoosier communities.

Explaining the Black Away

In 1987, the Black History Program of the Indiana Historical Society (IHS) started a statewide effort to collect information about Black experiences in Indiana. Sending a thirteen-question survey to public librarians, local societies, and historians in all counties, program historians hoped to paint a comprehensive picture of the Black experience in the state. The Carroll County historian's claim, "This survey about Blacks does not apply to this County as there has been only about one dozen Black Families that have lived in this County from the start of the County," as noted in the epigraph, is representative of many survey responses that provide little to no information, which warrants further exploration from a historical and contemporary standpoint. Despite historical phenomena like the Great Migration, some counties allegedly remained exclusively white, and the question is how. Given ample historical evidence of Black communities, as all but six of Indiana's ninety-two counties registered Black residents, according to the 1860 census, what mechanisms were in place that rendered some parts of the population invisible? Unearthing these mechanisms might explain the selective memory of residents who have traditionally perceived their communities as all-white spaces and allege so eagerly in public records, such as program surveys.

Receiving a survey from a state institution that inquires specifically about a group of people that never mattered in the county sparked varied responses across Indiana. Some county personnel blissfully ignored the inquiry for the entire time that the Black History Program archivist dedicated to collecting information.[9] Others, like the Carroll County historian, sent a one-liner explaining that this survey did not pertain to their county. Yet others responded differently to the IHS request. Pursuing various strategies, these responses range from apologies and different priorities to bestseller synopses, without giving us the full stories. The county respondents actively and selectively made their community archives. The "making of archives," anthropologist Michel-Rolph Trouillot notes,

> involves a number of selective operations: selection of producers, selection of evidence, selection of themes, selection of procedures—which means, at best the differential ranking and, at worst, the exclusion of some producers, some evidence, some themes, some procedures. Power enters here both obviously and surreptitiously.[10]

Regardless of the approach, the county respondents affirmed the overwhelmingly white nature of their respective communities while simultaneously absolving them from any involvement in creating such homogeneously white environments. Let's have a look.

Language, Lies, and Local Truisms

The choice of words in the survey responses often exposes the wide chasm between Black and white Hoosiers. The way the county personnel reflect on the Black experience often discloses that the writers are white people who do not concern themselves much (if at all) with the Black community in their counties. They present the contemporary and decades-long absence of Black bodies in their midst as a plain fact of life, as this Boone County example illustrates: "No Black family has lived in Thorntown for years until a year ago when the United Methodist Church hired a Black minister, Ivan Jenkins, and he is still here."[11] The insertion of "for years" indicates that this has not always been the case. We know that Thorntown once had a Black population if we recall Claybaugh's county history side note of Black folk being driven out of Frankfort at the end of the Civil War. The white residents actually "relocated" their Black neighbors to Thorntown. We do not know what happened to Thorntown's Black community between the end of the Civil War and late 1980s, and the survey response does not indicate interest in finding out the circumstances surrounding the Black population loss.

Similarly, the Huntington County respondent simply states, "As of 1985 there were only 6 families of Blacks in Huntington Co," accompanied by a handwritten note that attests to the county being known "for not having blacks." Though based on hearsay, the plain language states it as a fact of life; this is the collective memory of Huntington County. The survey responses of Warren, Whitley, and Scott counties ring similar:

> "We have never had any blacks as residents of Warren Co."
> "Only blacks in [Whitley] County at the time are a few adopted Children by White families."
> "Scott County Ind has never had a family of blacks make this County their home."[12]

The handwritten note sent along with the Scott County survey tries to explain that despite the lack of Black residents in their county, they are treated equally: "Blacks work in our town of Scottsburg when they work on construction for firms which are located in Jeffersonville or Louisville. They eat in restaurants and treated same as other customers. But never have they come here to live."

The respondent diffuses the county's structural racism by highlighting the access to public accommodations that echo bygone Jim Crow circumstances.

The three remarks prove more or less accurate for the twentieth century when consulting the U.S. Census. Between 1900 and 1980, Warren had one Black resident listed in 1930, Whitley had two (one in 1950 and one in 1970), and Scott County had one in 1960. In the late nineteenth century, however, all three counties registered double-digit numbers of Black residents. In 1880, Warren had nineteen, Whitley had 108, and Scott had ten African American residents. Scott County's prohibition of Black settlement has caught scholarly attention.[13] The other two counties and the history of how they "lost" their Black populations have yet to be told. Warren and Whitley county personnel did not attend to it. Instead, they stated the absence of Black folk in their vicinity as a local truism or, to quote Charles Mills again, "consensual hallucination . . . located in real space."[14]

Some survey respondents apologized in their written notes, either for not being able to provide more information on the topic or the fact that few or no Black folk have lived there. Yet they simultaneously found a way to absolve their counties from having anything to do with the status quo while documenting their efforts to trace Black history in their county. For example, a member of the Greene County Historical Society reached out to the former county historian in an attempt to provide more information for the survey. The attempt did not yield much, as the former county historian did not recall ever having encountered a Black person in the library. The county historian then reached out to the "only black still in the county," also unsuccessfully, as the person who was in her late seventies had different priorities: "I talked to her and she reiterated that she is not interested in 'the kind of thing' which you explained to her, for she is too busy." Case closed.[15]

Similarly, another county historian noted, "I have asked old timers, I have requested readers to respond to your request in the local publications . . . all to no avail. No blacks ever stayed around here, say the citizens in Starke County. We have every nation in the world—except blacks. So sorry."[16] The county historian seems to have asked for information in the local press, recorded the responses of the local residents, and used hyperbole to represent Starke County as a welcoming environment. Doing so, they reveal prevalent local attitudes that Black people are a "nation" on their own, thereby robbing them of their U.S. citizenship and national belonging.

Other respondents chose to document "creative" local truisms to explain the Black away and justify the survey's sparse completion. The LaGrange County response, for example, not only distracts from the Black experience by including information about the Amish, but it also introduces a boogeyman. The question inquiring about separate schools for Black children resulted in "Amish don't attend High School. There are 40 Amish one or two room schools in the county today. Grades one thru eight." Ignoring the Black experience altogether indicates Black residents' low (or no) priority in the community. The question about various county documents, such as deed books, tax records, and Negro registers, generated the following response:

> About 5 years ago a man supposedly from the State Historical Society came to the Court House and threw out 6 highway truck loads of old books + records which were hauled to the dump. Copies of our early census he took as well as other papers. Our county was the 35th one he did this to.[17]

The county historian is again evading the question. We still do not know whether a Negro register existed in LaGrange County, but the respondent made sure to indicate that it is through no fault of the residents. The survey was already sparsely completed, and a closer look at the answers reveals little about the Black experience in the county.

Nativity, or the absence thereof, is another indicator of white negligence in Indiana. It provided an easy way to dismiss the survey or justify the lack of information the respondents could provide. Clark County Historical Society respondents did not feel "qualified to complete" the survey because they were not natives of the town. County historical societies are meant to preserve, collect, and interpret county heritage and history, yet here we have a case where only an insider, a native resident, can complete the survey. Unlike other counties, Clark County has already been discussed in scholarship. Emma Lou Thornbrough notes that Clark County had one of the larger Black populations in Indiana throughout the nineteenth century, given its southern location. In the same breath, however, she documents the county's white hostility, noting places like Utica, which did not allow Black folk within its city limits, and the lynching of three Black men in 1871. Nativity obviously does not need to be a requirement to present Black experiences in the county, yet it is an easy way out to avoid researching and discussing less pleasant or low-priority topics.[18]

Such responses delineate white complicity in the erasure of Black experiences, depicting individual accountability as well as structural conditions, regardless of the effort undertaken to conduct research for the survey. For example, the Posey County historian stated, "I get the impression that many people either are *still* afraid to talk about their history or simply don't know." He continued, "Black History in Posey Co. could be emphasized in several directions. Some of it could be turned into a bloody, gruesome 'Best Seller' Historical Novel." At a different point, he indicated that he is "full of stories of the past," but he did not bother to elaborate further.[19] However, the fact that the county's history of the Black experience provides sufficient—yet "gruesome"—information leaves one wondering which incidents were not shared with the materials returned for the survey request.

One such gruesome incident that caught national media attention at the time took place 150 miles north of Posey County. Amid the first wave of the Great Migration, the *New York Times* reported "All Negroes Driven from Indiana Town" with the subheading "White Miners at Blanford Act after an Assault on a Young Girl" in 1923.[20] Elliot Jaspin discusses this Vermillion County incident at great length in his book. Let's recall, Jaspin discusses two such "successful" racial cleansings in Indiana. He clarifies that the county was a "Klan stronghold," enlisting "thirty percent of Vermillion's native-born, white males." The cleansing was the consequence of a report by a white girl of her alleged molestation by a Black man, resulting in an ultimatum for all Black residents to leave the town and county immediately. Vermillion's Black population dropped from 235 in the 1920 census to sixty-nine in 1930.[21]

Jaspin's account of Vermillion County is particularly relevant if one looks at the correspondence included in the Black History Project file. A note informs the reader that the county historian "can find no record of blacks in county. In my memory, I can name about 3 black families in [the] entire county for past 50 years." A follow-up letter by the Indiana Historical Society program archivist entailing some 1870 census information for the county and expressing curiosity about the county's history due to its "shape" resulted in a survey response later the same month, yet it was sparsely filled out. One learns from the survey that there were allegedly no Black property owners until sometime in the 1980s, when one family moved there; that they used to have a stop on the Underground Railroad "according to legend but unproven"; that the county is "strictly farm area [that is not] conducive to blacks"; and that the "coal mines were dominated by immigrant labor."[22] Local truisms explained the Black experience away. Twenty years later, Elliot Jaspin filled in many of the missing pieces.

The other racial cleansing Jaspin discusses concerned the 1864 county-wide expulsion of Black residents in Washington County, Indiana. Let's remember, Washington County's Black population dropped from 187 in 1860 to eighteen in 1870. Writing for the Early Black Settlements in Indiana project administered by the IHS, Martina Nichols Kunnecke acknowledges the growing anti-Black hostility in the county at that time, noting, "With threats, violence and aggressive 'colonization' campaigns, the 1850s ushered in tremendous pressures on Washington County's African Americans." She explains further:

> The successful crusade to drive African Americans away was followed by decades of erasing away any sign they had ever been there. What had made the settlement communities—its properties, institutions and cemeteries—were consumed, looted or otherwise destroyed.[23]

Here, Kunnecke explicitly identifies erasure as part of the white Hoosier identity. Along the same lines, Jaspin notes about numerous counties where racial cleansings took place, "while the fear remains, the histories are missing."[24] These authors help us understand how and why research in this regard is so challenging. Not only did white residents across the state spend decades ridding their county of people of color, but then they also dedicated their time to erasing traces of their existence while keeping their communities all white for many decades to come. To that extent, Washington County illustrates how residents indulged their white desires and *actively* forget about their minority residents.

Incomplete and Inconsistent: Census Data and County Records

Steep population drops in the U.S. census caught Jaspin's attention and led him to uncover countywide expulsions. In her attempt to elicit information about the Black experiences in Vermillion County, the Black History Project (BHP) archivist consulted the 1870 census records, which listed eleven households containing forty-eight Black residents in the county. Yet only a small percentage of the responsive county experts made use of such historical documents. Public records such as manuscript census schedules and city directories are invaluable in gathering data and formulating generalizations about the society across time. Early city directories clearly indicate Black churches, businesses, and residents by prefacing the former two with "colored" and by accompanying the latter with asterisks or the letter "C" at their entry. Rush County's city directories for 1901 and 1911, included in the BHP files, marked Black citizens with "col" next to each entry. Yet only in the rarest instances did county respondents present any of these materials.

Census data, for example, appears only sporadically in the Black History Project. Pulaski County was the only county to consult the 1980 census, the most recent census available at the time the survey was conducted. Census schedules from the nineteenth century were consulted slightly more frequently but still sparsely: Porter County uses the 1880 census to inform the reader that "We have no information of any black residents in our county. 1880 census shows none"; Clinton County also references the 1880 census in its approximation of "20 or more families/households" but shies away from specific numbers; Brown County references the 1860 census, which lists one sixteen-year-old Black waiter, who had been the only Black resident until the early 1960s, when a Black family moved into the county; Blackford County cites "14 negroes" according to the 1840 census; similarly, Miami County uses the 1840 census to mention that "Philip Pew, wife + son [were the] only blacks." Ripley County references the 1850 census to mention that there were Black people in Shelby Township, but it fails to mention how many; Randolph County also uses the 1850 census to list 111 Black heads of households. In total, only nine counties made scant use of such germane historical documents. Maybe they only listed the one census that listed Black folk in the county and expected it would suffice to tell the history of Black people in the county. Consulting one decade for the county population, however, does not reveal much about the population at all.

Let's return to *The 1979 History of Adams County, Indiana*, the county history that demonstrated how to present Indiana's race record in plain, simple language and detailed white hostility toward people of color in the county and the State of Indiana. It serves again as an example of how to document history more accurately—in this case, how census data can provide a more comprehensive picture of county residents, thereby shedding some light on community and race relations. Heller states that "blacks have been living in Adams County during ten of the preceding 14 censuses, starting with 1840, when the county registered 17, the most yet reported until 1970." After detailing names, characteristics, gender, age, and specific location for 1840, 1850, and 1860, Heller continues, "There were no blacks in the county in 1870, 1880, 1900, or 1920 census; two in 1890 and 1910." Of course, since the census collects population data only every ten years, one needs to fill in the stories of what happens in between those years. City directories and local newspapers come in handy for that. The *Freeman*'s coining of "Negrophobia" in describing that Black people were driven out of Decatur would have supplemented Heller's narrative, as the argument would corroborate the bad "race record" and the sundown town history he noted. As a side note, Heller discussed the incident with the help of local newspapers, though he did not connect it back to the revealed census overview.[25]

It was also through looking at census data that Elliot Jaspin came to realize and investigate the odd distribution of Black and white folks on a county level. He dug deeper and was able to pin down the decades in which counties resorted to mechanisms of expulsion and performed racial cleansings. Adopting Jaspin's strategy for Indiana counties, census data alone raises some questions regarding various counties across Indiana—besides Washington and Vermillion. Some other counties had large declines from 1890 to 1930, the nadir of race relations toward the end of the Great Migration's first wave. For example, Ripley and Dubois counties lost their entire Black populations in these forty years, from 74 and 93, respectively, in 1890, to zero in 1930. Jackson County had 270 Black residents in 1890 but registered only 67 in 1930 (-75 percent), and Parke County had 356 Black residents in 1890 and only 74 in 1930 (-79 percent). Similarly, Sullivan County lost 73 percent of its Black population during that time, from 182 in 1890 to 50 in 1930. Perry County also lost 75 percent of its Black population in these four decades (from 253 in 1890 to 64 in 1930), and Randolph County's Black population dropped by 78 percent from 606 Black residents in 1890 to 136 in 1930. Perry County's Black population dropped another 70 percent, down to 19 residents in 1940. So did Parke County's Black population, though only by 45 percent, down to 41 Black residents. Four of those counties would qualify for Jaspin's criteria of a "successful" racial cleansing. The 2000 census lists fewer Black residents than the 1890 census for Jackson, Randolph, Dubois, and Ripley counties: 227, 70, 56, and 13, respectively. These are only a few examples, and further research of these counties is needed to fill the void between those census decades to understand what exactly happened to the Black communities that once called these counties home. Here, they illustrate the power of census data in asking big questions.

From the survey responses alone, it is difficult to ascertain why the county historians did not consult historical and population data in a comprehensive way. It likely was a matter of priorities and time, as it takes some time to locate the sources for something they might not consider worthwhile. It is also possible that they did a skimming similar to the one I presented in the previous paragraph and did not like the impression it would give. The surveys do not shed light into these observations, but they do indicate an inconsistent consultation of historical documents. Aligned with Charles Mills's rule of "*white misunderstanding, misrepresentation, evasion, and self-deception*," county representatives generally overlooked county activities that intentionally or inadvertently caused a drop in their counties' Black population.[26]

Whose History? Sowing Omission, Reaping White Communities

The power of writing and recounting history lies with the public spokespeople of the county regarding the Black History Project and historical documents more generally. Above, I illustrated how some county respondents exercised their power by ignoring the subject matter altogether or by presenting their history, their narratives, and their justifications for the absence of Black folk in their midst. It is just as important to explore, if county historians decided to engage the survey in 1987, what they considered worthy of mention, and how community members approach the topic today, thirty years later. In other words, *whose* history is being shared? Are references to town- or county-wide expulsions included? Are Ku Klux Klan escapades noted, or would that have left the "wrong impression" of the county and its residents? Answering these questions will expose how county representatives share personal and collective memories as residents of their counties. A few examples from Tippecanoe and Clinton counties shall suffice to demonstrate the power of writing history. County respondents and local newspapers deployed the strategy of omission in celebratory community-building as well as in unpleasant, undignified moments. Omission became a powerful tool in erasing Black experiences in the county.

Throughout the twentieth century, segregation of schools, neighborhoods, and public spaces was a reality for many Indiana towns. Whereas the Tippecanoe County survey wholeheartedly paints a picture of segregated life in Lafayette, listing various Black fraternal orders, businesses, and schools, it almost strategically omits crucial entities and incidents that would present a more accurate picture of Black experiences in the county, both community enhancing and community depriving. For example, it fails to mention anything about the Hanna Community Center. Formally founded in 1943, the center was intended to be used for "educational, literary, scientific and charitable purposes, for the uplift and betterment of the Negro race." The Hanna Community Center still exists today, which made me stumble over its omission in the survey. Its mission until today has been to "celebrate the diverse cultures of Greater Lafayette while preserving Lafayette's African American culture, heritage, and history."[27] The survey failed to preserve that history.

The survey respondent also shied away from including anything regarding West Lafayette's enduring exclusionary history. Purdue University is located on the West side, and Black students were not allowed to live in student dormitories until the late 1940s. Purdue's campus integrated in the wake of the landmark U.S. Supreme Court decision *Shelley vs. Kraemer*, which prohibited housing and property contracts from discriminating on the basis of race. However, this court decision did not deter private householders from continuing their discriminatory policies. More than a decade after this monumental housing decision, in February 1959, Rev. R. F. Rehmer noted the following in light of the "Brotherhood Week":

> Through [*sic*] University housing, for example, is available to any Purdue student, faculty, and staff member, there are restrictions in West Lafayette against Negroes, also Negro faculty members. They are unable to buy a home on this side of the Wabash, and foreign students are sometimes more hard pressed to find housing than the native American is.[28]

In the mid-1960s, the university adopted a nondiscriminatory policy statement regarding off-campus housing and made householders of the listed facilities for rent aware of the changes. To be included on the off-campus housing facilities list, the university now demanded that "the householder indicates his (or her) intention of following the University policy statement regarding discrimination." Although the policy was rather weak in nature, the consequences of adopting it were drastic. The list of landlords shrank from about 500 to eighty in that year.[29] The list of off-campus housing ultimately ceased to exist, but housing discrimination persisted.

However, Tippecanoe County's most poignant example of willful amnesia, or the power of local historians to write history *as it matters to them*, happened right around the time the Black History Project was conceived. In late January 1987, the Black Cultural Center at Purdue University experienced a cross-burning on its lawn.[30] The community was aghast. Students, faculty, and community members protested, demanding strong action from the university's administration, so it definitely made the local news. The BHP survey was received in September of the same year. The Tippecanoe County Historical Association responded in October 1987, yet there are no traces of exclusionary policies or Klan incidents in the response. Respondents also chose to not enclose any newspaper articles that would have painted a direr yet more accurate picture of life for people of color in Tippecanoe County.

Omission functioned similarly in Clinton County—then and now. Here are some contemporary examples of how my informants erased the Black community in our conversations, to illustrate local white Hoosier town mentalities. Randy, a white native in his sixties, simply noted that there were no Black residents in town:

> Basically, this is a white Anglo Saxon Protestant community. It basically is this kind of a community. I know back in the sixties—back when the Black revolutions were taking place across America and the riots and so forth—people would come down from Chicago they would be aghast that there were no Black people in Frankfort. And so, they would say, 'We're gonna get 'em on a bus and load 'em out, put them down on the square and let them loose.' That was the attitude. Oh, my goodness, here's a city and there's no Black people here.

He adopts the plain fact-of-life tone that Heller demonstrated in his county history and introduces inflections only when he reflects on how outsiders of the community reflected on the absence of Black folk in Frankfort. He reinforces his white spatial desires by describing his community as WASP.

Frank, another white native of the community in his fifties, based his observation on his high school experience to assert the alleged absence of Black residents: "we had one or two Hispanics in my class and no African Americans." Not quite reinforcing the white fantasyland, he remembers other people of color, just not Black ones.

Thinking back to a community report he once completed, Richard, in his nineties, recalled that it required him to reach out to the local Black community. Since he had "never contacted the Black," he reminisced writing "my Black was on vacation." Laughing, he continued, "Can you imagine me say to somebody in Detroit or something, that the only Black we had was on vacation, so I couldn't get the Black to talk to me?" and speculated that the people reading his report "must've really scratched their head." In his lily-white ideal world, Richard starts off acknowledging that he had never talked to the Black community in town, not that there weren't any. Then he exclusively talks about Black people in the singular, leaving room for only one potential Black resident in his white world. Like Randy, Richard contrasts his white spatial imaginary with another metropolis, Detroit, known to have experienced a significant increase in its Black population as a result of the Great Migration.

Given their ages, time, and exposure in the community, the residents' recollections refer to the 1950s, sixties, and maybe seventies. Admittedly, the census numbers for the Black community in Clinton County are minuscule—fifty-three in 1950, thirty-eight in 1960, and twenty-four in 1970. But all these numbers are greater than zero, so they corroborate how Clinton County's collective memory contradicts reality.

The *Frankfort Morning Times* is instrumental in not only proving the omissions of residents' collective memory by filling in some facts but also in corroborating the community's sentiments. Staff writer Laura Barone attested to the invisibility of African Americans in her 1978 portrait of the Black community, observing that "as far as Frankfort is concerned, its black population was never that noticeable."[31] The sparse coverage, though a testament to the presence of Black folk, reflects that the community did not see their Black neighbors and, for the most part, did not care much about their achievements and events. I opened this chapter with the paper's side note of Black community members being drafted during World War I and the subsequent lack of coverage regarding any of their destinies during the war.

Like the Black service members, the Black schoolchildren—though present—remained invisible. So were their accomplishments. Black achievements were not worth commemorating, as Black people simply seemed to not belong to the Clinton County community. This is the racial logic of Indiana—one that is demarcated and dominated by the durability of whiteness. Black people—though present in the midwestern landscape—remained invisible to and in the communities they (temporarily) called home. Unsurprisingly, the Clinton County War Memorial, erected in honor of all Clinton County war veterans, does not include any of the Black service members native to the community, constituting one of the most powerful indicators of Black erasure and *non*belonging and illustrating how public space both reflects and (re)produces white racism (Figure 4).[32]

And like the Clinton County community at large, the *Frankfort Morning Times* adopted omission as a key strategy beyond simply ignoring its Black community members' achievements. The Travelers Protective Association (TPA) Park has frequently been mentioned in my interviews and surveys as one of the favorite public spaces in the city. Besides a petting zoo, the TPA Park houses an Olympic-size swimming pool. Every summer, the local paper ran numerous ads about the pool's opening, including opening hours and season prices. Not once did the ads include a restriction of *who* in the community was *allowed* to use the pool. Maybe it was an unspoken rule in Frankfort that local Black residents were not to use the pool. Or maybe a sign at the park or the pool gate clearly indicated who had access and precluded "outsiders" from using the pool. Either way, designating public spaces like city pools as white spaces and actively omitting these local realities in newspaper ads illustrates yet another way to make Black people invisible in the community. White pools are another community-enforced but poorly recorded mechanism of exclusion that demarcates the geography of hate.

We only come to know about Frankfort's discriminatory pool history due to a local white minister, who complained about the city's violation of Indiana state law regarding access to public accommodations in the summer of 1954. The ensuing community-wide discussion resulted in the pool being "Open to All." Frankfort was not alone in the white pool debate, as Marion, Grant County, Evansville, Vanderburgh County, and Muncie, Delaware County, were among the Indiana locales that fought to uphold or terminate the existence of white pools in the 1950s.[33]

Though this chapter overwhelmingly conveys an impression of absence and denied existence, it also provides a record of the Black experience in Indiana. At the same time, it provides a record of the white experience in Indiana, documenting contemporary and past white Hoosier attitudes to-

FIGURE 4. A panoramic overview of the Clinton County War Memorial in the heart of downtown, erected in 2007 adjacent to the courthouse on the downtown square. The centrality of the memorial indicates its value to the community. The central panel is inscribed with "All Gave Some. Some Gave All. Dedicated to All Clinton County Veterans," purportedly presenting a comprehensive overview of Clinton County residents serving in the wars—from the Mexican War to the Persian Gulf War. The website of the Indiana Elks clarifies that the memorial is dedicated to all local residents killed in action. Besides the Black granite that carries the names of county veterans for the respective wars, the red bricks honor certain individuals (based on donors). No Black service members are to be found anywhere in the memorial. Photo Credit: Marcela Poirier Maruenda

ward their Black neighbors. This chapter illustrates how selectively choosing historical documents conveys the impression of all-white communities. In the collective memory of Indiana residents, Black people were simply erased. Black folk never existed in their communities, so the story goes. Though historically inaccurate, this mindset prevails. The failure to include certain crucial institutions and incidents of the past corroborates that race-related issues occupy a lower priority on a county level. It also proves the subjective nature of history, as (local) historians point to "noteworthy" individuals, events, heroes, and testimonies that align with their worldview and their

FIGURE 5. This single-family home at the south side of Frankfort was once the Bethel A. M. E. Church, serving the Black community of Clinton County. Photo credit: Marcela Poirier Maruenda

racialized geography, which is dominated by the white habitus across Indiana. Their worldviews and personal experiences in society determine the relevance and importance of inclusion in the stories and histories they tell about their county and their state. A cross-burning that might terrify Black county residents might simply be a nuisance, quickly forgotten by a white resident, county historian, or survey taker accounting for the county's racialized history. Joseph Claybaugh determined who was "reputable" enough to be included in his county history's "representative citizens"—and Black residents weren't. Inadvertent or intentional, the survey responses, county histories, public landmarks, newspaper stories, and the like reflect that the white racial frame determined which information was ultimately included. Black Hoosiers have systematically been erased from Indiana communities, memories, and documents.

* * *

Frankfort once had a Black church, but no one remembers. Laura Barone from the *Frankfort Morning Times* described the church "as a silent reminder of what once was the Black history of Frankfort." The building still stood as of 2019 but had been converted into a family home (Figure 5).

There is no historical marker in the vicinity that indicates that this once was a place where the Black residents of Frankfort worshiped. Putting an end to the erasure of Black experiences in Indiana, this chapter ensures that this history will no longer be forgotten.

CHAPTER 4

Silencing Memories

White Desires and Black Terror

Ooh, Blacks . . . they was wicked on the Blacks.
—Tom, retired farmer and Clinton County resident,
October 2017

The Ku Klux Klan (KKK) and Black residents coexisted in Clinton County. Remember the Parkers—Joseph Parker was the one "old barber" who was not driven out of Clinton County when every other Black person was carted to Thorntown. When he passed in 1919, the KKK had not yet taken over every hamlet in Indiana. Times would change quickly. The week of his wife Rhoda Parker's death in mid-September 1923 was an eventful week for Klan members in the county. Klansmen conducted their first public funeral for one of their members—at the pulpit and the grave—earlier that week. After the announcement of Parker's death, which described her as a "pioneer of the city" and "the first colored woman" in Frankfort, a big Klan gathering in neighboring Carroll County resulted in high attendance of local Klansmen, which was followed by another Clinton County Klan gathering, including public speaking events and parades, on the day Rhoda Parker was laid to rest.[1] Just an ordinary week in Clinton County in 1923.

* * *

Black histories are not the only ones that are actively swept under the rug. Ugly white histories are as well, as they could spoil the bucolic image of their imagined white, nonviolent space. Unable to erase the enactment of their white desires across the state—some infamously known, others surreptitiously hidden, many of which resulted in Black terror—white Hoosiers collectively and actively silence any memories concerning said enactment, be they formal white supremacist organizing such as the KKK, or informal means such as sundown laws.

Foregoing chapter vignettes clearly manifest a Black presence in Clinton County, but they leave unexplored social realities that might have contributed to a decline in Black families in the area. After peaking with ninety people in 1930, the number of Black residents started to dwindle to a mere twenty-three in 1970 (-74 percent). As the peak and decline coincided with the Great Migration, we need to dig deep to investigate what changed in the community—values and attitudes? Is Hoosier hospitality actually rooted in Hoosier hostility? If Clinton County became a closed society toward new Black residents, the answer might lie in unearthing other sociohistorical events that took place in Indiana but did not make it into the residents' public memory.

Erasing the community's past racial and ethnic diversity might be easier than having to explain why most people of color left. Pondering the reasons might lead to disclosing the various mechanisms instantiated to enforce whiteness in these communities, including white supremacist organizations and sundown laws. Indiana has long been associated with the rebirth of the second Ku Klux Klan in the 1920s, but white supremacist desires long preceded and outlasted the Klan's heyday. Whereas the Klan history could easily explain the absence of communities of color across the state, this is not the whole story.

Again, I could exclusively use historical archives to demonstrate Indiana's commitment to white desires, documenting activities of white supremacist organizations like the White Caps, the National Horse Thief Detective Association (NHTDA), and the KKK, but this would fall short in capturing the silence that surrounds these white desires. Active erasing, silencing, and forgetting, or white complicity, seems to be a common trend in Hoosier history. The same mechanisms implemented to erase any traces of people of color in the collective memory of Indiana communities were widely applied and mastered across the state to hide these white supremacist desires. By silencing and negating this history, Indiana communities automatically absolve themselves from playing any role in their all-white surroundings and in creating Black northern urban enclaves. This chapter not only documents how Indiana figuratively and literally became white, but it also captures how people explain white supremacy away. What unfolds on the following pages are omissions and deflections of white wrongdoings as well as lackadaisical attempts to own the ugly parts of their white history.

Contemporary residents rarely acknowledge the existence of the KKK or the NHTDA in their community's history. Only four of my interview conversations (16 percent) specifically mentioned Indiana's connection to the KKK past, and one of them, from which the epigraph derives, did so more extensively. That conversation was also the only one in which the NHTDA surfaced. Despite the dearth of acknowledgment, a detailed discussion of both organizations is warranted, as the presence and communal support of such white supremacist organizations further illuminates white desires and might help explain why Black migrants did not permanently relocate in Clinton County during the Great Migration.

Omissions are a powerful tool in narrative county histories. The overall silence by most informants regarding KKK history in the county reflects the whitewashing trends in the Black History Project. What becomes clear in the survey responses is a widespread hesitation to name the inglorious realities and historical facts that illustrate white supremacist attitudes in Indiana. The failure to acknowledge and reflect on Klan history goes along with the trend to downplay or generally overlook county activities that intentionally or inadvertently caused a drop in minority populations in their counties. Adding to the discussion on county-wide expulsions in the earlier chapters, my discussion on people's silence on sundown town policies will further unearth how the pattern of white Hoosier hostility toward Black folk manifested across the state.

A Hooded Past: Whitewashing KKK History throughout the Twentieth Century

National print media articles on Indiana during the Great Migration were generally accolades about the state, praising the Hoosier economy, farming, land, culture, and people.[2] For these authors, the KKK and the NHTDA, as part of the state's white history, offered more of a discussion point than African Americans. The authors, including native Hoosiers, rarely mentioned Black Hoosiers or discussed the Great Migration. When native authors tackled the Ku Klux Klan, their approaches ranged from defending and absolving Hoosiers whom the Klan corrupted, to calling the 1920s a "tragedy" and a "holiday from conscience," to admitting the continuous presence of the KKK mindset in the state.[3] In the 1920s, articles that already drew attention to the Klan in their headlines usually tried to explore the reasons why the KKK was so successful in Indiana, which included that Hoosiers had a "follower" or "joiner" mentality, and that it was not about hate but Americanism and political power. Other authors declared the state as the true poster child of the KKK and labeled it as "a hotbed of hatred and suspicion."[4]

This level of outspokenness and contextualization demonstrated in the national press during and after the "reign of terror" was not reflected in the Black History Project, although the reign of the Invisible Empire was more than six decades earlier. Indeed, there is an overwhelming absence of Ku Klux Klan references in the survey responses. The fact that the responses include little reflection and acknowledgement of the KKK heydays in the counties is surprising, because it could have been a simple way to explain the absence of Black people.[5]

If KKK history is mentioned at all in the surveys, which was the case for the counties of Boone, Clay, Daviess, Johnson, and Morgan (9 percent of survey responses), it is addressed in passing. The Clay County historian's attempt to shed more light on the history of Black folk in the county illustrates this well: "I don't think there has ever been much conflict between blacks and whites. Maybe in the late 1920's when KKK law was riding high there were minor incidents—but nothing of major note. Mostly we all get along peacefully." Boone County's historian successfully creates some distance from its Klan history when he writes, "I have been told stories about the KKK both ways—they would cause trouble but according to the tape this does not seem to be true."[6] A volunteer at the public library conducted some oral histories (on tape) with several senior citizens in the area, which seemingly contested the accusation that the Klan stirred up trouble in the county. However, no further reference is provided.

Certain county representatives owned and acknowledged the white supremacist history and the KKK's existence in their county, but others accidentally revealed that dark stain on their county's past. Hamilton County serves as an example here. Through the survey, one learns about various Black businesses in the city of Noblesville. The county's newspaper, the *Noblesville Daily Ledger*, ran a weekly "Colored News" section from at least the 1920s through the 1940s. A 1924 newspaper clipping from the *Ledger* was enclosed with the survey returned. Due to the poor quality of the copy, it is unclear whether the article on the death of "colored" Edward Armstrong was part of the "Colored Section." However, two columns to the right on the same page, a Klan announcement was printed: "Klan meeting is said to be invitational" with the subheading "Big Event to Occur here tomorrow," documenting the coexistence of Black folk and the Klan in the county at that time.[7]

Though not mentioned in the survey, the vertical file for St. Joseph County also reveals the KKK past. The file contains a list of books and resources for the African American community in the county. The list is preceded by a little introductory paragraph, which notes the following about the history of the KKK:

> By mid 1923, Indiana's membership in the Ku Klux Klan led the nation, and St. Joseph County had an active Klan organization. However, because

> of the small number of African Americans living in St. Joseph County during the Klan's reign in the county, Klan activities appear to have been aimed mostly against Catholics and immigrants (many of whom were Catholic) and there was less violence against African-Americans and Jews than against Catholics in the county.[8]

The writer acknowledges the Klan's violent history yet shifts attention to their other targets because too few Black people were in the area. But the small number of African Americans in St. Joseph County was certainly no deterrent for the Klan. "South Bend Negroes Get Warning Letter," a front-page news article in the *Frankfort Evening News*, confirms that thought, as it "announced that the 'colored joints' would be 'cleaned up,'" signed by the "K. K. K."[9]

After its collapse in the late 1920s, the KKK continued to regain its political power and societal influence in Indiana throughout the twentieth century—and none of it was captured in the surveys. In 1940, for example, the *Frankfort Morning Times* reports rebirth efforts in the state and quotes the Imperial Wizard of the organization. He stated a drastic increase in Indiana membership over the last year and mentioned Klan activities in about thirty-five communities at that time. No longer with the same political influence it once had, it now directed its efforts to combat "subversive influences" and to organize the majority group, because "the Minorities—Jews, aliens, Catholics and to a lesser degree Negroes—are well organized."[10] The *Frankfort Morning Times* proves useful here to note other KKK revivals in the state that county respondents overlooked, including an anticipated rally weekend in Dearborn County in the fall of 1965, Klan parades in Morgan and Johnson counties in 1967, a cross-burning in Johnson County in the summer of 1967, and another Klan rally in Warsaw, Kosciusko County, in the fall of 1970. And as noted in the previous chapter, Tippecanoe experienced a cross-burning in 1987, as well as a Klan rally in 1994.[11] I note these incidents to show the breadth of white supremacist support in Indiana long after the 1920s heyday of the KKK in the state, as they corroborate that these beliefs are more intrinsic to Hoosier culture than residents and scholars might make us believe. These contours of the Klan history help us see how the geography of hate reproduces and is reproduced across generations.

A Hooded Past: Acknowledging the KKK in Indiana and Clinton County Today

Attitudes about owning Indiana's ugly history have changed in the state, though not drastically—on neither the state nor local level. Indiana recently celebrated its bicentennial anniversary as a state, among other events, with the "Indiana in 200 Objects" exhibition. With regard to including those "dark times in the state history" in the exhibition, Susannah Koerber, the Indiana State Museum's senior vice president of collections and interpretation, is quoted as saying that "the state should not paper over its past, and visitors viewing these items—including a set of Ku Klux Klan robes and photograph of the Aug. 7, 1930 lynching of Thomas Shipp and Abram Smith in Marion, Ind.—can reflect on where the state has been over the past 200 years and where it might be headed in the future."[12] Although the intent is laudable, the effect is questionable at best. The infamous photograph, here entitled "The lynching of Thomas Shipp and Abram Smith, 1930," was accompanied by a small, nonchalant paragraph, as displayed in Figure 6.

The description neither contextualizes nor explains the atrocity that took place. Of course, the genre of museum notes precludes a deep reflection on the history of racial violence, but it might give enough room to briefly comment on lynching photography and postcards—for example, on the fact that these artifacts were initially produced to reflect and uphold white superiority and supremacy. Instead of acknowledging the state's racist past, the description distracts the exhibit visitor with common lynching tropes and references such as "the South" and the song "Strange Fruit."[13]

The exhibit featured two other objects of Indiana's dark history to the left and right of the lynching postcard, both of which were accompanied by little to no historical context—the "Indiana House Bill 364, An Act to Prevent Procreation of Confirmed Criminals, Idiots, Imbeciles and Rapists, 1907," the nation's first compulsory sterilization law, and a red "Ku Klux Klan robe, circa 1979." Similar to the reflection on the lynching photograph, the Klan robe description misses the opportunity to acknowledge Indiana's extensive involvement in and empowerment of the second KKK. Instead, the succinct paragraph homes in on the "long period of decline" that the KKK endured in the 1920s and concludes with: "No longer the predominately anti-African American organization of old, the modern KKK evolved into a loose association of fundamentalist, gun-rights, anti-immigrant and white-pride adherents" (Figure 7). Visitors were left to their own interpretation in trying to connect the 1920s to 1979, the year the robe was worn in a public outing by a locally elected chief of police in Dubois County. But how to reckon the connection between the police and a white supremacist organization in a few words?

The biggest problem here is the difference in scale, or how the three objects were displayed at the exhibition. The Klan robe was given a full-body size space to display the red robe—visually pleasing due to the silk material

FIGURE 6. This photograph captures how the exhibition "Indiana in 200 Objects" attempted to publicly acknowledge the state's lynching history. The size of the caption provides an idea of the postcard's small scale. Photograph taken by author during exhibition visit in July 2016.

being used—whereas the lynching was merely displayed on a small photo postcard, about 6" by 8."[14] What could the effect have been if they had magnified the photograph, maybe hanging it from a papier-maché tree? These are but a few missed opportunities to publicly own and apologize for the state's wrongdoings. This way, however, the exhibition serves as an example of how Indiana's racist history is whitewashed and diluted on the state level in the twenty-first century.

These sparse and lackadaisical efforts of historical and cultural contextualization are also replicated in one of the permanent galleries of the Indiana State Museum, which is dedicated to the state's cultural history. Positioned in a transitionary corridor or pathway between bigger exhibition spaces stands a white Klan robe with no further explanation of its relevance to the state. The State Museum is a self-proclaimed "world-class institution," which is

FIGURE 7. Display of an Indiana Ku Klux Klan robe from 1979. However, the caption discusses the KKK during the 1920s. This robe was worn by the Huntingburg Chief of Police. The accompanying text does not close the gap between the 1920s and 1979; visitors are left to their own interpretations. Photograph taken by author during exhibition visit in July 2016.

"forward-thinking" and has the mission "to celebrate, explore and steward all that is authentically wondrous about Indiana." To position the robe spatially in a passage from one hall to the next questions Indiana's willingness to face its ugly past, or in the words of the state museum's website, to really "uncover Indiana's secrets."[15] Maybe the curator thought that the robe says it all, but it is rather unusual to let the artifact speak for itself, especially since the state's KKK history still is a raw sore. The lack of text and the scarcity of artifacts that would allow visitors to empathize with the victims of KKK violence is somewhat disturbing. It seems that the state and its citizens still try to minimize and repudiate—if not outright erase—this part of their sociocultural history. Publicly, Hoosiers then and now have saved face and shied away from acknowledging their respective Klan histories. Privately, it appears, Hoosiers act not much differently. As mentioned above, the KKK surfaced in only four of my interviews (16 percent). Though this part of Indiana's history was discussed by fewer than one in five of my informants, their abrupt dismissal once the topic came up caught my attention. They were quick to acknowledge the state's legacy of the Klan, but even quicker to denounce any Klan presence in their county. The one extensive conversation about both white supremacist organizations in Clinton County, however, contains a plethora of detail about the history, conveying a palpable atmosphere about the organizations' presence in the county. Let's have a look.

Shooing Away Klan Memories

Remember Doug from the vignette in the introduction—the local white resident who didn't "have a challenge with" the recent increase of Black people in the community as long as they "behave themselves"? Let's recall, he is a white native of Clinton County in his mid-sixties, and he ran a family-owned business in Frankfort for most of his life. Doug's key phrase during the interview was "all-white community": he used it to describe the town's identity and to explain the cultural and demographic changes Frankfort has undergone, as it now no longer is "an all-white community." As he repeatedly used the phrase, I inquired further on how it remained all-white until recently. He inserted the demographically homogeneous make-up of the community when he explained that it was a "small" "farming" and "railroad community" in the past that experienced migrant workers but remained "basically an all-white community." His reach to historical events allowed me to specifically inquire why African Americans did not move into the community in the past. Here is an excerpt of our exchange:

ME: But what about African Americans? You mentioned them. Are they recently coming here?

DOUG: Just recently.

ME: And they didn't come back then?

DOUG: There weren't any back then.

ME: Ok.

DOUG: And you know, I don't know why they didn't move to the community.

ME: And there wasn't anything that kept them out?

DOUG: I would think that. But the one thing, the reputation the community had way back, way back, was it had ties probably to the Klan, as Indiana was a big Klan state. And so that may have had some things to do with it. You know, reputation gets out. Your town reputation gets out. But I can tell you that through my age time, I didn't see any of that kind of activity going on. It was just a community that folks just didn't move to. I mean they just didn't. And I don't have the reason for that. I think now that's all changed.

Here, Doug inserts Indiana's historical ties to the KKK to explain the lack of people of color in the region. However, he protects his community immediately after that insertion, explaining that there have been no Klan activities in the community during his lifetime. In the same breath, however, he weakens his protective strategy by strongly asserting that it's just not a community Black people moved to, opening up the possibility that the community indeed embraced the KKK (though without his knowledge).

His frequent display of "no knowledge" illustrates Charles Mills's "epistemology of ignorance," which "produc[es] the ironic outcome that whites will in general be unable to understand the world they themselves have made."[16] Doug simply does not know and cannot conceive of any reasons why people of color did not move to the community. The repetitive nature of his lack of knowledge also suggests that our conversation might have been the first time he actually confronted this reality—thus far, his go-to moniker "all-white community" served to explain it all.

Frances, another native of Clinton County in her late seventies and a retired school employee, adopted a similar defensive strategy for the local community. During the interview on a cold wintry afternoon, she reminisced about "a lot of really neat things about [her] life." She expressed gratitude and love for her community, in which she once knew everyone who lived there, because "everybody was either related or had been here for years and years." Indiana Klan history did not surface during our two-hour conversation about the community until the very end. At the end of our conversation, I handed her my business card, so one of her acquaintances could get in touch with me for a potential interview. My card listed my research interests, including hate crimes, which prompted the following exchange:

FRANCES: I see this on here [my business card], too. Hate crimes. I don't ever remember the Ku Klux Klan being around here at all either. But I think they were in southern Indiana.

ME: Yeah, I haven't even looked into the KKK yet . . . but that's good to know.

FRANCES: And I just saw that. But that's never been around here.

ME: No?

FRANCES: Ever. No. Nothing like that that I can remember. Ever. Anything like that. Where somebody was . . . you know, I wonder if there are any Jewish families [here]. . . . Hmm. I dunno. If they are, they're ok. . . . Again, there has never been a place of worship for Jewish families.

My research interest in hate crimes triggered her defense mechanisms about her community. With a series of one-word exclamation and short sentences, she strongly negated any KKK presence in the area but hesitantly admitted to the presence in the state. Without finishing her thought, she immediately shifted the conversation to speculating about any Jewish families in the community. This ephemeral moment in which the words "hate crimes" prompted remarks about the KKK, which then triggered thoughts about Jewish families, illustrates confusion and discomfort on the one hand, and a potential connection of the KKK discriminating against religious minorities on the other.

The most recent acknowledgment of a Klan presence in Indiana was provided by Cheryl and Rick, a farming couple in their late sixties I interviewed on a rainy afternoon on their family farm in the fall of 2016. After conversing about the Great Migration that resulted in urban growth of the northern Black population, we speculated about why African Americans would not come to small-town Indiana. I recalled that some of my informants used the Klan as an explanation for why African Americans avoided Indiana, which triggered a personal memory among my interlocutors. Before committing himself to the farming business as a young small farmer, Rick was a teacher in the early 1970s in Putnam County, two counties south of Clinton County. He was aware of a Klan presence there because "Well . . . people talk." He clarified immediately that he would not have moved to that community as a Black man, which led me to inquire whether he was comfortable enough to work there as a white man. He responded: "Oh yeah. Oh yeah. I mean as a white person, there weren't any problem [*sic*]. But I do remember that there was a librarian that came to the school I taught at and she was a pretty hot little blonde but her husband was Black. And she didn't last but about three weeks." Rick resigned shortly thereafter, committing himself full-time to the family farming business. Whereas Cheryl and Rick acknowledged the most recent Klan presence in the state with a memory from the 1970s, they did not comment on Clinton County's Klan history.

"It Didn't Go Over Very Good": Hushing Memories Confirmed

There is no doubt that at least two white supremacist organizations existed in Clinton County: the National Horse Thief Detective Association and the second Ku Klux Klan. The local newspapers' coverage attests to the wide-ranging support in the community for both organizations. The two groups aligned their agendas in the 1920s, blending white supremacy, vigilantism, and politics. The marriage of these two white supremacist organizations could explain why people of color then and now have avoided settling in the Hoosier state. It could explain the silence, omission, and avoidance of discussions about race.

In that regard, one interview stands out in affirming the presence of both white supremacist organizations in the county. Tom and Robert, both elderly white gentlemen and native to Clinton County, are interested in their county's history. Their dedication to preserve local history led them to many auctions and postcard shows in the area, where they acquired memorabilia from the county. I was honored to spend a wonderful afternoon with them, as they opened up their house and memories for me.

Sharing a wealth of county memorabilia, from postcards and newspaper prints to "Gem City" shot glasses and bottles made in Frankfort, they stumbled across badges from the NHTDA in their collections (Figure 8).

The badges triggered a lot of memories and knowledge about the vigilante organization. It was almost as if they forgot my presence in the room, as the two men were mainly talking to each other. My intermittent comments and questions appear more like a reminder to contextualize the association. Here is one excerpt of our conversation (identifying information of other community members has been removed):

TOM: Oh, oh. . . . You know, I have been told Frankfort had two [chapters].
ROBERT: Yeah, they had the Gem City and the regular Frankfort.
TOM: Regular Frankfort. Somebody said this was a rare one, the Gem City, the Woodside, I guess.

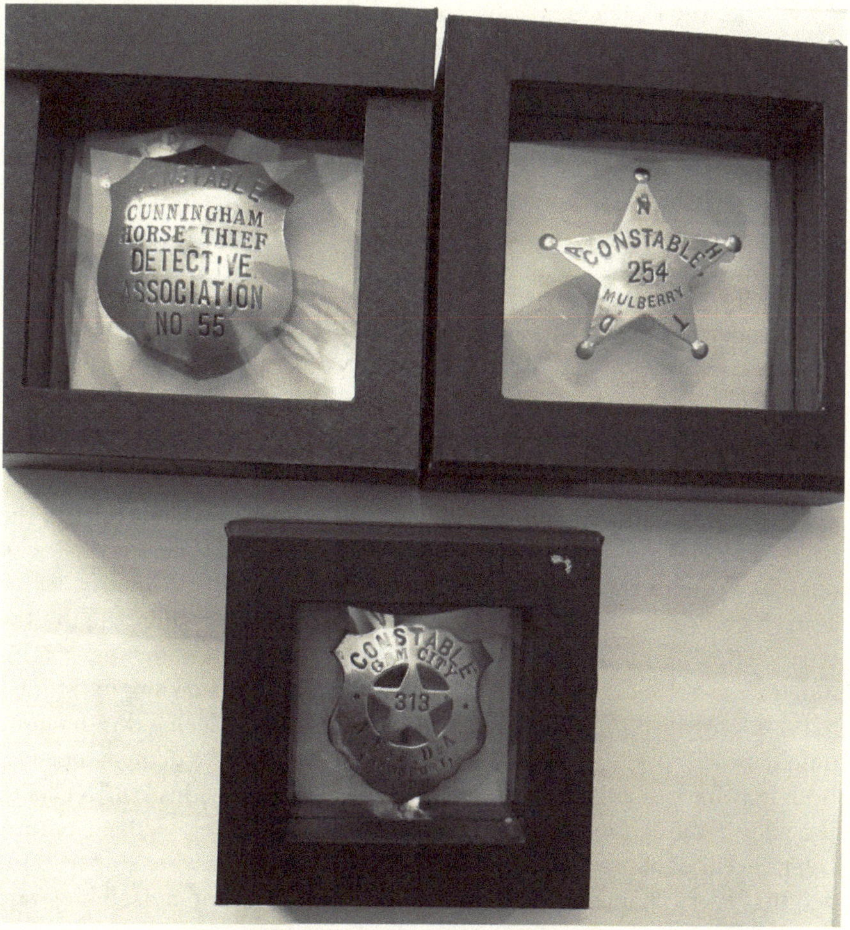

FIGURE 8. Badges of some of the NHTDA chapters in Clinton County. They represent constables, or chapters, in Cunningham, Mulberry, and Frankfort.

ROBERT: I've got the Gem City, the Mulberry, and the Cunningham [badges].
TOM: I had Cunningham, Rossville, and Mulberry.
ME: What are you talking about?
TOM: That's for the Horse Thief badge . . . they had horse thieves.

. . .

ME: So Frankfort had two? Like clubs?
ROBERT: Like a chapter.
TOM: Avery had one [chapter], and [a common friend of theirs] had one of Geetingsville. I never saw one of Geetingsville.

ROBERT: And that's exactly what they did, too—chase horse thieves.

TOM: Well, they did to an extent. [A common friend of theirs] said there was a fella in Mulberry who got too familiar with his neighbor's wife. So, one day he went out and they had tied a bundle of switches with a note that said "you better stay home or you get these used on you."

ME: You get what?

TOM: You better stay home or we use these on you—switches, whip.

ROBERT: It probably would have been a good thing for him.

ME: Switches are whips, aha.

TOM: [A common friend] laughed, [he] belonged to the Mulberry, he laughed, he said they went a little bit beyond horse thieves.

ROBERT: Yeah. Oh yeah, yeah, they were more like a vigilante group actually.

TOM: See [a common friend], he was the captain of Mulberry. And I often wondered. See this is a constable, I wondered if these were here.

They recalled community members who had badges of other locales in the county as well as some names of neighbors, friends, and acquaintances who once were members of the association, including former captains. While Tom shared some activities of the group, Robert tried to contextualize the organization for me. Tom spoke from his experience, given that he is in his nineties, and Robert spoke from what he had acquired during his studies of the county history, as he is thirty years Tom's junior. Seeing this dynamic unfold underscores the value of having interviewed the two of them together. Both may have instilled the confidence in each other to admit the NHTDA presence in the community and even attest to their violent, vigilante nature. Later, we talked about the badges' different styles, which is when Robert clarified that every chapter had its unique style and Tom emphasized how rare these badges are. We also stumbled upon a "window sticker" of the NHTDA: "If you were a member, this one went in your window," and a "pin." "You would wear that on your lapel," Robert explained. In that realm, they dwelled on having owned an enlarged panoramic photograph of a big meeting of the NHTDA in 1925 that took place in Frankfort, which captured all the "guys" and "they all had their badges on. It was a great picture," Tom remarked. Robert inserted that more than 200 men were shown in the photograph. Their collection also spanned stock books and journals of the NHTDA (Figure 9).

The various NHTDA memorabilia triggered from my two interlocutors a wealth of information that attests not only to the organization's strength in the community but also to the fact that they knew people who belonged to the organization. The members were not strangers or invaders but their neighbors and friends.[17] Consequently, in their minds, the NHTDA was group of "guys"

FIGURE 9. Journal of NHTDA from the 1924 annual meeting in Terre Haute, Indiana. The poor quality of the photograph captures the nonchalant way the journal "peeks" out of a pile of local history booklets.

mainly concerned with "chasing horse thieves." Whereas both confirmed the NHTDA presence, they also illustrated how vigilantism in Clinton County is whitewashed—willingly or subconsciously.

Whitewashing as a geography of hate mechanism explains white supremacy away. Robert described the NHTDA as "more like a vigilante group," maybe because the organization was sanctioned by the State of Indiana as a legal (though unpaid) force for upholding the law ever since the passing of the "Horse Thief Detective Company" Act in 1852. Membership was exclusive to "free, white males, 21 years old, with superior character and property."[18] Aligning themselves with the Klan leadership in the state in the 1920s resulted in the NHTDA having the same powers as the police. Regardless of whether the organization was state sanctioned, African Americans and other outsiders might have rightfully been concerned to know that groups to which they could not belong could take the law into their own hands, and they might have reconsidered relocating to Indiana during the Great Migration.[19]

Robert, Tom, and I talked about the National Horse Thief Detective Association at various points during the afternoon, yet never did either of them make the leap to associating the organization with the Ku Klux Klan. Already in 1924, Max Bentley, journalist for *McClure's* magazine, noted the connection between the two organizations. He argued that through D. C. Stephenson, the Grand Dragon of the Indiana Klan, the Klan "resurrected the Horse Thief Act and made it the law-enforcement arm of the Indiana klan [*sic*]."[20] Erik Wade expands on this aspect, detailing the intertwined nature of the two white supremacist organizations. Wade argues that the "Klan and the NHTDA emerged from and converged during moments in national and state histories when anxieties about race and citizenship ran high."[21] In that regard, it was no coincidence that both of these white supremacist organizations were popular in the immediate aftermath of the Great Migration's first wave and World War I (Maps 6 and 7). Indiana experienced its fair share of immigrants and southern Black migrants settling in their midst. Joining organizations that stood against such demographic influxes was one way for white Hoosiers to express their displeasure about such demographic changes. As the history of the KKK in the state is still a sore subject, it could explain why most of my informants kept their memories and knowledge hushed. And even when admitting the existence of such white supremacist organizations, my interlocutors presented a tame or distanced version of the KKK and NHTDA, which does not place agency with Clinton County's white residents. Inadvertently, however, their refusal to admit having knowledge about the NHTDA, the KKK, and their intersection contributes to perpetuating an idyllic small-town environment full of whitewashed history operating under a white racial frame. This is white complicity par excellence in preserving their white reality.

Tom and Robert were the only ones who openly acknowledged the Klan's existence in Clinton County.[22] While we were engaged in a conversation about the few Black families that lived in the community in the past, Robert inserted, "you also had the Ku Klux Klan that was busy in all those areas for a number of years that would have kept the Black population out." Here he

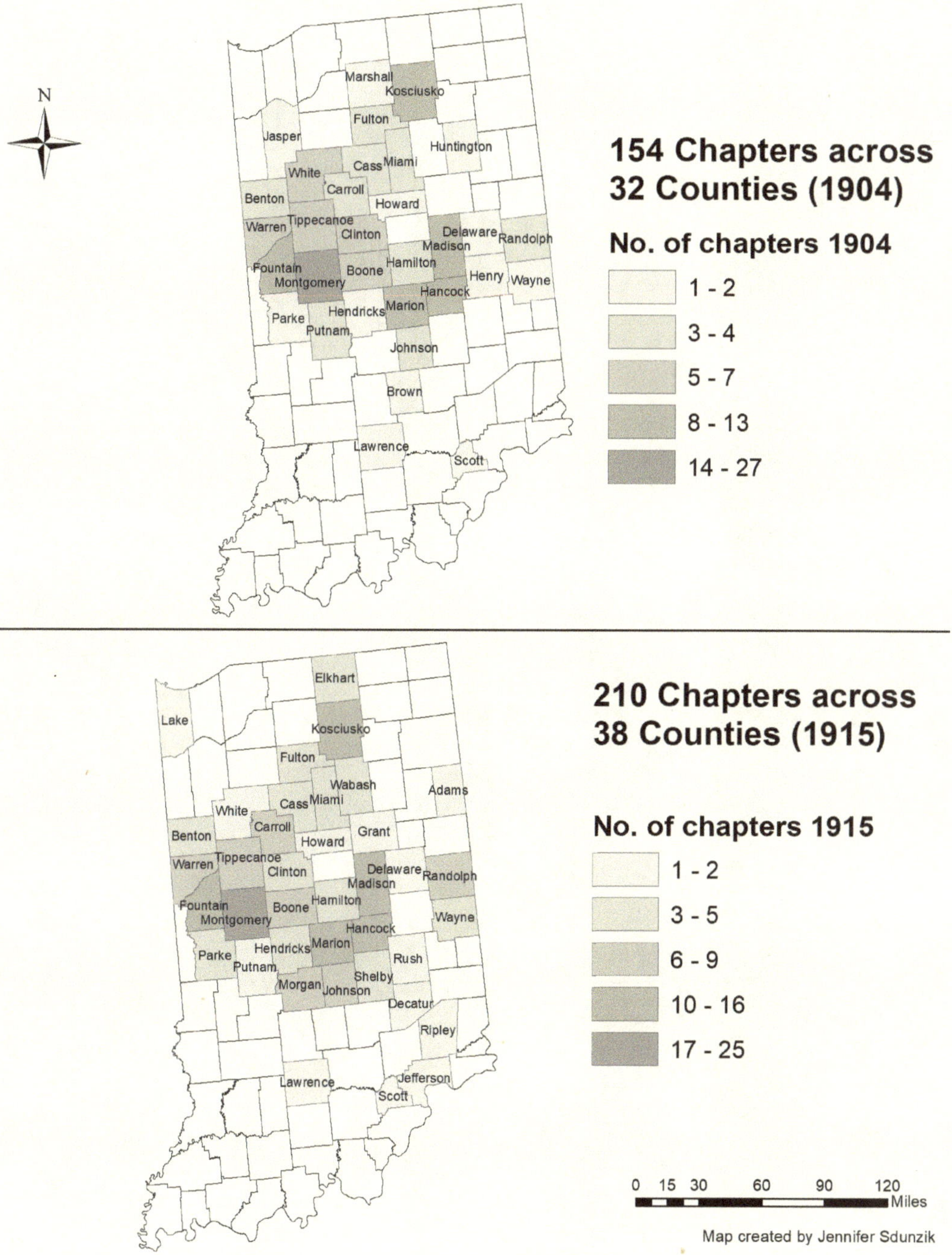

MAP 6. Growth of NHTDA chapters in Indiana between 1904 and 1915

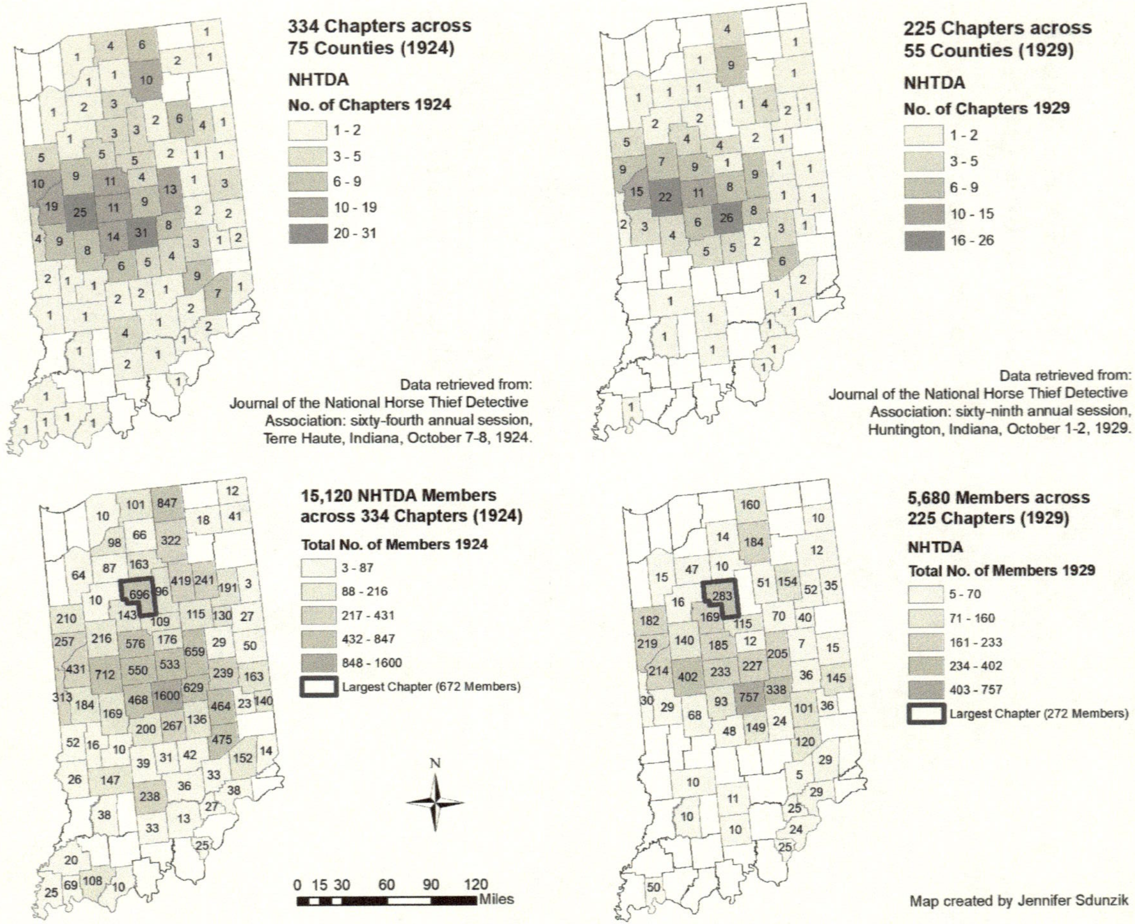

MAP 7. Growth of NHTDA chapters and membership in Indiana in the 1920s. Maps 6 and 7 indicate that the increase in chapters preceded the reign of the Invisible Empire in the 1920s and overall seems to have coincided with the first wave of the Great Migration (1915–1930).

follows a strategy similar to Doug, correlating the Klan presence with the Black absence in the community. Robert's comment was met with a loud "Oooooh yeah. Now that stuff" by Tom. While Robert reiterated that Black families "were kept out," Tom recalled the following:

> They were anti-Catholic, anti-Jewish. We had a fella that opened up an ice-cream parlor . . . the Rainbow Inn, it was a little ice-cream parlor, it had little rainbows and little chairs. . . . They had a big rainbow at the balconies on the west side of the square. And it was a Greek that run it. And he had a brother-in-law, I think it was his brother-in-law, he ran a candy kitchen on the north side of the square. Well, that rainbow, in World War II, or World War I, he was in the 42nd Division, which was the Rainbow Division, a very highly honored division in World War I, and to commemorate that, he painted a rainbow over the balcony over that brick . . . that's how he got the name Rainbow Inn. And they, them Ku Kluxers made it so tough on him, he finally just quit business and left town.[23]

Although Tom started his recollection of Klan activities with the organization's anti-religious stance, his example also attests to its anti-immigrant stance in Indiana.

Frankfort city directories affirm the ownership of Candy Kitchen for Harry Kussurelis in 1913 and the Rainbow Inn for Thomas Kussurelis in 1924. The *Indianapolis News* ran advertisements for Frankfort's Rainbow Inn in 1919. In March of that year, they were looking for an "experienced chef for first class café" and the contact reference was Harry Kussurelis, and in October the advertisements desired a "second cook; necessary to have good experience; white or colored."[24] The Greek brothers openly advertised for personnel to hire regardless of color, constituting the only example I found during my research on Clinton County. Because Black folk did not constitute part of the larger Clinton County community, it is fair to assume that not many establishments in Frankfort hired across the color line. Though the local establishment remains unidentified, the *Frankfort Morning Times* reported on a "Colored Chef Leav[ing] Frankfort in Hurry" two months after the advertisements. Whether the Black cook worked for the Kussurelis brothers, we do not know. The fact that he was driven out of town before the Klan dominated Indiana politics and ideology corroborates that the social environment was hostile toward Black Hoosiers in Frankfort. Small-town Indiana found civic value in exclusion, which the KKK knew how to exploit. That said, the KKK in Indiana and Clinton County was not an aberration but rather an extension of the tendencies the community engendered.

Tom's recollection about the Rainbow Inn left me puzzled. I felt the need to confirm that the Klan, indeed, was in Clinton County. Tom doubled down, affirming, "Ooooh, it was strong!" Though a youngster, Tom was alive when the Klan was in power. He had vivid memories of the Klan "marching around the square in Frankfort, must have been hundreds of them." He remembered the "sheets, regular bed sheets. They'd pin it around; they had pointed hats." Both Tom and Robert recalled that the local museum once had one of the robes on display. "We put it on a mannequin up there," Tom chuckled, "it didn't go over very good," alluding to the community's unwillingness to face its own racist past—on a mannequin. I could sense that Tom was appalled by the Klan history, and then he continued: "I think they was ashamed of themselves, that's why they had to put sheets over themselves."

Tom's recollection about the Greek restaurant owner being driven out of town led me to inquire whether African Americans were also "requested" to leave town. "Ooh, Blacks . . . they was wicked on the Blacks," Tom remarked. His recollection here is important, as it further illuminates why few African Americans settled permanently in Frankfort during the Great Migration.

Robert and Tom are collectors of historical artifacts and proud of owning rare memorabilia. Our conversation transitioned into Klan collectibles, upon which Robert commented, "Yeah, it's highly collectible" and "yeah, but you don't show it." The same might apply to NHTDA badges, which Tom above described as "rare" (though he recalled quite a few in the community who had some). Collectors of these artifacts may simply decide not to openly advertise their collection, further corroborating the bitter taste the white supremacist history still leaves in the community.

Among their Klan collectibles, Tom and Robert had a pocketknife and postcards[25] showcasing local Klan members (Figures 10 and 11).

We were unable to locate the application for membership in the local KKK that they had among their local history treasures. But Tom recalled some information from the form, noting:

> What I couldn't understand, the people, they were supposed to be religious, you had to be a Protestant, religious Protestant, that was on the application. And guess what, they'd go around in people's yard and burning crosses. So now what kind of religious belief can you have and burn a cross?

Robert engaged this remark with: "Yeah, they got sidetracked pretty early on what they were supposed to be doing," ending with an embarrassed or uncomfortable chuckle.

This moment marks one of the complexities and contradictions I encountered in the various hours of interviews conducted in the community. As local

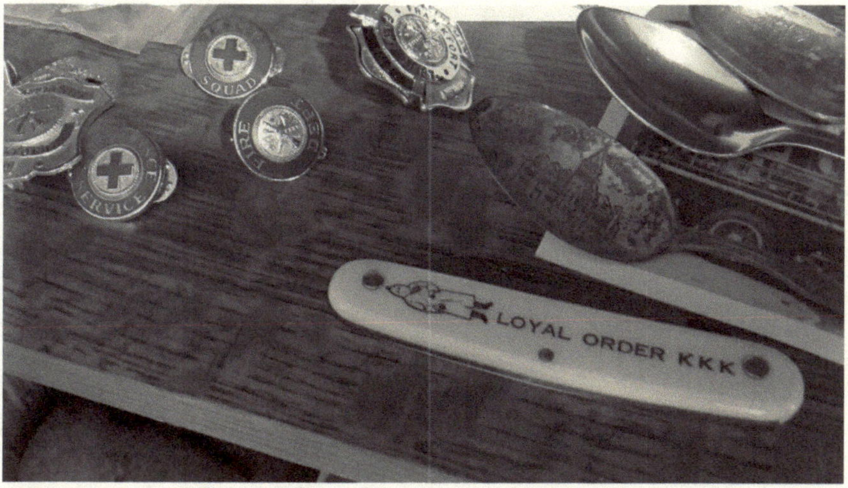

FIGURE 10. This pocketknife was among the memorabilia from the county. Robert contextualized the item, noting "They did all of their advertising, so you could keep . . . and they would sell that to membership and they would either show that and they would take the money on whatever they spent the money on, and they promoted. . . . [T]hey sold that, paper weights, everything that had . . . typically just the KKK on it."

historians, they had memorabilia and stories, which they willingly shared with me. In the comfort of their own home, they both acknowledged the county's burden of history to me. In an attic full of historical artifacts that reflect county and state history, it might feel appropriate to discuss less glamorous moments from the past. Although Robert acknowledged the importance of preserving the materials and sharing history, he admitted that I was the first one to whom he opened his house. I hope that going forward and expanding on his collection, he is courageous enough to share some of the artifacts and stories publicly—with the help of the public library or the county museum. The wealth of knowledge and collectibles could transform Robert from a mere collector of artifacts to an educator about the county history. The need to publicly reflect on the less-ideal history of the county is there, so that incidents of exclusion and intolerance can be avoided in the future. However, this might take some time if we recall Tom's remark that the display of a hooded mannequin a couple of years ago "didn't go over very good."

Tom's and Robert's accounts were by far the most comprehensive I could gather on the matter from Clinton County residents. Per sheer coincidence, I bumped into the former Clinton County historian who had filled out the

FIGURE 11. Two of the Klan postcards Robert and Tom were able to acquire over the years. Robert estimated that the photographs were from 1924, speculating that it must have been the Klan's heyday in the county, as "for anybody to take their mask off, that just didn't happen." This statement is slightly exaggerated, as the Library of Congress holds a plethora of photographs of a 1926 Klan parade in Washington, D.C., many of which feature marchers with their hoods down. See, for example, Alex Arbuckle, "Hate on Parade: When the KKK Marched on Washington."

BHP survey in May 1989 during one of my research visits to the Indiana Historical Society.[26] At some point in our conversation, he shared with me in great detail how he recalled his aunt reflecting on a Klan funeral she attended when she was young. The aunt, so the story continued, vividly remembered the moment because of the full regalia in which the dead body was buried. The white hoods, the KKK's trademark, made an impression on the young aunt just like they did on young Tom. This example not only corroborates the county's Klan history but also proves my point that the power lies with those county representatives who write history. There is no single mention of the KKK in the survey response.

Hiding and hushing white horrors is a powerful tool in narrating the county's history. Most of my interlocutors followed the motto "If we don't mention it, it never happened." Their memories are silenced. The handful that acknowledged the Klan presence in Indiana whitewashed the history, shooing away any memories close to home or too gory. Negating, silencing, and forgetting this history of the KKK and other white supremacist vigilante groups in Indiana and Clinton County does not make it go away, but it is troubling. The consequences are far-reaching and problematic, because covering up and glossing over historical wrongdoings prevents reconciliation, healing, and progress. It fosters ignorance and reignites stereotypes and animosity. It emboldens white Hoosier residents to perceive their neighborhoods as "naturally" white spaces, which they claim to defend against "encroaching" immigrants and migrants of color.

"Invisible" Sundown Towns: Silencing Memories of Enforced Whiteness

The pinnacle of hidden racism and epitome of silenced white history and hushed memories is the existence of sundown towns and sundown counties. Historian Emma Lou Thornbrough already noted stagnation and declines in the Black population in some places despite "a fivefold increase between 1860 and 1900" in the state's total Black population, attributing it to economic causes as well as "a deliberate anti-Negro policy." Besides noting Washington and Crawford counties as African American–free zones, she identified Perry and Spencer counties as already pre–Civil War sundown counties. Thornbrough also named various towns that barred Black folk: Utica in Clark County, Aurora in Dearborn County, Scottsburg and Lexington in Scott County, Linton in Greene County, and Bluffton in Wells County. She also observed that the riots in New Albany, Floyd County, in 1862 and Evansville, Vanderburgh County, in 1865 resulted in temporary exoduses and an overall intensification of racial animosity.[27]

County respondents in the survey were less forthcoming thirty years after Thornbrough's account was published. There were only two remarks across all files that alluded to a sundown town past. Responding to the inquiry about potential Underground Railroad sites, the Allen County historian mentions in passing: "Unlikely, Ft. Wayne enforced no-Black ordinance."[28] A hand-written letter by the Boone County historian identifies Whitestown as a location that "would not allow any Black people to stay there," suggesting a sundown history.[29]

Not a single survey response provided any concrete information or explicit acknowledgment regarding sundown town history. Heller's excerpt from the *1979 History of Adams County, Indiana*, a copy of which was sent instead of a detailed survey response, builds the only exception here and establishes one important fact. Heller notes, "Decatur and other towns in the county are commonly referred to in Indiana as 'sundown' towns."[30] Heller's insertion "in Indiana" here is crucial, as it corroborates the expansiveness of the white spatial desires enforced through sundown town policies. The phenomenon is not particular to Adams County, and residents across the entire state label these towns as such. As this county history was published in 1980, it proves that people knew of such towns and policies.[31] It was not until 2005 that sociologist James Loewen published his seminal work *Sundown Towns*, constituting the first major attempt to unearth this history on a larger regional scale and raise awareness of the phenomenon nationwide. Until then, sundown towns had evaded a historical record.

Sundown towns are tricky, though. White people can easily deny the existence of sundown towns if they choose to, as sundown towns have never been the *official* law of the land in Indiana. AP reporter Bem Price describes them as exclusion "through community pressures," as noted in Chapter 2. Many places had unwritten yet socially sanctioned rules regarding minority settlement and service in their midst. Heller explains the epistemology of the term:

> By sundown every Negro is expected to be out of town. Of course, *this is not law, nor never has been, literally*. But it has been enforced many times; waitresses, as late as the 1950's and 1960's, refused to serve blacks, in restaurants, well-known black performers have been refused motel rooms, customers, even actual foreigners visiting here from another country, have been refused service at counters in the stores.[32]

Heller did not exaggerate, if we recall the unwritten policies of exclusion in vacation resorts and housing markets from Chapter 1 or the incident at the gas station in Michigan City from Chapter 2. The Rush County historian also recalled when a Black friend was not permitted to enter a local restaurant, upon which they all left the establishment.[33] The law is an interesting case in Indiana. The state ratified an anti-lynching law, yet lynchings of Black Hoosiers continued to take place without the white perpetrators being punished. Sundown towns have never been official law in the state, yet they were widely and rigorously enforced.

So how does one enforce such racist practices over decades and yet evade the history books? One way to enforce such unofficial but socially sanctioned law was an agreement by a group of property owners or real estate operators to not sell, lease, or rent their property to members of a specific race, also known as racially restrictive covenants. Housing segregation and restrictive covenants were already identified in Chapter 2 as one of the key mechanisms to keep Black people out of town and their community all-white. West Lafayette in Tippecanoe County had an expansive web of racially restricted property and neighborhoods. During my research, I came across housing deeds that still, in 2019, contained the language of the northern Jim Crow days (see Figure 12 for a typical example). It appears not to have been a priority in the county to amend the deeds' language.

The ownership and occupancy section displayed in Figure 12 clearly spells out white desires—spatially and socially. It reads:

> The ownership or occupancy of lots or buildings in [this] Subdivision are restricted to members of the pure white Caucasian race and no persons except members of the pure white Caucasian race shall acquire, title to or occupy any lot or building or any part of any lot or building in this subdivision as owner, tenant or roomer or otherwise. This restriction is not applicable to the domestic employees of owners or tenants or residence in this subdivision.

The abstract for this particular lot was last amended in 1967, yet the exclusionary language was upheld—a strong indication that the previous property owners were white. These housing-related documents in West Lafayette are unique, as they include (rather than exclude) parties eligible to purchase, rent, or occupy property, namely "members of the pure white Caucasian race." In other words, these deeds exclude by inclusion (and vice versa). Before discovering these deeds and abstracts, I encountered "white race" or "Caucasian race," but not the more emphatic "pure white Caucasian race." And I encountered more deeds that excluded people, frequently "Negroes," than deeds that named eligible groups.[34] Deeds became one of the subtle mechanisms to cement Hoosier whiteness and white supremacy in physical spaces for decades.[35] Racist practices hidden in property abstracts enabled white people to enforce exclusion while publicly maintaining the friendly and hospitable face.

Whereas no racially restrictive covenants were confirmed for Clinton County, we still know that the community enforced residential segregation at some point and discriminated against its Black residents, from the *Frankfort Morning Times*. Martha V. Maxey's letter to the editor marks the first Black

NOTE: Iron pipe stakes set at all corners except NW corner of 8, NE corner 18 and NE corner 20 in which are set 2" x 2" x 18" pine stakes. No stake set NE corner 16 due to a building.

SCALE 1" = 40'

I, Claude M. Draper, a Registered Civil Engineer of the State of Indiana do hereby certify that this plan correctly represents the lots, streets and alleys.

Claude M. Draper
Reg. Engr. 1425

Approved by the City Plan Commission of the City of Lafayette this 20th day of March 1946.

F.A.Tedford
Chairman
Harry B. Overesch
Secretary

Approved by the Board of Public Works & Safety of the City of Lafayette, Indiana this 25th day of March 1946

Jack R. LeFevre
City Clerk

Geo H Devault
Harry B. Overesch
E Burke Walker
Board of Public Works (Seal)

CLEGG PARKWAY ADDITION

WE, EDWIN R CLEGG and MATHILDA E CLEGG, of Tippecanoe County, Indiana, owners of the real estate herein described and shown, do hereby dedicate forever for public use for highway purposes the streets and alleys shown on this plan.

Lots as shown on this plan, and the use thereof by present and future owners or occupants shall be subject to the following restrictions and conditions which shall run with the land, to wit:

1. OWNERSHIP or OCCUPANCY - The ownership or occupancy of lots or buildings in Clegg Parkway Subdivision are restricted to members of the pure white Caucasian race and no persons except members of the pure white Caucasian race shall acquire, title to or occupy any lot or building or any part of any lot or building in this subdivision as owner, tenant or roomer or otherwise. This restriction is not applicable to the domestic employees of owners or tenants of residence in this subdivision, If any deed, instrument or arrangement shall be made attempting to convey or permit the occupancy of any lot or building in said subdivision to or by any person not of the pure white Caucasian race except as therein provided, the execution of any such deed or instrument or arrangement shall cause the forfeiture, except against a bona fide mortgagee, to the undersigned respective owners, their heirs, devisees, assigns or successors of said lot or building so attempted to be conveyed, leased or subjected to such occupancy and the title thereto shall at once revert to the undersigned owners, their heirs, deviees, assigns or successors. If any person not of the pure white Caucasian race shall occupy or attempt to occupy any lot or building or part thereof in this subdivision as owner, tenant, roomer or otherwise except as herein provided such occupant may be enjoined from continued occupancy by any court of competent jurisdiction at the suit of any owner or owners of any lot or lots or buildings in this subdivision without being required to show any damage to such owner or owners of any kind whatsoever.

2. BUILDING - No dwelling costing less than $6000.00 or containing less than 6000 cubic feet shall be erected in this subdivision. No building or part thereof shall be constructed within 30 feet of the front

23

FIGURE 12. Example of racially restrictive covenant of West Lafayette abstract. Restrictions and conditions, outlined under "Ownership and Occupancy," were added to the property in March 1946. Photograph taken by author in May 2018.

voice printed in the paper—in 1970. The recently received "fine treatment" at the local hospital inspired her to write the letter.[36] Yet, as a lifelong resident, Maxey also attested to segregation in the community generally, noting for example that "some of our churches were never segregated." In other words, some were.[37] Maxey's experiences with the local housing market reflect the extent to which housing discrimination affected the Black community. She wrote:

> The main trouble I ever experienced was in finding a house to rent or live in—but I always had some good white neighbors who helped me find a place and they usually succeeded. Afterwards, I found it was not my race so much as the fact that they had never rented places to colored people and did not know anything about them.

Maxey was born in Frankfort as Martha Kersey in 1898 and lived there through the Great Migration. Yet she experienced landlords in her own hometown who had never rented to Black residents.[38] Maybe the landlords recently joined the Frankfort community, but maybe they also actively contributed to the fact that they were shy of that very experience. Maxey's letter, however, is a testimony that housing discrimination was part of the lived experiences for people of color in Frankfort—native or not. This is yet another "invisible" barrier the white community of Frankfort put in place to make their surroundings an inhospitable place of *non*belonging for people of color that could explain the decline of its Black community.

Sundown town policies are no longer openly enforced in Indiana. West Lafayette, home to a world-renowned university, integrated around 1970, allowing people of color to occupy, rent, and purchase property as a result of the Fair Housing Act.[39] City limit signs were removed, but discriminatory language in residential deeds and housing titles was not. The chapter of Indiana's sundown history was closed without ever righting the wrong. As white Hoosier communities (all but one) never apologized for nor acknowledged their white wrongdoings, caution in those towns by people of color is still the best approach.[40]

Because sundown towns were based on unwritten laws, it is difficult to pin down white residents' efforts to expel their Black neighbors. There is no record of possible threats and warnings given to Black residents, and newspapers usually covered other, more "newsworthy" events.[41] Sometimes, however, violent threats turned into violent actions, making it impossible for newspapers and residents alike to deny their biased attitudes and actions. Some heinous incidents in white communities catch the nation's attention. The moment the national spotlight is on those communities marks the moment when sundown towns become visible. White supremacist organizations like the KKK come in handy to deflect blame when white desires can no longer be hidden.

When White Desires Result in Death

Besides the reputation as a hotbed of the second KKK, Indiana's notoriety as a racist state, if at all perceived as such, surrounds two gruesome incidents that resulted in the death of three young Black people in 1930 and 1968. The former concerns the lynching of Abram Smith and Thomas Shipp in Marion, Grant County, in August 1930, one of the most gruesome lynchings to take place in the North, which produced an iconic photograph of the incident, discussed above.[42] The latter concerns the ghastly screwdriver murder of Carol Jenkins in Martinsville, Morgan County, in September 1968. The twenty-one-year-old African American was in town after dark selling encyclopedias. This crime was also too heinous to be hidden, yet white Hoosiers still found a way to hide their white desires. This incident threads together various previously discussed topics: sundown towns, the KKK, and racial cleansing, the phenomenon in which the local communities rid themselves of their Black neighbors entirely, unearthed by Pulitzer-prize-winning journalist Elliot Jaspin.

Indeed, Jaspin appears in the Black History Project. He started researching the phenomenon of county-wide racial cleansings in the late 1990s. Besides documenting Vermillion and Washington counties' exclusions, he also considered Morgan County for potential inclusion in his monograph, as one comes to find out when studying the BHP files. The Black History Program archivist referred Jaspin to Coy D. Robbins, who has written extensively on the history of African Americans in various counties across the state, including a 1991 monograph on Morgan County. A photocopy of the email exchange between Jaspin and Robbins in 2002 is included in the Morgan County vertical file. Jaspin inquired about the "sudden drop in the black population in Morgan County," as the county lost 92.5 percent of its Black population over the course of three decades, and the census listed only eight Black people in 1930. Though he negated Jaspin's assumption of a racial cleansing in Morgan County in the early twentieth century,[43] Robbins confirmed the exclusionary attitude toward Black folk in the state. He remarked:

> White citizens here—as in most other Indiana counties—supported the long standing U.S. practices of their racial superiority and the segregation of non-whites until very recent years. Throughout much of its history,

> Indiana created successfully a social, economic and political atmosphere that discouraged the emigration [*sic*] of non-white residents.[44]

Here, Robbins asserts the culture of exclusion as an intrinsic characteristic of Indiana, noting the structural, institutional, and discursive barriers that pushed communities of color to the margins of Hoosier society and manifested the geography of hate. In contrast to the outspoken chastising of white Indiana at large, Robbins attributes the negative reputation of Martinsville and Morgan County solely to the KKK, thereby exonerating the ordinary local white citizens:

> Martinsville, from a racial standpoint, has achieved its negative image nation-wide, particularly since the 1920s when "The Invisible Empire" invaded Indiana. The KKK is said to have gained strong support among white Hoosiers. Two racial incidents are believed by many to have involved some Klan members and their local supporters: [1] August 1943 mob disturbances to prevent the employment of about 20 Jamaicans who were agricultural workers and British citizens of African ancestry sorely needed due to the shortage of men during WII [*sic*] to pick ripe fruit in Morgan County. The downtown mob finally dispersed when the Indiana State Police moved these visitors out of town "for their own safety." [2] The street murder in September 1968 of Carol Jenkins, a 21-year old door-to-door encyclopedia salesperson of color from Rushville, Indiana. After 34 years, an elderly white male murder suspect from Indianapolis was arrested and jailed in Martinsville this summer.[45]

Robbins extends the existence of the Ku Klux Klan in Indiana way beyond the 1920s—unlike many other Hoosiers—by contextualizing two racist incidents from the 1940s and 1960s and affirms the local mob mentality prevalent in white Hoosier minds. The connection between these two incidents and the KKK notwithstanding, we should remember that the racist attitudes and prejudices preceded Indiana's Klan era and lingered many years thereafter, in parts up until today. Both of Robbins's examples corroborate this point, as they took place long after the KKK heyday of the 1920s. It is also striking that Robbins chose not to mention the two KKK rallies that took place in Martinsville in 1967 and 1968. Maybe it would have weakened his argument that the KKK that "invaded Indiana" was responsible for those hateful incidents in 1943 and 1968, respectively, and not the ordinary white Hoosier. Maybe it would have alluded too closely to attitudes in the area that seem to condone displays of hatred toward people of color.

Jenkins's murderer was arrested in 2002 but died before being tried in court. He did confess to the murder on his deathbed. Whereas he lived in a nursing home in Indianapolis by the time of his arrest, he lived in neighboring Hendricks County in 1968, when he passed through Martinsville and committed the murder. While Martinsville residents were relieved that it was none of "their own" who committed the atrocity, accounts from local residents confirm that it easily could have been. According to historian James H. Madison, there is no concrete evidence that "Martinsville is a dangerous place for blacks," but "What matters, he said, 'is that people think it is.'"[46] Here, Madison invokes what Doug earlier described as "your town reputation gets out."

The Carol Jenkins murder put Martinsville on a national stage in terms of being a small, white, midwestern, racist town. Newspaper coverage from three different decades proves this point: 1) newspaper clippings from 1989, when the city started to fight its "racist reputation," which had been left untouched for decades, 2) accounts from 2002 after Jenkins's murderer was arrested, and 3) most recently, articles from November 2017, when the town mayor dedicated a memorial stone at city hall to Carol Jenkins. All the newspaper articles quote town leaders and long-term residents about their firm beliefs that Martinsville "is no more racist or bigoted than any other place," sometimes with the caveat of any other "almost totally white town in south-central Indiana."[47] That might be true, but that does not absolve Martinsville from the legacy of its racist past. The similitude between residents admitting in 1989: "sure we have some bigots and rednecks" and in 2017: "we have idiots. But everywhere you have idiots" indicates that residents' mindset has not changed overwhelmingly. On the contrary, the descriptor "idiot" obscures the nature of the issue and perpetuates the denial of real or apparent intergenerational bigotry and racism. The defensive stance that the residents took also reflects the idea that prejudice is "natural" and widespread, allowing them to deflect racist practices onto other towns rather than their own.[48] That said, the 2017 article recorded numerous other racist incidents in the last two decades, at times involving town officials such as the assistant police chief, that corroborate Martinsville's image as a place intolerant of and hostile toward nonwhite people.

In 2017, town leadership presented a formal apology and a memorial stone to the Jenkins family—almost five decades after the crime. Martinsville had become the scapegoat for racist Indiana attitudes ever since 1968. And even though it did not face its ugly history for many years, it did so now—unlike all the other small, formerly all-white towns across the state that did not have any incidents that catapulted them onto the national stage as examples of intolerance. Yet, as illustrated herein, Martinsville is not alone in Indiana with its residents' deeply held beliefs and attitudes.

Given the magnitude and infamy of the crimes committed and the subsequent nationwide news coverage they received, survey respondents from Grant and Morgan counties were unique in sharing news coverage pertaining to the legacies of the 1930 lynching and 1968 murder, respectively. Whereas the respondents sent many clippings that attested to those crimes and their aftermath, neither Grant County's survey response nor Morgan County's letter response (that county did not return a survey) acknowledged the crime in writing. In this regard, they demonstrated a similar silence as most other counties, regardless of the scope of materials received. And as this book lays bare, a plethora of expulsion examples exists to draw from. The Orange County survey, for instance, documents the two separate societies in the county but fails to acknowledge that white French Lick residents "instructed blacks to leave" at the beginning of the century.[49] The Vermillion County representative did not own the county-wide expulsion of 1923 that Elliot Jaspin uncovered in *Buried in the Bitter Waters*. The list goes on and on.

A Sore That Didn't Heal

When the *Frankfort Morning Times* discussed the potential rebirth of the Ku Klux Klan locally in 1965, a concerned community member responded the next day with an editorial. Titling the response "Revived Ku Klux Klan Should Not Be Allowed to Exist in Hoosierland," the writer condemned the 1920s "advocacy of white protestant supremacy" and called on fellow Hoosiers to not let this happen again. Speaking out against the KKK's ideals, this letter provides the first example of public resistance in the Clinton County community.

The writer also noted that the "Klan left a canker sore across Hoosierland that didn't heal for many years."[50] Based on the general evasion of this very topic in my countless hours of conversations with Indiana residents, I am not certain the sore has healed yet. Inquiries about local histories tended to highlight positive attributes about their railroad past and being a farming community, but the responses rarely included references to the KKK's impact. The silencing of history and memories might be one legacy of a potent geography of hate.

The local paper's inconsistent coverage of Klan activities, the lack of a strong stance against the organization, and the overwhelming silence on Klan matters from most of my interviewees warrants caution. The lack of coverage, for example, does not mean the Klan or the ideologies that defined the organization were absent. The limited exchanges I had on the topic affirmed the Klan's strength in the community back then, as well as the organization's continued existence in other parts of Indiana and the country. As demonstrated throughout this book, racism and prejudice are more intrinsic to Indiana than is commonly acknowledged. In Clinton County and elsewhere in the Hoosier state, the Klan exploited rather than generated white supremacist notions and beliefs. White Hoosiers were KKK members, but by fostering the narrative of a Klan invasion, they use language of evasion, relieving them of any guilt or responsibility.[51] The omission of ugly county history and residents' continued discomfort in confronting it might indicate an attempt to forget what happened or to perpetuate the prejudice and biases toward the Other—nonwhite, non-Protestant, non-native. Current sociopolitical events and attitudes revealed in the community might suggest the latter.

Silencing the Klan connection and hushing the existence of sundown policies were clear trends in the Black History Project surveys thirty years ago. Diving deeper into one county's history revealed the same whitewashing strategies among my informants: if you don't mention it, it never happened. Indiana residents might hope that by avoiding conversations about Klan activities in the county or the state, the stain might just go away. This lack of reflexive public memory and county history enabled Clinton County to reimagine its past and commemorate moments of pride, such as the railroad boom, without reflecting on politics and communal attitudes that prevented Black southerners and other people of color from settling and staying in their town.

Maybe Rhoda Parker was fortunate that she passed away in 1923. Had she not, she might have been forced to leave Frankfort like Thomas Kussurelis or bear witness to yet another county-wide expulsion in her lifetime. The departure of the Parker children hints at an unwelcoming racial climate in Clinton County. Carol Jenkins's murder in 1968 clearly demonstrates that anti-Black sentiments did not leave the state with the demise of the KKK. In contrast, the way Indiana communities at different times in history keep negating white supremacist desires in their midst, minimizing and negating the racist nature of countless incidents in the state, demonstrates that not much has changed in Indiana. May the Parkers rest peacefully.

CHAPTER 5

When Black Folk Make the Record

We had one that was a doctor here,
Dr. Hill, he had a white wife.
—Tom, retired farmer and Clinton
County resident, October 2016

Frank went on to marry the white girl.
And she was a preacher.
—Walter, retired farmer and Clinton
County resident, April 2017

Dr. Hill and Frank were both Black men who resided in Frankfort, Indiana. Here are their stories.

Dr. Hill lived in Frankfort and practiced medicine for more than half a century. His parents were born in North Carolina and Virginia, but he was a native of Indiana. Clarence Hill was born on Christmas Day in Logansport, Indiana, in 1874. Around the time he graduated from the Medical College of Indiana in 1898, he permanently settled in Frankfort.

Were one to rely solely on the obituaries printed about his sudden death in March 1954, Dr. Clarence Hill married Henrietta W. Folkerts in 1930, his "white wife," with whom he had a son, Clarence Harrison. Henrietta Wilhemina Folkerts was a native of Germany, born in Wilhelmshaven in 1896, who immigrated to the United States in 1923, joining uncle Lubbo Pennbacker and his wife, Meta, both immigrants themselves, in Frankfort. She brought a daughter into the marriage with Clarence, also named Henrietta. When she gave birth to her daughter in 1927, Dr. Clarence Hill certified the birth of then-named Meta Folkerts. This may be how they met. Son Clarence Harrison, born to Henrietta and Clarence in 1931, and daughter Henrietta both attended Frankfort High School and graduated in the 1940s. Son Clarence joined the U.S. Air Force during the Korean War. His time in the military may have taken him away from Frankfort physically and mentally, as he decided after the war to relocate in Jacksonville, Florida, which, unlike Frankfort, had a vibrant African American community in the twentieth century.

But Henrietta was Dr. Hill's second wife. Clarence got married before—to Anna, or Annie, Collins, a Black native of Ohio in 1897. It is Annie who lived with Clarence in their house on 502 West Sullivan Street from at least 1900 until 1930. Whereas many of the Black families in town owned their houses, theirs was by far the most expensive home, worth $5,000, according to the 1930 census, at a time when the median value of owned nonfarm homes in Clinton County was $2,715. Sometime in 1930, Annie was hospitalized in the Central State Hospital, a mental health institution in Indianapolis, where she ultimately died at the age of 89 in 1954, a few months after Clarence had passed away. Annie was a resident of Clinton County for more than three decades, yet she has been entirely erased from the record. And Clarence? He is remembered for having a white wife.

Frank—the second Black Frankfort resident remembered for having married a "white girl" in the epigraphs—is Franklin B. Jones Jr., born in Indianapolis in 1920. He grew up in Frankfort, as his father was a pastor and was appointed to the Frankfort Bethel A. M. E. Church in the 1930s. After graduating from Frankfort High School in 1939, he joined and served in the U.S. Army during World War II. And like Clarence Hill Jr., Franklin did not return to Frankfort but relocated to nearby Kokomo, Indiana (about 35 miles away). There he had a long and active career in politics and in the community, as commemorated in his obituary in the *Kokomo Tribune* in the summer of 1999. For example, he became the first Black Howard County Council member in 1978. Advancing life for (Black) Hoosiers in the community, he served as a member of the Howard County Child Abuse Council and the Howard County Mental Health Advisory Board. He also founded and served in various executive roles of the A. Phillip Randolph Institute, Kokomo Chapter, and the Franklin B. Jones Community A. M. E. Church. Furthermore, Franklin was a member of Veterans of Foreign Wars Post 177, the 21st Century Education Program, the Steelworkers of America Retirees, the Minority Health Care Coalition of Kokomo, the Howard-Tipton Central Labor Council, the Mayor's Advisory Board, and the Governor's Coordinating Council. He also worked on the Indiana State Alcoholic Beverage Commission and served as an Alcoholic Beverage Excise Officer. Politically engaged, he organized meet-the-candidate forums and voter education programs, as well as voter registration drives. Franklin B. Jones Jr. was ultimately honored as a Distinguished Hoosier, an award granted at the Indiana governor's discretion to Hoosiers who have earned respect and admiration through their accomplishments and character. Besides noting his expansive and impressive list of service, the obituary notes his marriage to Rev. Mary E. (Ray) Jones in 1977.[1] A racial denominator was not included. Another article in the *Kokomo Tribune* includes a photograph of Rev. Jones, which is inconclusive regarding her race.[2] In her application for Social Security, she identified as white, corroborating Walter's memory of a "white girl."

Clarence and Frank lived regular small-town lives in Indiana. Both men were remembered not for their personal achievements and accomplishments, for saving lives and defending the nation, but for having married white women. They were memorable *because* they had white wives. In Clarence's case, this aspect is particularly striking, as Indiana had its anti-miscegenation law on the books until 1965. Yet the fact that Henrietta was a German immigrant might explain how they were able to live as an interracial married couple in Frankfort.

* * *

Some Black residents were not forgotten, as the opening vignette illustrates. In these rare cases, however, *how* they are remembered and *how* they were perceived matters. How do long-term white small-town community members notice Black residents? Clarence and Frank left their footprints in the communal memory. Other African Americans also made an appearance in the historical records, but not quite in the same way. Unlike the previous chapters that detailed mechanisms on how best to erase and forget past nuisances, this chapter illustrates how Blackness is recorded and imagined in small-town Indiana.

Of course, white people in Clinton County do not live in a utopian ideal environment but in the real world, in which vice, crime, and people of color exist. Imagining, presenting, and acting as an all-white community, however, gives license not only to erase people of color but also to create, disseminate, and perpetuate myths and stereotypes about the Other. Presenting minorities as "problems" by attaching racial denominators in coverage of crimes is one way to achieve this. Minimizing (or erasing) positive contributions of people of color while emphasizing negative contributions simultaneously reinforces the (desired) whiteness of the community. It leaves the boundaries of the ideal white small-town world intact—in which people of color do not belong. Local journalists reflected, fostered, and reinforced communal attitudes toward African Americans in their coverage, creating a clear distinction between those who belong and those who don't. The local paper attests to this strategy's permanence over the course of the twentieth century; my interviews suggest that the same mechanisms apply today to a great extent. The geography of hate makes visible yet another mechanism designed to sustain white supremacy and Black subordination: the durability of white desires.

This permanence can best be understood by exploring how white Hoosiers come to think in stereotypes that positively correlate people of color with crimes and violence, which obviously makes them unfit for peaceful small-town coexistence—then and now—and thus justifies upholding their white spaces and white realities. How white people write about Black visibility demonstrates the cultural work historical records can do, showing how contaminated white minds are created, nurtured, and maintained. White Hoosiers engaged Blackness in three particular ways: they recorded it, mimicked it, and criminalized it. This chapter lays bare how African Americans have been objectified, dehumanized, and criminalized, which justified their being treated with suspicion and loathing.

A Black Record—Recording Blackness

We know that African Americans lived and thrived in Indiana and stamped its history, though thus far, their impact has been little explored and even less celebrated within the state. One official historical record is Negro registers. As mentioned in Chapter 1, the Black Codes in 1831 required Black newcomers to register with the counties, and twenty years later, Article XIII of the 1851 Constitution demanded all Black residents register. Whereas census data were referenced only nine times in the BHP, the survey results disclosed the existence of fourteen Negro registers.[3] With the help of Coy D. Robbins's *Indiana Negro Registers, 1852–1865*, researchers can complement these findings with an additional seven counties.[4] Thornbrough specifically adds Clark County to the list, totaling twenty-two counties, but also mentions that "registers were begun in most counties." She corroborates the statement in her footnote: "Negro registers were found in many of the courthouses of the state" during the 1930s, when the Works Progress Administration conducted a survey of county archives in the state (Map 8).[5]

We cannot be certain how many registers existed in Indiana in the nineteenth century, as historical record preservation depends on the approach and attitude of those who account, describe, and interpret county histories.[6] Based on the extant Negro registers, here is what we can learn. I want to highlight the content, as it paints a dull, more eerie picture of the environment Black Hoosiers found themselves in during the mid-nineteenth century. It is this Black record that tells us a great deal about white attitudes.

Most counties listed Black individuals in table format, but some wrote little paragraphs about their Black neighbors and residents.[7] Regardless of format,

MAP 8. Map displaying counties known to have maintained Negro registers

each entry includes name, age, description, place of birth, residence, name of the witness, and sometimes the date of registration, as required by the act that introduced the provision of Negro registers in 1852.[8] The reductions to physical markers and the level of detail in the "description" column are striking and strongly resemble characteristics noted in newspaper advertisements for runaway slaves. These advertisements often captured the "runaway's most noticeable physical and psychological characteristics, while commenting on his origin, work, and use of English," including characteristics such as "height, posture, skin color, habit of grooming and dress and emotional peculiarities—for example, speech defects and uncontrollable movements of hand and face."[9] The same scrutiny of detail was applied in Indiana Negro registers. Jackson County records note examples such as "11-year-old a boy of dark complexion," "scar on the right temple," "yellow complexion," and "a copper coloured woman." Harrison County records list "moderately black, a little stiff in walking and five feet ten inches high," "very black," and "of bright copper color, the skin on the back of his right hand is scared [*sic*] from a scald, well made and about five feet three inches high," "Has rather a young look for her age," and "of a good countenance and rather intelligent, quick spoken, when spoken to."[10] During times of slavery, this level of detail might have been "helpful" to pin down potential runaway suspects by identifying physical markers. In Indiana communities, in contrast, reducing Black people to phenotypical, physical, and behavioral characteristics might hint at white people's preference of knowing a person by appearance rather than by name, occupation, land ownership, or religious affiliation. The level of objectification was not unique to Negro registers but surfaced in newspaper coverage across time, illustrating how Black Hoosiers were perceived in white Hoosier communities: nameless and objectified, as they did not belong.

The fact that almost three times as many county representatives acknowledged the existence of Negro registers compared to the county's involvement in the Ku Klux Klan is worth noting (fourteen versus five). One explanation could be that the former is further back in history, 130 years compared to *only* sixty years that distanced the county from its possible Klan engagement. Some people on potential membership lists may have still been alive at the time the survey was conducted—and if not the individuals themselves, immediate descendants of former NHTDA and KKK members, whom the communities took it upon themselves to protect. Negro registers, in contrast, recorded Black existence in the respective counties, not white supremacist tendencies. The scrutiny and dehumanization of Black neighbors in the registers could easily be justified as demanded by the law of the land at that time, but justifying membership in the Klan and NHTDA is more difficult, because it was voluntary.

NHTDA journals in the 1920s kept a detailed record of its members, listing the number of members as well as names and positions of the presidents, secretaries, and captains in the respective chapters. They did not, however, capture any physical or behavioral characteristics. I wonder if Klan "registers" contain any phenotypical descriptors about their subjects, similar to the ones found in the Negro registers. I doubt it, but as most Klan membership lists remain hidden, we may never know.

Negro registers ceased to exist with the Civil War,[11] but the level of objectification persisted. The us-versus-them boundaries were strongly upheld. Black residents did not belong, were driven out, and were overwhelmingly erased from the records. It is important to understand how white Hoosiers learned about African Americans, since the number of Black residents dwindled across the state. In the (almost entire) absence of Black community members, how were these negative stereotypes formed and fostered, and how did they come to dominate (and contaminate) white minds?

Ostracizing Blackness: "Tales of Rape and Revenge, of Stupidity and Docility"

Local newspapers present another way to gauge white Hoosier attitudes toward Black Hoosiers and Blackness in the past. "Hounds Chase Negro" reported the *Frankfort Morning Times* on October 22, 1904. Based on local coverage, this incident constitutes the first local racial controversy documented in the paper. The article details the account of a white twenty-year-old palm reader, a native of Ohio, who alleged that a Black man she had met in Indianapolis followed her to Frankfort, threatening her, beating her, and stealing her money. The local police, however, "accused her of being intimate with the negro, but she denied this." The Black man was able to escape the police twice, once despite the bloodhounds. His destiny was not revealed until the next issue of the paper a week later.[12] Under the sensationalized heading "Negro Fugitive Captured after Desperate Struggle," the article described in great detail the arrest of John Johnson. According to Johnson, the two had been intimate and "that in cities where they were allowed to do so they passed as husband and wife." The article reveals two crucial points. First, Johnson "sought refuge in the home of Rev. Harper, the colored minister."[13] That is, the *Frankfort Morning Times* tacitly acknowledged here that the city had a Black church as early as 1904 yet did not dedicate any coverage to it in the paper then. Second, the article confirms the insecurity and vagueness of race relations north of the Mason-Dixon line. This aspect becomes clearer in the article later on: "When asked why he did not surrender to the officers if he had done nothing more than to be intimate with the woman, he replied that he wasn't certain just how strong the race prejudice might be around here." And Johnson's concerns were warranted, as Indiana had an anti-miscegenation law on the books since the mid-nineteenth century, although the article did not acknowledge it.[14]

Suspicion, criminality, and abnormality accompanied *Morning Times* coverage of Black folk in the years that followed, feeding and nurturing contaminated white Hoosier minds. In his midwestern small-town study of race relations in the early twentieth century, James DeVries also analyzed local newspaper coverage about people of color, arguing that "the newspaper chains found that the public had a genuine interest in negative stereotypes about blacks. Tales of rape and revenge, of stupidity and docility regarding the Negro titillated the imagination of the public and sold papers."[15] This is true for Clinton County as well, where the white residents lived their segregated lives, or as Charles Mills noted, "in an invented delusional world, a racial fantasyland," dominated by "white mythologies" that influenced their coverage of Black people.[16] Oddities like a Black girl with her heart located on the right side of her chest became newsworthy in 1905, as did a "mysterious" Black man hiding in the local woods, for whom arrest was suggested to explain his mysterious behavior. In May 1906, a Black boy was arrested and charged with larceny for having stolen a watch—which, according to him, he traded. The following year, the conviction of John Lewis, "a Negro Burglar," became a cover story.[17] The sole emphasis on oddity and crime when covering Black folk in the county created a distinction between those who belonged and those who did not.

The *Frankfort Morning Times* also responded to demands for tales "of stupidity and docility," reinforcing stereotypes about Black people through pictures and words, thus providing additional insight into Black people's subordinated status in the community that the white habitus engendered. The paper never featured photographs of local Black residents—throughout the twentieth century.[18] Instead, it featured demeaning caricatures of Black people and blackface. These visuals served to advertise minstrel shows and cotton mattresses, or they simply provided general entertainment value in comic strip format featuring stereotypical southern dialect and big-lipped, ignorant Black people and southern mammies, such as the cartoons entitled "Taking the Hurdle" and "Bean Sprout" (Figures 13[19] and 14[20]).

FIGURE 13. Example of caricature featuring ignorant Black man on a horse carrying a piece of the fence because he didn't lift his feet when he jumped over the fence.

When a Black migrant arrived in Frankfort in the 1920s, the *Morning Times* reported on a "Colored Lad [Who] Eats Thirteen Watermelons in Six Days on Trip from South to Frankfort." A *Morning Times* reporter interviewed the boy, and he disclosed that he was on his way to Indianapolis to live with an uncle. The reporter described his interviewee as "a bright little chap who has been in the grade schools, can read and write and talk intelligently." The boy's level of education and physical and behavioral characteristics (as in the Negro register) became noteworthy. Earlier that month, the *Morning Times* featured a photograph of a small Black boy who enjoyed his "melon time in

FIGURE 14. Example of caricature featuring white perception of Black people. The way the white individual positions the Black individual, Ick, trying to "hide" the donkey, results in the donkey's ears appearing to grow of out Ick's head like "Bean Sprouts."

Georgia" and did not worry about "politics, the high cost of living and so on" on its front page.[21] Photographs in the paper usually featured Black people from "far away," depicting them involved in city riots, as lynching victims, criminals, or "happy-go-lucky" people from southern farms. In this regard, the *Morning Times* coverage stayed true to its philosophy of covering Black crime and Black stereotypes. And this is how the Clinton County community learned about African Americans. The legacy of such skewed exposure can be seen today, such as in interviews with local community members, which subtly reproduce such stereotypes in conversation (see below).

Accounts of lynchings, or as DeVries called them, "tales of rape and revenge," were another way Black people made an appearance in the local paper. Ever since the beginning of the twentieth century, the *Morning Times* sporadically covered lynchings, most of which occurred in the South. A lynching in Georgia in August 1904 constitutes the first example reported in the *Frankfort Morning Times,* when the local paper announced "Two Negroes Burned by Mob" in Statesboro. Whereas most of the lynchings were described in gruesome detail, they usually were not accompanied by a photograph. The closest lynching to home featured in story and picture was the lynching of Abram Smith and Thomas Shipp in Marion, Indiana, on August 7, 1930.[22] Covering the news reporting in detail is beyond the scope of this chapter, but it is worth noting that the *Frankfort Morning Times* did not openly condemn the violence enacted on the three Black teenagers, two of whom were lynched just sixty miles east of home. Instead, it featured voices such as Prosecutor Harley H. Hardin, who himself attended the lynching spectacle and then was put in charge of investigating the mob violence. In the quotes featured in the *Morning Times*, Hardin blamed the Black victims and exculpated the white community.[23]

In the aftermath of the Marion lynching, coverage returned to Marion sporadically to report on the end of the investigation, the non-indictment of mob members, and the local sheriff's exoneration. Of course, though not prominently displayed, the local paper did not fail to report the fate of then-seventeen-year-old James Cameron, who was convicted of being an accessory to voluntary manslaughter and was sentenced to imprisonment for two to twenty-one years.[24] The article also gives insight into the different ways of reporting and describing crimes and criminals. Cameron, though by the time of the verdict only seventeen, was referred to as a *man*, but white criminals simultaneously got the benefit of youth attached to their character, no matter the crime. For example, in this front-page coverage from February 7, 1932: "Richard H. Gladden, 22-year-old Frankfort *youth*, today stands formally charged with murder of his wife."[25] Unlike draft-related news that labeled Black men as boys to go and fight the war, as mentioned previously, crime-related news robbed Black teenagers of their youth.[26] There is nothing strange about that for a white polity that lives by white misrepresentation and self-deception.[27]

Lynching coverage can help gauge the local white attitude toward Black people, as the *Frankfort Morning Times* frequently demonstrated apathy or sided with the perpetrators of the crime. The last coverage of a lynching was the heinous murder of Emmett Till in 1955 and the ensuing travesty of a trial against the two murderers. Similar to its coverage of the Marion lynching, the *Frankfort Morning Times* wrote nothing that condemned the violence enacted on fourteen-year-old Emmett Till. Instead, it tacitly seemed to agree that Till deserved to die, as its first reporting of the reason for the lynching noted that Till died "because he made 'ugly remarks' to a white woman"—without inserting "allegedly" or "supposedly."[28] Upon discovering that this murder—unlike the many previous ones reported in the *Morning Times*—sparked an outcry across the nation, the tone shifted toward more empathy and included key words like "allegedly" when noting Till's "crime." Simultaneously, however, the paper repeatedly printed the Mississippi sheriff's conspiracy theory that the body retrieved from the river appeared like a grown man and was too decomposed to have been in the water for such a short period of three days.[29] When the *Morning Times* decided to cover local voices that strongly defended the community and doubted the crime, it demonstrated once again that it sided with the perpetrators of violence rather than the victims.

In the spirit of racial unrest and continued mob violence throughout the nation in the 1940s, the *Morning Times* claimed that Frankfort was on the verge of its own little riot in town in 1947. The front-page news coverage "Five Negroes Jailed; Police Halt Trouble" starts with "Quick action by city police averted a possible riot about 11 o'clock last night following a fracas on Main Street near Freedman's Store." Eyewitness accounts described the Black men's behavior as "acting belligerent and apparently in search of trouble." An encounter between the group and a white couple caused the situation to spiral out of control, eventually resulting in the arrest of all five non-resident Black men. Follow-up coverage featured the white man's version only, noting the cause was an exchange of "hot words" after "the Negroes had walked between he and his wife in a swaggering manner." It emphasized how local "whites who were attracted to the scene" came to the white man's "rescue." One of the Black men arrested was "adjudged not guilty" as he remained in the car when the other four "became engaged in a brawl." The remaining four were fined for assault, battery, and disorderly conduct. Though labeled a brawl, only one party was to be punished: the Black criminals who did not belong to the community.[30]

Coverage of local incidents involving people of color frequently echoed these sentiments. In 1919, transitory people were arrested by a local constable "pending word from the Danville police as to their identity and character," and local Black folk were being chased out of town because one of them had asked a white girl "to take a trip with him." When the *Morning Times* eagerly followed the uproar in Marion in the aftermath of the Shipp and Smith lynching, it also reported on the local arrest of three Black men after a chase through the cornfields. All three were charged with vagrancy, "admitted they were trespassing and annoying residents west of the city limits, and were held guilty by the court."[31]

Vagrancy and trespassing ordinances and their strict enforcement signify a popular means to control access to Frankfort. In Chapter 2, I noted the fate of Black southern migrants arriving in Frankfort mid-twentieth century. Among other southern arrivals, native Louisianan Bennie Rogers, native Kentuckian Virgil C. Hamilton, and native Arkansan Essec Ree Walker were all described as "negro transients" arrested for having violated Frankfort's trespassing ordinances.[32] I noted further that if the word spread, such coverage might have deterred southern Black migrants from settling in their midst. Law professor Timothy Zick notes, "for a substantial time in our nation's history local territories were largely under the discretionary control of the police and other local officials," such as Nickel Plate special agents or NHTDA constables, who "were empowered to create purified territories."[33] This way, the community determined who belonged in the community and reinforced its identity as an all-white town. Clinton County operationalized such community discretions, if we recall the "colored chef" in 1919 as well as the two "negro transients" in 1949, all of whom received ultimatums to leave town to avoid further troubles or court fines. The *Morning Times* demonstrated an impeccable consistency in othering and ostracizing these Black migrant arrivals, continuously referring to them as "negro transients" and invoking criminality, homelessness, and thus *non*belonging.

Although Clinton County drove out the Black community and Black individuals at various points in time, Frankfort never officially enforced residential segregation when Black residents lived there, to my knowledge. Martha Maxey's letter to the editor from 1970, discussed in the previous chapter, hints at privately enforced segregation. The 1930 census documents that, with the exception of three families that lived adjacent to one another, the vast majority of Black residents had only white neighbors. However, that doesn't mean that "voluntary" segregation did not occur or that neighborly coexistence was peaceful. For example, in July 1934, "Color Lines Drawn in Neighborhood Rumpus" spanned the cover page of the *Frankfort Morning Times*. Though it appears to have been a quarrel among neighbors with accusations on all sides presented in the courtroom, the journalist seemingly wanted to attribute the blame to the Black children involved, prefacing the description of what ensued in court with "a neighborhood quarrel in which little colored boys played an important part." The journalist shifts his tone between Black and white descriptions:

> Whites were accused of pushing colored children off the sidewalks and accusations were also made that on numerous occasions, stubby, brown-skinned thumbs have often strayed periously [*sic*] near flat proboscis and the chubby brown hand to which the digit was fastened is said to have wobbled and wavered, especially strong in the direction of whites.[34]

Instead of noting who complained on behalf of the Black family, the reader receives descriptions of Black body parts that might belong to a Black boy. The reduction to physical markers objectifies the Black family in a way similar to the Negro register entries discussed above. More important, the journalist concludes that it was Black kids who threatened to punch white kids in the nose, which stands in stark contrast to the actuality of white kids pushing Black kids off the sidewalk.

The most heated moment in the courtroom "occurred when a white man, the only male member of the troubled families present, told the gentleman of color that he should be back 'down south across the line.' The colored man replied that 'I suppose you are a tough guy, I guess you are a regular Dillinger.'" It remains unclear whether the Black family actually was a migrant family from the South or how long they had lived in Frankfort; property ownership is the only information we can retrieve from the article about the Black family. Clearly, however, the white male complainant believed all Black folk should live below the Mason-Dixon line, invoking further a sentiment of unacceptance and *non*belonging.

The presiding circuit judge also offers insight into the white residents' inhospitable and exclusionary community mindset. He said he hoped that the families, upon returning to their homes, can "try to iron out the disagreeable situation," seemingly siding with no one. But he continued, "In the meantime I will talk to the two colored boys and warn them of what they should not do. White families should likewise warn their children to remain on their premises and mind their own business." Here the judge apparently trusted white parents to know how to discipline their children but did not extend the same benefit to the Black parents involved.

African Americans coexisted in these white Hoosier communities—yet they didn't belong. Local newspaper coverage ostracized Blackness by reporting on Black crimes and, to a lesser degree, on other Black stereotypes. To that extent, this printed record exemplifies how white Clinton County community members learned about African Americans and came to associate African Americans with negative stereotypes, including their inclination to criminality, without having had personal interactions. *The Frankfort Morning Times* coverage emphasized crimes committed by people of color while justifying crimes against people of color, establishing a lily-white world in which the culprit remains the same: the nonwhite person. People might argue that these were individual journalists with preconceived notions when reporting about incidents involving Black people. That they, indeed, indicate the overall communal mindset will become more obvious in the next sections that discuss further how Hoosier communities engage and co-opt Blackness.

Displaying Blackness, Mimicking Blackness

Besides KKK and NHTDA memorabilia, the local historians Tom and Robert also possessed some rare community collectibles that displayed Black people in disparaging ways. In *Mammy and Uncle Mose*, Kenneth W. Goings explicitly links Black memorabilia to white America, as "White Americans developed the stereotypes; white Americans produced the collectibles, and white American manufacturers and advertisers disseminated both the images and the objects to a white audience." Thus, they reflect "the history of white American acceptance of the stereotypes embodied in black collectibles."[35] Besides salt and pepper shakers and miniature dolls, Tom and Robert had some trade cards that merchants had lying on their counters back in the day. Trade cards are like business cards and flyers today. Goings connects the increased popularity of trade cards to the development of consumer culture in the late nineteenth century, as businesses eagerly tapped into racial stereotypes to promote their goods, because "What better way to attract attention, arouse humor, and provide the consumer with a sense of racial superiority than the stereotypical Old South/New South myth of the loyal, *happy* servant just waiting to do the master's—now the consumer's—bidding?"[36] Tom highlighted one card in particular and even recalled the wording on it due to the incendiary language it contained (Figure 15).

The trade card helps gauge the white community's attitude toward the Black community in the early twentieth century. By displaying a trade card as shown in Figure 15, the local dry goods store Southard & Swan sent a clear message to any potential customer of color at the time, as they advertised their store deriding Black folk in word and picture—with a southern tongue resembling Black character speech during slavery, calling themselves a derogatory term, and displaying three big-lipped, funny-looking people.

Clinton County's mindset parallels attitudes elsewhere in the state. Examining the words in the BHP surveys further reveals strong divisions between Black Hoosiers and white Hoosiers in Indiana counties. Among the most potent examples were the respondents' reflections on various public spaces whose names reveal white attitudes and signal exactly where Black folk be-

FIGURE 15. An exemplary trade card that circulated in the community around the turn of the twentieth century.

long in the county. Responding to the third question on the survey, which inquires about historical landmarks that are associated with the presence of Black people, Howard County's respondent from the county museum lists, among other sites, "Colored or Nigger Pike (now called Smith road)" and explains further that it referred to the "road that ran through the colored settlements."[37] Similarly, Perry County had a road in their county records called "Nigger Hollow" for decades, sending a message of knowing one's place and what attitudes to expect to any Black person attempting to settle in the area. The Perry County Commissioners approved a name change of the road to "Bell Hollow" in 1989, in honor of "a Black family that lived on the road for many years."[38] It does not only prove the low priority of Black sentiments in the county, but it also attests to white attitudes across the state that it was acceptable to display their hostility and animosity openly and publicly with such derogatory language.

Ironically, the name attests to the fact that Black folk once resided in Perry County, 253 in 1890, apparently enough to "dedicate" a neighborhood to them, signaling via public landmark where Black people belonged. However, keeping the name of the road until 1989 might be one reason why the 1980 census registered only twelve Black residents in the county. Who would want to live in a neighborhood or town where white Hoosiers' attitudes toward people of color are reflected so publicly?

The foregoing examples are subtle, community-encompassing ways of displaying white Hoosier attitudes for Black and white folks alike. Whereas Black people might decide to relocate to a more welcoming environment, white people might realize and reproduce similar attitudes. Other community-wide initiatives that attest to white Hoosiers actively engaging Blackness are the performance and support of minstrelsy.

Organized by social organizations, clubs, churches, and schools in the community, minstrel shows were a popular form of entertainment for Frankfort residents for many decades. James DeVries, who investigated race relations in a Michigan small town at the beginning of the twentieth century, notes the following about the entertainment value of minstrel shows:

> It is generally recognized that as an entertainment form, minstrelsy far outdistanced any of its rivals until the 1890s. So important was this "folk and popular form" in the nineteenth century that one authority on the subject has viewed it as a *key to understanding the thought and social realities of America's common people in this era*. A truly national medium, it reached virtually every town and hamlet in America in the late nineteenth and early twentieth centuries. In fact, it could be accurately stated that most northerners of that time period learned about "Negroes" from the minstrel shows.[39]

Frankfort, indeed, was one of these northern hamlets entertained by minstrelsy, and it continued the tradition way past the time frame DeVries gave. The earliest announcement of minstrel shows in the *Frankfort Morning Times* came in 1905 and the latest in 1950. Blackface in school performances was

FIGURE 16. This photograph, by far the largest across all yearbooks featuring minstrel shows, spans across pages 44 and 45 in the 1952 *Cauldron*.

common until the early 1960s if one looks at the high school yearbooks. Figure 16 provides an exemplar illustration of how blackface was celebrated and commemorated in the yearbooks.

In *The Wages of Whiteness*, American Studies scholar and historian David Roediger labels blackface minstrels "the first self-consciously *white* entertainers in the world. The simple physical disguise—and elaborate cultural disguise—of blacking up served to emphasize that those on stage were really white and that whiteness really mattered."[40] Thus, whiteness mattered in Clinton County even though it was never publicly acknowledged or labeled. Frequent county-wide announcements of such entertainment sent a clear signal to the local Black community, as well: whiteness mattered. Besides shows designed by local community members in Clinton County, the local paper celebrated minstrelsy on radio shows and nationally acclaimed minstrel teams, reinforcing the power yet invisibility of whiteness.

Minstrel shows exemplify how community engagement functions to perpetuate racist and stereotypical ideologies. Local social organizations and churches planned and hosted minstrel shows, which the newspaper usually celebrated as successful, detailing showings for multiple days with exuberant audiences. In 1935, the Rotary Club announced a special afternoon matinee of its minstrel show inviting about 350 "underprivileged youngsters of the city" to watch and experience their show. In its second-to-last day of its six-day coverage of the show, the *Morning Times* noted: "With the exception—that of George Goodnight, interlocutor—the ensemble works in blackface." In 1949, the Lions Club took it upon itself to revive the minstrel show and return it to "the peaks of popularity." Fully committed to the mission to bring back minstrel shows, "even the doormen and the ticket seller will smile blackface." A 1950 announcement of a minstrel show of the Lincoln School confirms that parents actively participated in the minstrel cast. Some Clinton County parents wore blackface as late as 1950 and, as role models for their children, helped reproduce racist attitudes in the generations after blackface had disappeared.[41]

These local minstrel shows demonstrate the white habitus of white small-town residents. The extent of and language in covering the shows in the local paper illustrate their successful and entertaining nature—despite having a small community of color in Frankfort at the time and despite the paper's own claim in 1939 that everyone reads the *Morning Times*. After all, the high school used to have its own minstrel performances each year—Black students and classmates notwithstanding. Frankfort no longer entertains with minstrel shows, but maybe, after all, the durability and nature of the community's white culture of exclusion provides one explanation why the Black population steadily declined in town over the course of the twentieth century, turning the white spatial imaginary into a white spatial reality. The legacy of and problem with these white spatial realities are the feeding and breeding of contaminated minds.

Contaminated Minds

The longevity and power of such negative stereotypes came through in my interviews and the BHP surveys. Remember Doug from the introduction's opening vignette, who subtly associated crime with Black newcomers moving into town? Let's revisit his comment on the current demographic changes in Frankfort in a larger context:

> But I know that there has been an increase of . . . African Americans into our community. I don't have a challenge with that, as long, you know, they behave themselves. I'd say that with the Caucasians, the white folk. You know? If you can't behave yourself, I don't want you to be here. But as I said earlier, or just a little while ago, that the population now—and I'm not saying that the people who are coming in are not law-abiding citizens, but the people who have been resident here for a long period of time, who were law-abiding, they kind of mingled out and have gone and has left us with a larger number of people who are now trying to regroup their life because they have had challenges with the law. And so it's been, that's been . . . a struggle with the community. I think it has been a struggle with the community.

On the one hand, Doug affirmed the recent growth in Frankfort's Black population. On the other hand, he didn't object to that growth as long as "they behave themselves." Here he subconsciously associated African Americans with trouble, which is corroborated in the remainder of his remark, in which he attempted to generalize (and deracialize) the struggles in the community with recent newcomers who do not respect the law. By inserting a series of "buffer statements," he emphasized and ascribed the law-and-order mentality to the local community. "A group's failure or difference," political scientist Robin Dale Jacobson notes about contemporary conceptualizations of new racism, "is explained by its members' failure to act in accordance with the social and cultural values of the larger society or simply by the failure to respect such values."[42] Doug juxtaposed the recent newcomers with long-term residents based on their proclivity for law and order, thereby camouflaging his prejudice toward people of color.

Traversing and transgressing the geography of hate gives us an idea of how Doug—or anyone else for that matter—associates African Americans with crime and trouble in the first place. Doug was not alone in this line of thinking. Despite the lack of daily interactions with people of color in the "all-white community," to use Doug's terminology, many of my informants still formed negative opinions of African Americans. For example, there was Bob, the one who remembered that Frankfort once had a Black church, noting the community's association of Black folk with laziness: "We knew when a Black person came and the mentality was, well they're on welfare. They don't work. They drink. They drive Cadillacs. And they're useless. And that's the mentality." The tropes he uses ring of former loafer descriptions from newspaper snippets discussed in previous chapters. The reflection of Penny, a white long-term resident in her late sixties, rings similar: "Black people, it's like they are out for themselves. They wanna get ahead, they want their family to get ahead. They are friendly and all that stuff, I don't mean anything bad about that, but they are just not an organized group. There are always factions. They don't jell very well." Starting her remark off with dreams common in any family "to get ahead," she inserts her "but" to express her true opinion that they are actually not quite "organized" and "don't jell very well." And like Doug, Brad, a white man in his sixties, associated people of color with crime, noting:

> We are seeing a growth in Black—mainly because we're seeing a lot of people coming from Gary and there's just so less opportunity at some of these other communities like Gary, Indiana, and Lake County. High crime and so we had unfortunately picked up some of the gang banger

type people and they're looking to get away from their situation. Whether they're trying to do it for the right reasons or just doing it for the wrong reasons and looking for new territory, I don't know, but we're seeing some of that. And that's been difficult.

Bob, Penny, and Brad mention various negative stereotypes about the Black community, some in more general terms and some specifically regarding Frankfort. Though Bob starts his remarks in past tense, he ends in present tense. This shift in tense could indicate that this mentality did not shift—the community may continue to think that way. Penny's and Brad's remarks indicate that. Brad's remark, in particular, echoes Doug's association of African Americans with crime. Unlike Doug, Brad does not do so subconsciously.

Indifference and ignorance toward any (potential) Black residents characterize the environment today. Unfamiliarity and anachronistic terminology, for example, revealed the limited interactions white Hoosiers had with African Americans. The way survey takers reflect on the Black experience in the Black History Project often discloses that the writers were white people who did not concern themselves much, if at all, with the Black community in their counties. These exclusionary attitudes, reflecting an us-versus-them mentality, can be seen throughout the survey responses, such as in the following remarks:

> We have tried for 5 years to do a history on the Elkhart (city) blacks but have gotten little or no help from them. *They* tell us there is nothing good in this history so why talk about it.[43]

> I suggest that you contact Mrs. Bentha Ballow. She is the oldest colored lady in the community. She is a descendent of the Ballow slaves. Her mind is very clean [*sic*] and knows a lot of her people's history.[44]

In both cases, the survey takers established a clear boundary between their own community and the other community, echoing Anthony Cohen's community and identity awareness that takes place at the boundary, as well as his concept of community assertiveness.[45] The second example is particularly striking, not only because of the segregated possessive pronoun "her" in "her people," but also because the resident was described as "colored" in 1987. The same descriptor is used by the respondent from Pike County, who has "talked to a lot of people and seems no one knows if we have colored people living in Pike County now." A similarly anachronistic description can be found in the Floyd County file, where the survey respondent refers to Black families as "Negro families."[46] Such antiquated language and the demarcating use of possessive pronouns illustrate the boundary-making process when the survey respondents realized their white identity and their white communities, cementing a fence around them.

The unfamiliarity with nonwhite community members shone through in multiple interviews corroborating African Americans' presence yet *non*belonging. I can see how a gentleman in his nineties recalled having had "three colored people" in his class and continued to refer to African Americans as "colored" throughout our conversation, but I struggle to extend the same understanding to a community-engaged family with both parents in their late forties/early fifties: "I don't know like the history of any colored—Black people." Though she corrected her speech right away, it felt like she did it because of my presence as the researcher in the room. Other people mentioned the Black community as "the Blacks" or recalled once having had a Black pastor as "black as the ace of spades," indicating unfamiliarity if not condescension. And if we look back to Map 8 and the discussion of the Negro registers that existed in Indiana, the language echoes the physical descriptions used to describe their Black neighbors. Here, it is their pastor.

Obliviousness and ignorance are passive mechanisms white people use to express their white desires. Reminiscing a little more about the Black pastor, Rick concluded his thought with "And it's kind of funny you think well, there should be some prejudice there in rural Indiana. But I sure never saw any of it." The remark clearly begs the question: what made Rick think that there "should be some prejudice" in rural Indiana in the first place—that he then felt the need to vehemently deny? Forty years earlier, a white teacher in Laura Barone's portrait of the Black community in Frankfort similarly claimed that "There was never the least feeling in the community against them." Both remarks illustrate the "epistemology of ignorance," which precludes white folk from genuinely understanding the social realities in their imagined white world.[47] Catherine Lewis, Black Hoosier and a former student of the very teacher quoted in Barone's piece, actually clarified that prejudice is exactly "the reason the few Black families in the town left. . . . But the whites don't realize it because they weren't Negro."[48]

Denouncing racism—even in light of actual physical violence—became another common mechanism in Indiana's racialized geography. Let's recall that Prosecutor Hardin, the investigator of the Smith and Shipp lynching in Marion in 1930, "did not believe the violence was a demonstration against the negro race, but that it was aimed against the individuals and the charges involved" before conducting his investigation. When Black Clinton County resident Charles Kersey "was beaten and robbed," and "had had three teeth knocked out and was cut and bruised about the face" in February 1964, the investigating sheriff noted that "he was convinced that there was no racial difficulty involved in the beating." It remains unclear where the sheriff's conviction came from, as the investigation was still open and the suspects were still at large at the time of the news coverage. Unfortunately, the case was not closely followed in the *Morning Times*.[49]

The trend of building and preserving the county's image as a non-racist environment was also palpable in the Black History Project. Survey takers pursued two noticeable paths to negate any appearance or charges of racism despite the lack of diversity in their midst—claiming a connection to the Underground Railroad and presenting "token" Black residents. Indiana has had its fair share in the Underground Railroad.[50] Levi Coffin probably is the best known among pre–Civil War historians. But survey respondents provided proof (references, diaries, documents) regarding the extent of their Underground Railroad involvement only in the rarest cases. As one survey question specifically inquires about Underground Railroad sites, county representatives were inclined to emphasize the county's *potential* involvement in Underground Railroad activities. The fact that they based their knowledge on rumors did not matter, as the following examples demonstrate:

> "Many, many rumors but have not documented actual existence and buildings involved."[51]
>
> "Yes. I've read this someplace but I've searched the five history books of Co.—nil. Neither can I locate it in newspaper clippings. Sorry."[52]
>
> "supposedly three Underground Railroad stations"[53]
>
> "according to legend but unproven"[54]

By noting the county's connection to the Underground Railroad, regardless of whether it is fact or fiction, county representatives tried to absolve its residents from any racist past. At times, it was the only question answered in the survey, upholding what historian Larry Gara called "America's favorite legend."[55] It allowed them to share Black experiences in their counties without revealing any of the ugly truths surrounding or following those years. The Underground Railroad reference allowed survey respondents to assert "yes, we have a Black history" and "despite a sizable minority population, we did help them in the past." However, I need to make an important point here. The fact that a community was involved in Underground Railroad activities, no matter how extensive, does not prevent it from turning its back on its African American neighbors later in history, as Washington County demonstrates. Helping runaway slaves before the Civil War, it drove out its Black population during the war—out of fear that they would become voting and contributing members in the community, as discussed extensively in Chapter 1. Similar arguments could be made for various other counties that excluded Black residents in subsequent decades.

Likewise, remembering at least one Black resident in their midst—as was the case with Franklin Jones and Clarence Hill in the chapter opening—provides a contaminated white way of countering assertions that their counties are and have been racist and purposely all-white communities. This trend can be noted beyond survey responses, as county histories and local newspapers followed the same strategy. If counties had a "famous" Black resident, who may have been their only one in the county for decades, they emphasized the very existence of their "token" Black resident. Here I am not referring to the famous Black sons and daughters who were born in those towns, such as Hazel Harrison, renowned Black pianist born in La Porte County, but rather the community "tokens" like Dr. Clarence Hill and "Uncle Joe" Parker, the "Oldest Colored Man" in Clinton County in 1919. Mrs. Elizabeth Smith from Michigan City, La Porte County, for example, was known in the community only as "nigger Liz."[56] "Black Ben" in Cass County is another example. The 1913 county history features Benjamin Talbot as probably the first Black person in the county, who was "familiarly known as 'Black Ben.'"[57] Henrietta Surgh, an herb doctor in Ripley County, is described in the survey as "Aunt Nettie." She was reprimanded by the "Ripley Circuit Court for practicing medicine without license."[58] White people's reflections on why they can recall the name of one particular person or the nickname the community has "fondly" given them are missing, however. In word and print, I did not encounter any afterthoughts, such as: How come not more of them came—why so few that I recall each name?

There are traces of Black visibility in Indiana, yet these communities exude white desires and white realities. Dr. Clarence Hill and Franklin B. Jones Jr. are the exception. They are remembered—not for their achievements and contributions to and beyond the community—but for their white wives. Other African Americans also made the Black record in Indiana, yet their lack of a white connection resulted in feeding the white imagination about Blackness in two specific ways: crime and derision. The complete erasure of the local African American community failed through simple means: the belief and perpetuation of Black Americans as violent criminals and lawbreakers. In general, the newspaper considered coverage involving African Americans newsworthy only if they were spectacularly violent and geographically distant (lynchings, riots, school boycotts), or it painted the people in the story in a negative light (trespassing, welfare). At the same time, the deployment of "exceptional" Black people makes the town seem welcoming.

Criminalizing Blackness helps justify white desires and white communities vis-à-vis undesirable nonwhite Others. Objectifying, deriding, and mimicking Blackness helps maintain the us-versus-them boundaries in case the all-white reality is breached. Through such coverage, the *Morning Times* affirmed a Black presence in the community and the community's contempt toward this presence. Contemporary remarks by white Hoosiers affirm the potency of such skewed imagination and reproduction of Blackness. Yet this contaminated mindset is the white record of Indiana.

CONCLUSION

The Geography of Hate—Mapping Whiteness

> She's a stay-at-home mom with pink roses blooming outside her spotless home. Her husband's steady factory job helped pay off the modest house. Their five children speak flawless English. For these newcomers, life in this old railroad city could be a cozy scene of middle-class serenity but for one glaring fact. President Bush would send her and her husband back to Mexico. So would many Frankfort officials. Being deported is often on her mind. The reason: They are not legal U.S. residents.
>
> "You live in fear because you aren't ever calm," said the woman, who requested anonymity because of her illegal status. Playing out in this Clinton County city of 16,662, where one in four residents is Hispanic, are the fears and hopes brought on by America's immigration surge.[1]
>
> —Ted Evanoff and Tania E. Lopez, *Indianapolis Star*, 2007

Clinton County's white desires resurface in every generation since Black residents were first driven out. Let's remember, Clinton County drove out its Black population in the late nineteenth century. White residents actively contributed to their all-white county by "relocating" its Black population to Boone County, except for Joseph Parker and his family.

A generation later, the community acted on its white desires yet again. We learn about it from the *Frankfort Morning Times*, which reported "Colored Chef Leaves Frankfort in Hurry" in December 1919. The local paper notes the "voluntary" departure of one of its local Black residents, explaining that "Lawrence W. Brown, colored chef at a local hotel, has brushed the dust of

Frankfort from his feet for the last time. At least that is the promise he has given city officials in exchange for his freedom. It is charged that Brown wrote a note to a white girl employed at the hotel asking her to take a trip with him."[2] Through this little snippet, we learn a lot about racial conditions in small-town Indiana. By 1919, Clinton County residents still firmly upheld and enforced the state's anti-miscegenation law, undermining any attempts of race mixing. Let's keep in mind that Lawrence Brown was forced out of the community before the Klan came to dominate Hoosier life and politics in the 1920s. By the time the Klan officially took power in Indiana, Hoosiers had already created a culture of exclusion that embraced and validated whiteness as an ideal, if not a prerequisite, for life in Hoosierland. The success of the KKK and other white supremacist organizations in Indiana is therefore not an aberration but an extension of community values and ideals.

Thirty-five years after Lawrence Brown was "asked" to leave Frankfort, the local paper reports "Pool Is Open to All"—effective immediately. A local white minister lambasted the community for violating Indiana's state law regarding access to public accommodations, as the city operated its local pool on a "whites-only" basis. In other words, the community had consistently enforced its all-white desires in public. It manifested its white desires in reality without documenting how—through unspoken and unwritten rules. Only through the bravery of a local minister do we learn about it in 1954, as his complaint was newsworthy enough to be reported in the *Frankfort Morning Times*.

Another thirty-five years later, the local county historian documents the history of race relations in Clinton County in the Black History Project survey. He discloses neither of the foregoing incidents nor any of the other events shared in this book. We are back at the question of *who* is writing and preserving our histories, particularly our local stories. This question becomes even more pertinent when we contextualize unpleasant moments of the past.

Discrimination, criminalization, invisibility, and non-representation still characterized the daily lived experiences of people of color during the time I conducted my research in the community three decades later, from 2015 through 2018. With the rapid and continuous growth of the Latinx population since the late 1990s, Clinton County residents once again operationalized the mechanisms of exclusion to re-enforce and preserve the all-white, Christian, *and* now also English-speaking nature of their community. Manifesting its culture of inhospitality and sending a message of *non*belonging to outsiders, the Clinton County community made state-wide news in 2007 when the *Indianapolis Star* reported that "Frankfort Rolls Up Its Welcome Mat." It appears that white desires are indeed a constant in the community. We have evidence for each generation in Clinton County since the Civil War, demonstrating the durability of such contaminated and exclusionary mindsets that demarcate the geography of hate.

* * *

The geography of hate rejected the absence and invisibility of Black Hoosiers in the history of Indiana. Tracking Black experiences across the state over time attests to not only a Black presence but also white supremacist ideologies in each county. Indiana's white desires left their mark and secured a white spatial reality for decades. We know that Clinton County was not alone in its pursuit to turn the white spatial imaginary into a white spatial reality. This book has documented a plethora of socially sanctioned mechanisms and enforced practices that undermined a peaceful coexistence between whites and people of color in Indiana communities. It has illustrated the long legacy of a culture of exclusion that came to dominate lived experiences in Indiana. Living and breathing this culture, white Hoosiers knitted a blanket of whiteness around their white communities—surreptitiously and otherwise. This conclusion will end the invisibility of these white spaces and make Indiana's white animosity toward Black newcomers—which marked each of the foregoing chapters—visible. I will revisit the Black History Project and previous chapter arguments in my discussion to make visible these invisible practices and mechanisms and to map Indiana's geography of hate.

Black History Project: A Treasure Map for the Ugly

The Black History Project was designed as an in-house project of the Indiana Historical Society (IHS) in 1987. Considered "experimental" for that time, IHS staff members did not have an ultimate goal for the project in mind but rather wanted to see "where it was going."[3] For one, it serves to preserve the collective memories of Indiana counties as they pertain to the Black experience. It sheds light on laws and policies as well as white values and attitudes regarding Black Hoosiers. As this book affirms, the Black History Project became my treasure map to trace many ugly moments in Indiana's white history.

The counties were given two months to respond to the survey when they were first contacted in September 1987. As the first to return the survey, the Jasper County historian responded to the request within less than a week. By February 1988, forty-eight counties had responded. Three months later, the number was up to seventy-three counties. The unresponsive nineteen counties were contacted again. The Black History Program archivist remained patient. A year later, in May 1989, she sent an update on the status of the project to all responsive county representatives and contacted the remaining nineteen counties yet again. This time, she received nine additional responses from the counties—five surveys and four letters. The remaining ten counties—Steuben, Newton, Wells, Jay, Madison, Putnam, Switzerland, Lawrence, Delaware, and Martin—remain unresponsive to date. On the first look, the project seemed successful after two years of gathering information on Black Hoosiers in Indiana, with a response rate of 89 percent (Map 9).

However, a closer look at the project files paints a different picture. First, only roughly two-thirds of the BHP files from the responding counties contain an actual survey response, curbing one's enthusiasm about the treasure trove by thirty percent (Map 10). Some counties responded in the form of letters, and others sent documents pertaining to what the survey was inquiring about. Still others solely sent a referral sheet. Most of the alternative documentation provided contained little information regarding the Black experience in Indiana.

Keen observers of Indiana (Black) history and current political buffs might actually find Map 10 surprising in at least two instances: Vanderburgh and Monroe counties, both located in the southern third of the map. Vanderburgh County, home of Evansville, is well known for having a long history of Black folk in the county, as it was one of the first locations to which southern Black migrants relocated. The history can be described as troublesome, as Vanderburgh's race record culminates in infamous instances like the 1865 and 1903 race riots or massacres. Monroe County, on the other hand, is home to Bloomington and is perceived as one of the more liberal bastions in the state, as it houses Indiana University at Bloomington. The most recent examples of the common understanding of Monroe as a liberal bastion would be the 2016 and 2020 presidential elections, in which it was one of four and five counties in the state, respectively, that voted for the Democratic Party. In both cases, no survey responses were received. Instead, typed and hand-written notes were sent, referring to recently and then forthcoming monographs devoted to the history of Black folk in their respective counties: France V. Halsell Gilliam's *A Time to Speak: A Brief History of the Afro Americans of Bloomington, Indiana, 1865–1965* and Darrel E. Bigham's *We Ask Only a Fair Trial: A History of the Black Community of Evansville, Indiana.* These two authors dedicated extensive studies to these two communities, and the survey respondents consequently ignored the survey questions, which asked for specific details in a succinct manner. Some respondents indicated keywords with reference to specific chapters or page numbers in books they consulted, which would have been a great solution here. But neither Vanderburgh nor

MAP 9. Map displaying responses received to Black History Project request. The counties in white are the ten unresponsive counties.

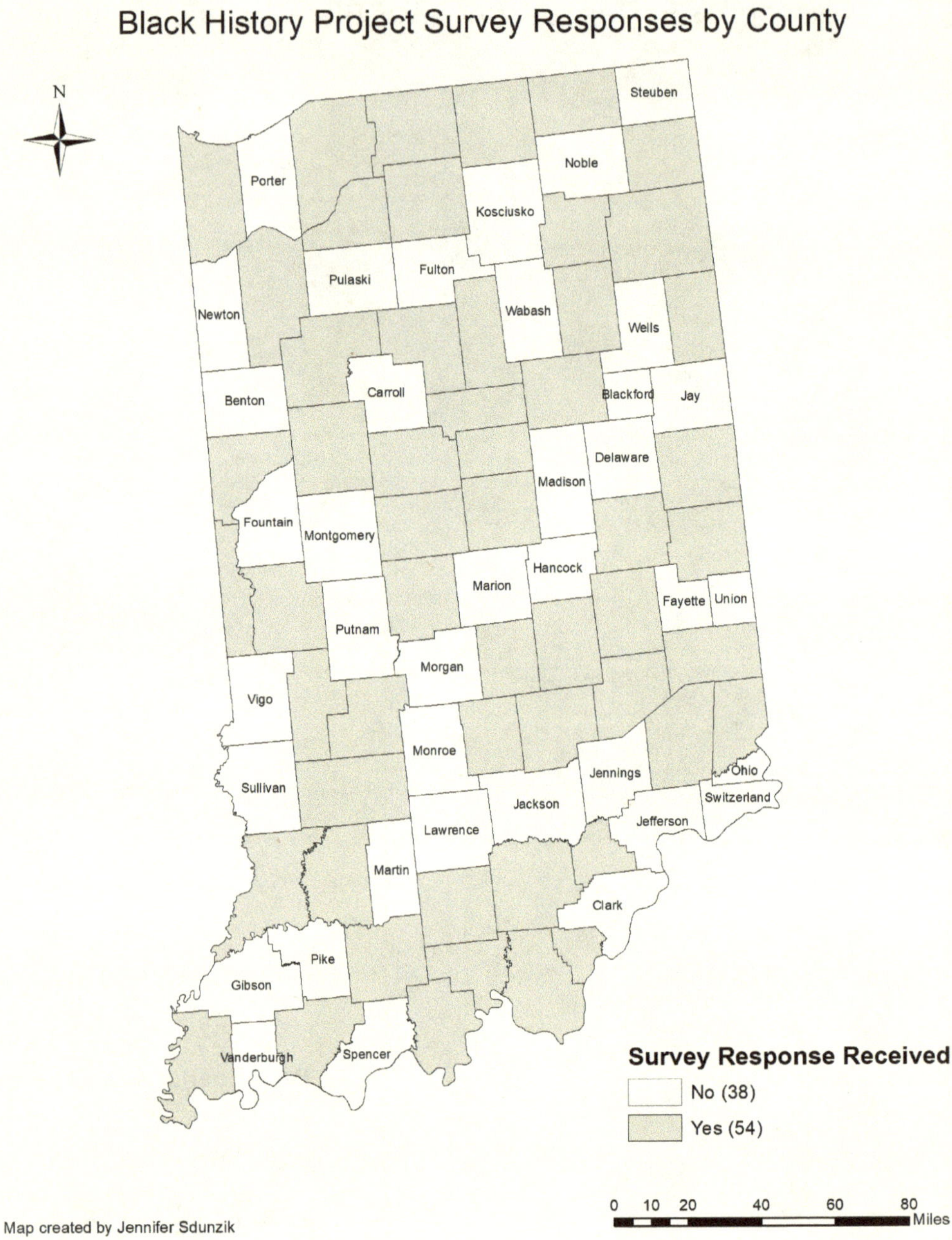

MAP 10. Map displaying actual survey responses by county. The counties that did not send a survey response are identified by name.

Monroe's spokespeople considered documenting Black history worth their while as far as the BHP survey is concerned. This, once again, underlines the importance and power of those writing and preserving history—as it matters to them.

Second, of the fifty-four actual survey responses in the BHP, nineteen were sparsely filled out. Often, only one or two questions on the survey were attempted, or the empty spaces in between the questions, designed for the respective responses, were used to write a quick note about not having much knowledge about the topic. I have discussed various examples in the preceding chapters. The survey response from White County serves as a good reminder here, as question 1a) *To your knowledge, what is the earliest occurrence of Blacks in your county and where were they located*? was the only question with an attempted answer: "Checking with the census records of White County also voting registration records there have never been Blacks located in White County."[4] I will return to this example in a bit.

Thus, after the first look at the Black History Project files conveyed the impression of a successful inquiry into the Black experience in Indiana counties, the second look reveals a more accurate representation of the available materials. Despite a response rate of 89 percent, only thirty-five counties, or 38 percent, completed the survey in detail (Map 11). These 35 surveys paint a dire picture of the African American experience in the state. Segregated life, as indicated through Negro registers, Black cemeteries, and separate schools and neighborhoods, many of which I referenced in the preceding chapters, constituted reality for Black Hoosiers in the *northern* state of Indiana. And this is important because of how we script the South as the location of racism in general and in Great Migration discourse specifically.

Let's return to the White County statement about the proclaimed permanent absence of African Americans in the county and question whether the respondent was cherry-picking historical documents, one of the identified strategies of erasure discussed in Chapter 3. We quickly learn that the statement is indeed inaccurate. Even though the writer does not specify which census records they have consulted, the 1970 census lists four Black people in the county and the 1980 census lists ten. Though proven inaccurate, a statement like this quickly addresses the survey and may eschew any further interrogation into the county's history concerning the issue. Thus, White County operationalized erasure, similar to the other twenty-odd counties I discuss in Chapter 3, making "active forgetting" a viable strategy among white Hoosiers. Some communities mastered erasure to the degree that many county residents, survey respondents included, seemed to have actively forgotten that they have (had) a Black history.

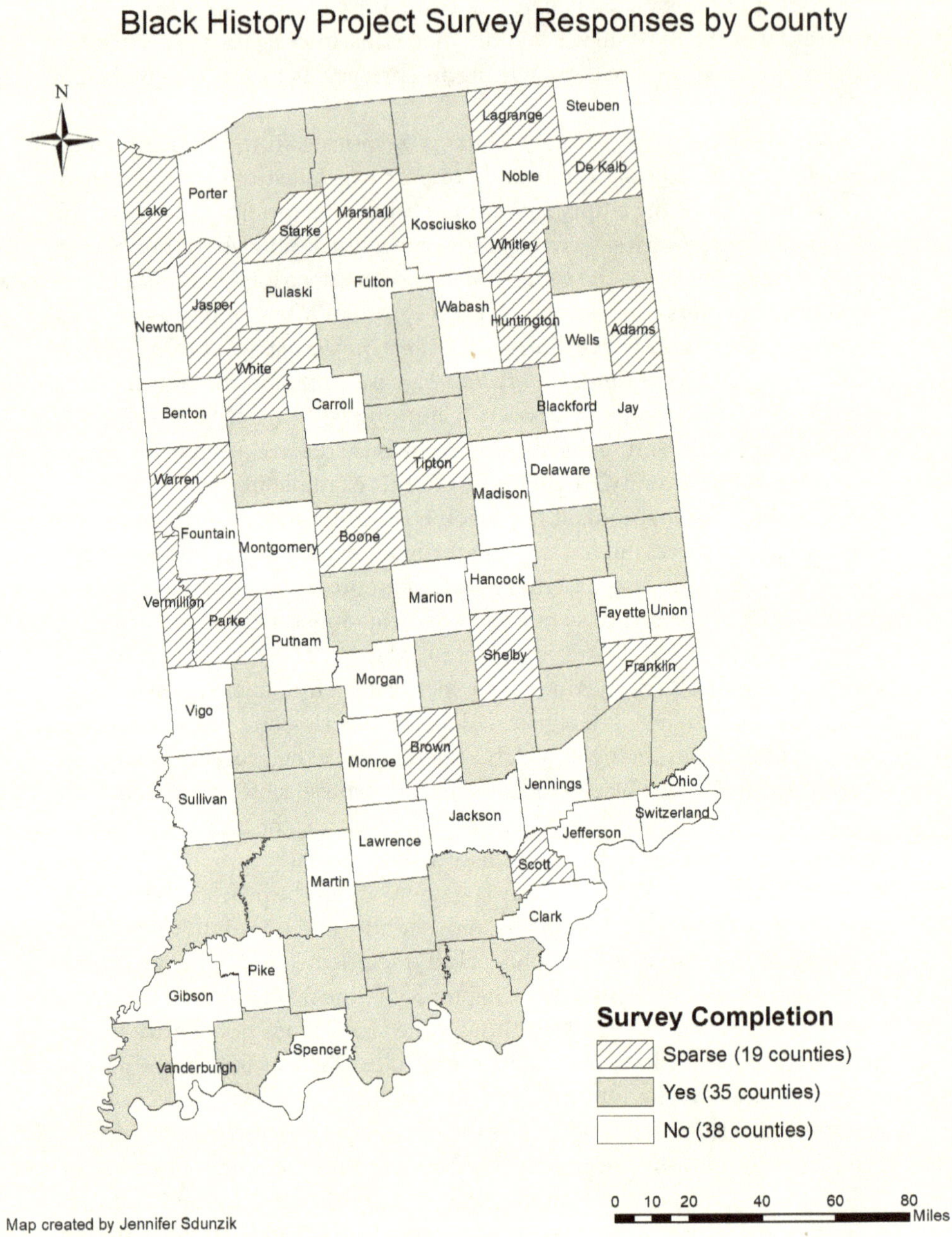

MAP 11. Map displaying county survey responses for the Black History Project. The different shades capture the extent to which the surveys were completed. The map provides a more accurate visual of the BHP request's success, as only thirty-five counties completed the survey in more detail.

The White County statement also serves as a reminder that personal memories and collective memories are constructed, so they transmit selective knowledge about their county past. The White County respondent simply may not have encountered a Black individual in the county during their lifetime, yet we do not know enough about the survey taker regarding age, place of origin, and other identities. We do know, however, that the person is non-Black, most likely white, and has the knowledge to consult census and voting records to answer historical population questions, as well as the authority to speak on the county's behalf. And we know that the statement is inaccurate, as the 1970 and 1980 censuses proved. "Inherent in the transmission of historical memory," writes historian W. Fitzhugh Brundage, "is the active labor of selecting, structuring, and imposing meaning on the past rather than the mere reproduction of inherent historical truths."[5] Linking the concept of collective memory to cultural authority and the exercise of power, Brundage declares memory an "essential component of [groups'] social identity," arguing that

> Remembering consequently becomes implicated in a range of activities that have as much to do with identity, power, authority, cultural norms, and social interaction as with the simple act of conserving and recalling information. Groups invariably fashion their own image of the world and their place in it by establishing an accepted version of the past, a sort of genealogy of identity.[6]

Exercising cultural authority as the county spokesperson for the survey inquiry, the respondent shared White County's "accepted version of the past"—a version that supports their white spatial imaginary if not reality.

The sparsely completed surveys frequently attest to the geography of hate prevalent in Indiana. Responses to most of the questions ranged from "no" to "none" to "not to my knowledge," as was the case in the White County survey. Again, there is a chance that Black people have resided in those counties, yet if they did, there was no priority in capturing their life experiences in the survey. Neither were there, for the most part, efforts to consult local newspaper archives, biographical county histories, or church histories. Instead, like White County above and Carroll County in Chapter 3, survey respondents claimed Indiana's all-white and whitewashed history for their respective counties. Here are some more examples:

> "Noble County has had little or no Black inhabitants during its 150-year plus history, hence there is no documentation of the type you are seeking."
>
> "We have never had over 5 Black families living in Ohio Co. Sorry I have no knowledge of any Black History available."[7]

However, by inserting "little" and "never had over 5," both responses actually insinuate that Black people resided among them at one point in their county's history. The number might have been deemed too insignificant to provide more detailed information on the residents themselves, or where and when they lived in their counties. Having applied a "white racial frame" to the survey, the respondents successfully whitewashed the county's history and maintained its white image publicly. This way, they actively contributed to the social construction (and perception) of their counties as all-white. Without further inquiry, selective memory and knowledge-sharing in the survey enabled survey respondents to uphold the common perception of their counties as "natural" white spaces.

The cultural authority that comes with the position enables county personnel to note seemingly insignificant numbers as a fact of life, with no desire to explore the topic further, another strategy discussed in Chapter 3. Brown County's survey—also sparsely completed with two brief remarks—notes a sixteen-year-old "waiter" in a household in Nashville, its county seat, as the only Black resident of the county (according to 1860 census) until about twenty-five years ago, which would be in the early 1960s, when a Black family moved in.[8] The second remark on the survey refers to the situation in Brown County in 1987: "Today there are only 5 black children in the entire County school system." No further context is provided regarding the twelve decades between the two comments, leaving us wondering whether Brown County successfully enforced and maintained its white desires for more than a century. The same is true for Blackford County, which its survey response revealed had "13 negroes" according to the 1840 census and "Now we have only 1—Tom Shade—He works for 3 M and is a leader in our city parks program for Hartford City and has done a great deal for and with our young people and in our Heritage Days program."[9] Not questioning the decades-long absence of African Americans, the county personnel acted within their white racial frames and simply reaffirmed the perception of their counties as white spaces.

The sparse survey responses inspired the Black History Program archivist to follow up with some of the respondents, most likely via telephone. She had one such conversation with the Noble County historian in early 1988, which resulted in her jotting down that he "Does not plan to complete the survey due to the fact 'there is no documentation of the type you are seeking.'" Other follow-up attempts resulted in "does not plan to complete survey—no information available," as was the case for Porter and Pulaski counties.[10] The program archivist confronted the county personnel with an inconvenient reality. They in turn shooed away her follow-up inquiries, brushing them off with terse remarks about the unavailability of information. To that extent, the inquiries were met with the same strategy that county residents applied to KKK memories, another inconvenient history, discussed extensively in Chapter 4. Both Black history and KKK history are inconvenient realities—memories and documents of which may simply disappear the longer they are actively forgotten.

Consequently, empty county folders and sparsely completed surveys[11] in the Black History Project reveal more about the county's attitude toward ethnoracial minorities than their history. The empty folders of the ten unresponsive counties, for example, may not necessarily mean that these counties do not have a trace of Black life in their history. Yet frequent follow-up forms over the course of two years, to gauge information about the Black experience in their counties, were ignored. Suffice it to say that the lack of any response at least implies a very low priority of the Black experience locally, as none of the county entities—local historical societies, county historians, and public libraries—bothered responding, not even in a manner that acknowledged receipt of the request, nor in a quick and superficial way as some others did.

"Faced with an inconvenient history, the first defense is silence," Elliot Jaspin reminds us in his monograph on racial cleansings.[12] A community's need "to either deny or shade its history" may partially be "a way to protect the memories of their fathers and grandfathers who took part in these expulsions," Jaspin explains further. Shading serves the purpose of "protecting [and continuing] the legacy of the cleansings," while denial allows townspeople to "claim that their racially 'pure' world is a coincidence."[13] The silence on sundown towns and KKK memories indicates that. Jaspin's interpretation corroborates my identification of various strategies people deployed in Indiana counties to preserve the reality and/or perception of their counties as "natural" white spaces.

Thus, despite the overwhelming absence of information regarding the Black experience in the state of Indiana across time, we learn a lot from the Black History Project files—about Black Indiana and even more about white Indiana. I embarked on this journey with the desire to understand why southern Black migrants decided not to permanently relocate to small-town northern America, which stands in stark contrast to their expressed desires in the migrant letters. I tracked down Black experiences in Indiana counties, documented their (mostly) ephemeral stays in the communities, and recorded their dwindling numbers over time. Locating and drawing on Black histories and Black subjects excavated white (spatial) imaginaries and realities. Black Hoosiers existed in white Hoosier communities—alongside white supremacist ideologies. This journey has led me to uncover a map of white hostility and animosity toward Black Hoosiers, or the geography of hate.

Mapping Whiteness

The Geography of Hate unanchored the common perception of "natural" white spaces, emphasizing the constructive nature of Indiana towns. White Hoosiers actively contributed to and enforced the all-white nature and perception of their communities as white. On a county level, white Hoosiers successfully sent the message that this was white territory and white property, where Black people simply were out of place. If not driven out, Black folk seemed to have been merely tolerated in various Indiana counties. The Black History Project confirms Black residents' marginalized and low-priority status across Indiana counties. Their small numbers, if any at all, seemingly justified county personnel's denial of having a Black history in their counties altogether. Although they were present, Black Hoosiers remained invisible in the Indiana landscape.

The Geography of Hate captures the persistence of these exclusionary attitudes over time, thereby drawing attention to the perpetuating nature of white supremacist ideologies. In Chapter 1, I surveyed various county histories published in Indiana over time, which allowed me to document the consistent and continuous nature of white Hoosier hostility toward African Americans in historical records. At times, the writers explicitly conveyed the county people's attitudes and opinions. In other instances, they adopted the prevalent tone to reflect on Black experiences, leaving many things unsaid. Regardless of the extent of openness, the tone of the writing, and whether the shared opinions reflect the writers' personal attitudes, we learn from the county histories how preconceived notions and degrading stereotypes were nourished in Indiana and perpetuated over time. We begin to see a pattern that creates an unwelcoming environment for people of color.

The county narratives are but one example of the blanket of exclusion that covers the state of Indiana. The foregoing pages describe this exclusion, drawing careful attention to the connections between space, place, and power. Mapping the legacy of white desires, Map 12 juxtaposes the numerical increase in the Black population with the numerical increase in white counties in Indiana from 1890 to 1970.

Spatializing the history of white desires then allowed me to make violence—and the spaces in which it occurs—visible. Throughout the book, I detailed the maelstrom of exclusion, violence, threats, insults, fears, and problems that people of color face in a state that embraces whiteness and a

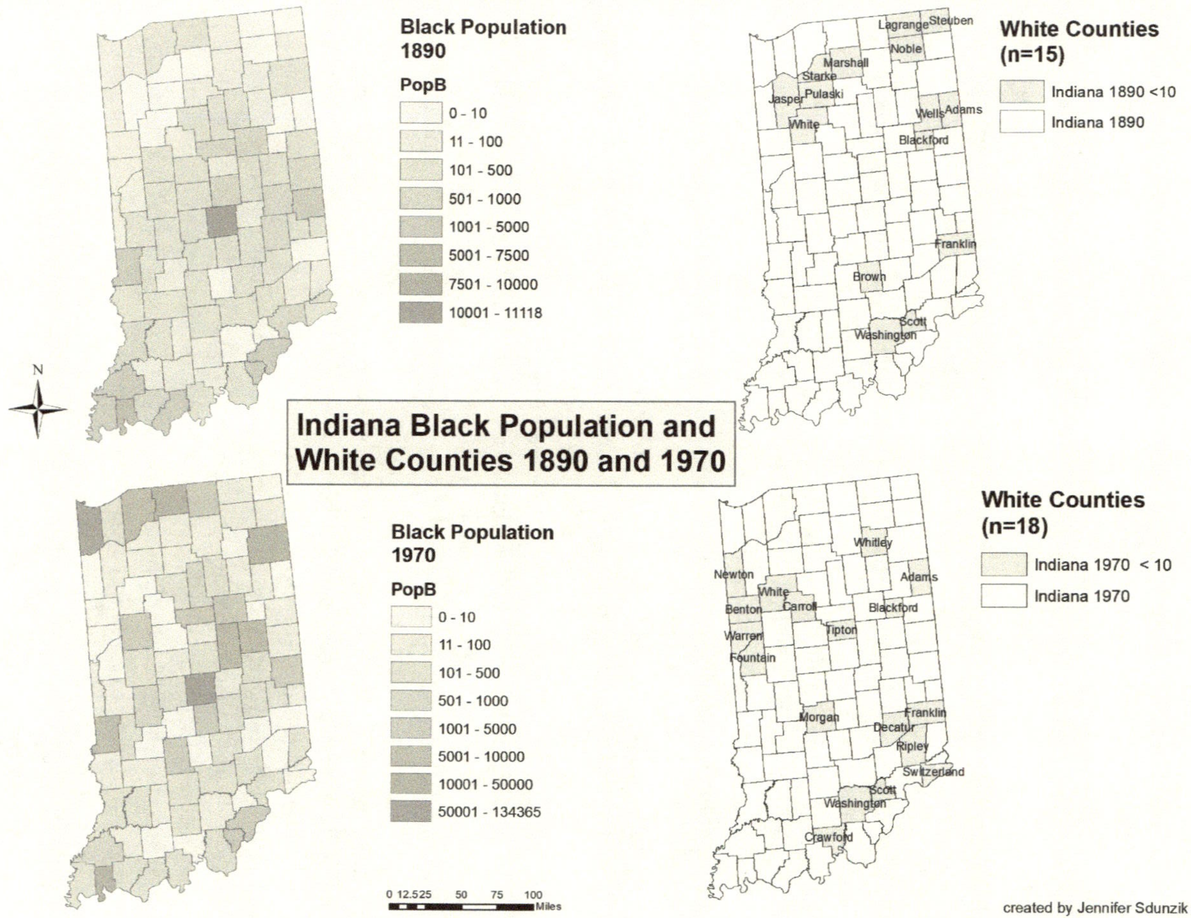

MAP 12. Maps on the left capture the Black population numerically in Indiana in 1890 and 1970—decades preceding and following the Great Migration. Maps on the right visualize the number of counties with a minuscule (<10) or nonexistent Black population in 1890 and 1970.

culture of exclusion. Map 13 illustrates all seventy-nine counties discussed in this book that demonstrated hostility and inhospitality toward Black Hoosiers in their midst explicitly. Counties were included on the map if I recorded and documented in the book incidents of violence, expulsion, exclusion, segregated life, Negro registers, and the like. I did not include the ten counties that did not respond to the BHP survey request at all, if that was the only county reference in the book, which would have increased the number of counties to eighty-one.[14] Their unresponsiveness, though an indicator of the low priority of Black lives in their midst, does not provide enough grounding for incidents of intolerance and hatred. I also did not include counties mentioned exclusively in the context of possible Underground Railroad connections.

Map 13 perfectly illustrates how a cartography of hate upends efforts to use one town as a scapegoat—to demonize that white space after a violent crime has been committed and has drawn national attention. If conversations around racism and exclusion occur, white Hoosiers do not shy away from scapegoating Martinsville in Morgan County as the *one* racist location in the state, frequently in reference to being a Klan hotbed and the site of Carol Jenkins's murder, both discussed in Chapter 4. Map 13, however, clearly visualizes the pervasiveness of acts of violence, bigotry, and intolerance in the state. It corroborates that neither Morgan County nor Clinton County, on which I lay the magnifying glass in this book to document race relations, were an aberration in the state—they were rather the norm.

By making visible such violent, intolerant, and hateful acts and attitudes across the Indiana landscape, this book opens a space to include excluded voices and erased experiences in these very communities. The opening vignettes in each chapter manifest the lived Black experiences into Clinton County history books. They serve as a testament to Black resilience in Indiana and celebrate the successes and achievements of African Americans who once called Clinton County home. They personalize broader sociohistorical circumstances in Indiana, one of the in-between spaces along the migratory corridor from the American South to the North. While affirming Black migrant desires to settle in small-town America during the Great Migration, the vignettes document the hardship, obstacles, and difficulties of Black southerners attempting to do so in small-town Indiana.

Ultimately, *The Geography of Hate* interrupts and challenges the culture of denial that has overlooked and thus exonerated these "invisible" and "normalized" spaces, and it demarcates them as white spaces that are built on and reproduce white supremacist ideologies, white desires, and exclusionary mechanisms, hidden behind the veil of midwestern friendliness.

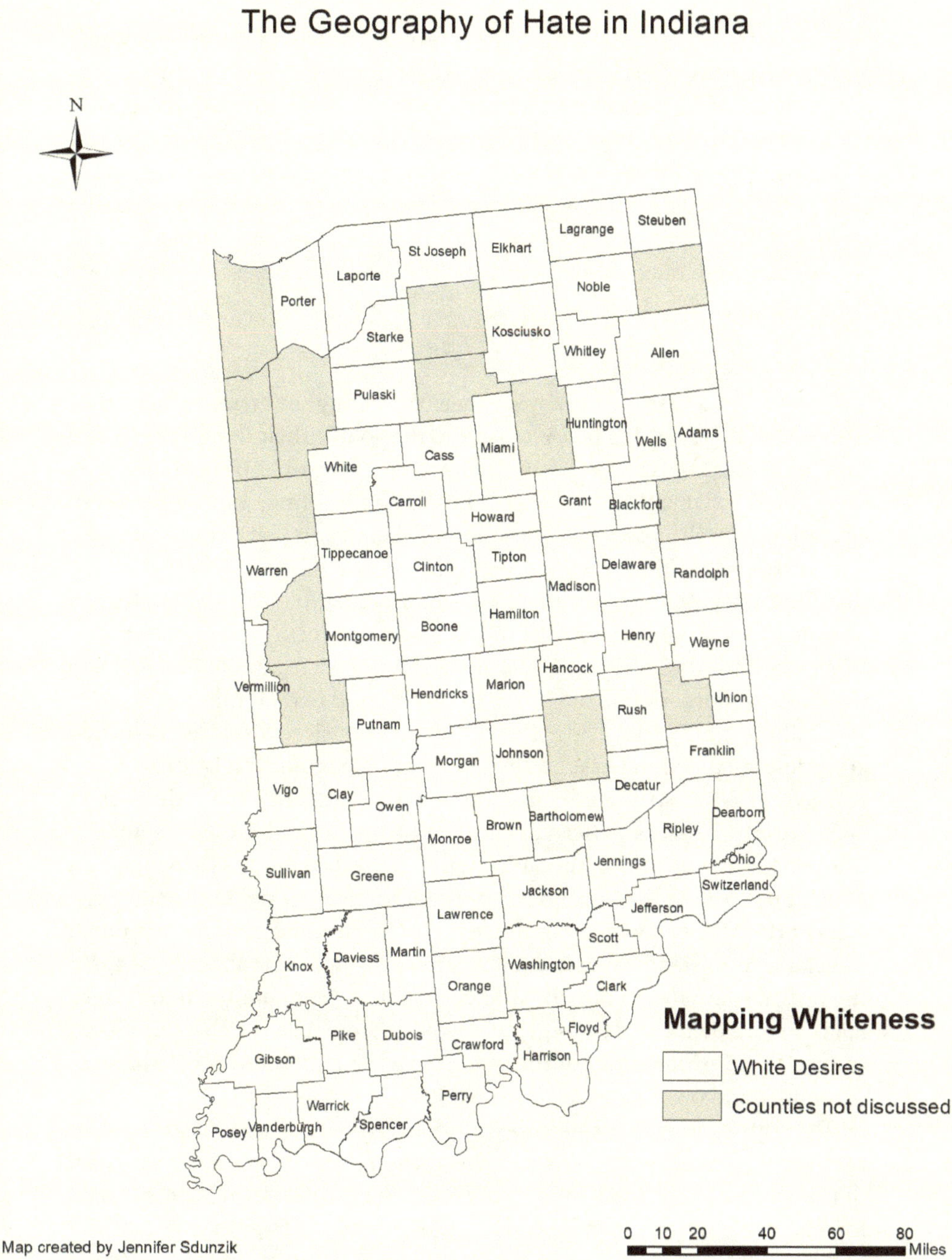

MAP 13. Mapping Whiteness. Map displays all counties discussed throughout the book, recording examples of resentment and animosity toward Black residents. Seventy-nine of Indiana's ninety-two counties (86 percent) have a proven tainted race record and have subscribed to the culture of exclusion. More research is needed to assess the race record of the thirteen remaining gray counties.

Most Black experiences are narrated through the lens of white violent acts and racist actions. This book castigates these acts of violence, intimidation, inhospitality, and erasure, and it documents the extent to which they (almost) succeeded. Indiana's race history is not pretty. White Hoosiers created not a Promised Land for southern Black migrants but rather a racialized, if not racist, geography, in which the ethnoracial newcomers faced insurmountable and invisible walls that prevented them from reaping the promises of the American democracy—equal rights and pursuit of happiness in small-town America.

* * *

One hundred years ago, many southern Black migrants packed their bags, determined to pursue happiness outside of the South. Their desires to relocate were motivated by an interest in different practices of citizenship, including property ownership, access to a living wage, voting, and high-quality education, as well as control over their well-being and that of their families. The historical archives they left behind with the migrant letters confirm that their relocation desires included small-town America. In small-town America they sought tranquility, robust social networks, and good schools. What they found was a hostile and unwelcoming environment inhabited by white midwesterners who did not want "their" kind in their midst, economic and cultural similarities aside. The culture of exclusion, displayed in hostile attitudes, local ordinances, exclusionary practices, and racist discourses, secured the white spatial imaginary and white spatial reality for decades.

These days, many southern migrants, this time from below the southern U.S. border, migrate north, similarly motivated by the pursuit of a living wage, good education, and control over their and their families' well-being. The fears of the Mexican woman in the opening vignette suggest that not much has changed in small-town Indiana. Her experiences corroborate yet again the potency and durability of white desires that dominate the midwestern landscape, as delineated throughout this book. Together, the chapters record the racialized geographies of Indiana, providing a nuanced understanding of identity and belonging in the Midwest.

Through its focus on small-town Indiana, this book demonstrates how normative racism is to the nation. Small-town Indiana serves as a microcosm of the United States in its failure to own its racist past. Instead, it silences, forgets, and erases. Until Indiana and white America at large openly confront and honestly own their history of prejudice, discrimination, and violence, race relations in small-town America and the nation will continue to be a source of contention and instability. Until then, the beat goes on.

Notes

Preface

1. Spickard, *Almost All Aliens*, 416.

Introduction

1. Discursive buffers like "I'm not racist, but . . . " are semantic phrases of color-blind racism that white people use to avoid "dangerous discussions" and express their ambivalence on a "controversial" social policy or, in Doug's case, changing reality, which Bonilla-Silva labels "yes and no" strategy (*Racism without Racists*, 57–63).

2. Lipsitz, *The Possessive Investment in Whiteness.*

3. McKittrick, *Demonic Grounds*, x. In general, my approach to geography is informed by the work of scholars like Katherine McKittrick, Laura Pulido, and George Lipsitz. Their critical race perspectives reveal how race, space, and power intersect. At a different point in her seminal work *Demonic Grounds*, McKittrick elaborates, noting that "Geography, then, materially and discursively extends to cover three-dimensional spaces and places, the physical landscapes and infrastructures, geographic imaginations, the practice of mapping, exploring, and seeing, and social relations in and across space" (xiii). All of these layers encapsulated in her definition are unfolding in this book.

4. See, for example, Spear, *Black Chicago*; Osofsky, *Harlem: The Making of a Ghetto*; Drake and Cayton, *Black Metropolis*; Grossman, *Land of Hope*; Gregory, *The Southern Diaspora.*

5. Gregory, *The Southern Diaspora*, 23–38.

6. Reich, editor, *The Great Black Migration*, xxi; Grossman, *Land of Hope*, 19; Gregory, "The Second Great Migration: A Historical Overview," 21. For scholars interested in the second wave of the Great Migration, see Isabel Wilkerson's *The Warmth of Other Suns*, in which she weaves the cultural-historical underpinnings of

the Great Migration around the experiences of three southern Black families leaving the South in three different directions in three different decades, highlighting migrant desires and dreams.

7. For example, Spear, *Black Chicago*; Osofsky, *Harlem*; Grossman, *Land of Hope*; Lemann, *The Promised Land*; Tolnay, "The African American 'Great Migration' and Beyond," 209–32.

8. For example, Gregory, *The Southern Diaspora*; Dochuk, *From Bible Belt to Sunbelt*; Luther Adams, *Way Up North in Louisville*; Pruitt, *The Other Great Migration*; McCammack, *Landscapes of Hope*; Walker and Wilson, *Black Eden*. For an excellent and more comprehensive literature review of Great Migration scholarship and the emerging trends, see, for example, Tolnay's "The African American 'Great Migration' and Beyond" and Reich's introduction to *The Great Migration. A Historical Encyclopedia of the American Mosaic*. Tolnay also contextualizes the return migration to the South after 1970 (223–24).

9. Adams, *Way Up North in Louisville*, 2; emphasis added. Adams's remarks echo Henri Lefebvre's representations of space, invoking the power and dominance with which (public) spaces are socially constructed (see Lefebvre's *The Production of Space* and McCann's "Race, Protest and Public Space"). Black Studies and Gender Studies scholar Katherine McKittrick also discusses domination with regard to geography; see *Demonic Grounds*.

10. Loewen, *Sundown Towns*, 8, 127.

11. Gregory, *The Southern Diaspora*, 117.

12. Myrdal, *American Dilemma*, 186–87; emphasis added. *American Dilemma* was published on the eve of the second migration wave, which relocated more than five million southern Black migrants to the North and West of the country. Myrdal's observation held true, however, as the time span overlapped and correlated with the spread of sundown policies across the nation; see Loewen, *Sundown Towns*, 127. The late Myrdal admitted some errors in his attempt to understand American society, including and most relevant to this study, "underestimat[ing] the degree of bias in the North." See "Gunnar Myrdal."

13. Blocker, *A Little More Freedom*; Blocker, "Black Migration to Muncie, 1860–1930," 304, 309–10. Muncie also is the only exception among Blocker's four case studies, as it did not witness an outbreak of racial unrest around the turn of the twentieth century (such as the race riot in Springfield, Illinois, in 1908). Such racial unrest often is credited with exacerbating race relations to the extent that Black residents left for good.

14. Cayton et al., editors, *The American Midwest*; Shortridge, *The Middle West*; Lauck, *The Lost Region*; Hurt, "Foreword."

15. Cayton et al., editors, *The American Midwest*, xxiv.

16. Taylor and McBirney, *Peopling Indiana: The Ethnic Experience*; Reid, "'The Whitest of Occupations'? African Americans in the Rural Midwest, 1940–2010," 204–54; Lee Moore, *Re-Examining the 'Heartland': Korean American Religious and Ethnic Identity Formation in the Midwest*.

17. Cayton and Gray, editors. *The American Midwest: Essays on Regional History*, 24–25.

18. *A Stronger Kinship*, 6. Cox has written extensively on the Black migration into the Northwest Territory ever since the American Revolution and describes the nineteenth-century Black migration as the "region's first Great Migration" ("When Anti-Immigration"; see also *The Bone and Sinew of the Land*).

19. Reid, "'The Whitest of Occupations,'" 208.

20. Bourdieu, "Habitus," 43; emphasis in original.

21. Hillier and Rooksby, *Habitus: A Sense of Place*, 21.

22. Bonilla-Silva et al., "When Whites Flock Together," 233.

23. Bonilla-Silva, *Racism without Racists*, 104.

24. Ibid.

25. *Race, Whiteness and Education*, 79. Leonardo describes "these strategies of whiteness" such as housing and school segregation as neither "innocent" nor "harmless" (ibid).

26. Critical Whiteness Studies have become a vibrant field over the last two decades. For example, see Gerstle, *American Crucible*; Omi and Winant, *Racial Formation in the United States*; Razack, *Race, Space, and the Law*; Lipsitz, *How Racism Takes Place*; Nelson, "Racialized Landscapes: Whiteness and the Struggle over Farmworker Housing in Woodburn, Oregon," 41–62; Bebout, *Whiteness at the Border*.

27. Olson, *The Abolition of White Democracy*.

28. Frankenberg, *White Women, Race Matters*, 231.

29. Leitner, "Spaces of Encounters"; Lipsitz, *How Racism Takes Place*.

30. Spickard, *Almost All Aliens*, 27.

31. Feagin, *The White Racial Frame*, 10.

32. Bucholtz, "The Public Life of White Affects," 489; see also Matias, *Feeling White: Whiteness, Emotionality, and Education*; Bonilla-Silva, "Feeling Race"; or Leonardo, *Race, Whiteness, and Education*.

33. Cox, *A Stronger Kinship*, 6.

34. Admittedly, the U.S. Census is not without its issues, such as for homogenizing whites and dividing people of color into multiple subgroups, as anthropologist Jane H. Hill points out, but it is still the best way to approximate the demographic make-up of communities across the country; see Hill, *The Everyday Language of White Racism*, 13–16.

35. Wiegand and Wiegand, *The Desegregation of Public Libraries in the Jim Crow South*, 190.

36. *Demonic Grounds*, xiii.

37. *Demonic Grounds*, xi–xii.

38. Curtis, *Colored Memories*, 9.

39. Gittins, "Oral History, Reliability and Recollection," 92; emphasis in original.

40. Feagin, *The White Racial Frame*, 17; emphasis in original.

41. Trouillot, *Silencing the Past*, xxiii.

42. Madison, *Hoosiers*, 192.

43. For example, see Painter, *Exodusters*, 68; Grossman, *Land of Hope*, 6.

44. Mapping Prejudice and Segregated Seattle are two digital archives that capture residential segregation in Minneapolis and Seattle, respectively. Both are participatory archives, in that community members actively contribute to the research, unearthing and digitizing thousands of restrictive covenants in now-known whites-only areas. They are housed at the University of Minnesota and University of Washington, respectively. Mapping Inequality, conceived at the University of Richmond, visualizes redlining on a national scale by digitizing redlining maps of the Home Owners' Loan Corporation from the 1930s. The Southern Poverty Law Center's Hate Map captures contemporary organized hatred and extremism, serving as an annual census of active hate groups and their activities in the United States since 1990.

Chapter 1. Manifesting White Indiana

1. That is slightly below the median value of owned nonfarm homes in Clinton County, which was $2,715 in 1930, according to the census.

2. Claybaugh, *History of Clinton County, Indiana*, 178–79.

3. Leonardo, *Race, Whiteness, and Education*, 88.

4. Spickard, *Almost All Aliens*, 27.

5. "Oldest Colored Man Here, Dead," *Frankfort Morning Times*, Aug. 16, 1919, 1.

6. Admittedly, Clinton County's Black population was small, comprising 0.4 percent and 0.3 percent of the total county population in 1900 and 1910, respectively. But the first arrival of Black people in Clinton County preceded the Civil War and thus could have been included in the earlier accounts of county families.

7. Thornbrough, *The Negro in Indiana*, 55.

8. Julian, *Speeches on Political Questions*, 127–28.

9. Andersen, *Negro Education in Tippecanoe County*, 5.

10. Wilson, "Indiana," 29, 102.

11. Lyda, *The Negro in the History of Indiana*, 14–15. This book underlines the durability of white Hoosiers' unfavorable yet commonly held perceptions of African Americans.

12. Thornbrough, *Indiana in the Civil War Era*, 13–14; Madison, *Hoosiers*, 109; Hine, *When the Truth Is Told*, 10. It is beyond the scope of this book to explore Indiana's treatment of, negotiations with, and policies against Native Americans. I provide a brief overview of Native Americans in the state elsewhere (Sdunzik, "Indiana"). Suffice it to say that white Hoosiers pushed for the removal of local tribal nations as early as the state was founded, and particularly after the Indian Removal Act was passed on a national level in 1830. The white man's conquest of Indiana lands, which belonged to Miami, Potawatomi, Kickapoo/Mascouten, Delaware, Wyandot, and Shawnee Peoples, among others, culminated in the forced removal of Potawatomi from Indiana to present-day Kansas in 1838, known as the Trail of Death. As of 2021, Indiana did not have any federally recognized tribal nations in their midst,

though at least sixteen different peoples reside in the state, with the Cherokee being the most common tribal nation. Native Americans comprise 0.4 percent of the total state population, according to the 2020 census. Scholars discussing Native American resilience and experiences in Indiana include Rafert's 1996 work *The Miami Indians of Indiana*, Hicks et al.'s *Native American Cultures in Indiana*, and Glenn and Rafert's 2009 monograph *The Native Americans.*

13. Though outlawed, Thornbrough notes that illegal indentures existed in the state, as the constitutional ban on involuntary servitude did not encompass indentures. See *The Negro in Indiana,* 25–30.

14. Indiana was the second territory from the Northwest Ordinance to gain statehood. Ohio became a state in 1803 and did not limit voting or militia rights to white male citizens in its first constitution.

15. However, Thornbrough notes elsewhere that it did not become official law of the land until 1840, when an interracial couple breached the law, causing uproar among the citizens and public officials in Indianapolis, resulting in cementing and harshening the law. See *The Negro in Indiana,* 125–26. Other scholars do not agree with Thornbrough's interpretation that the 1818 law was not officially enforced until 1840, but they do cite the same 1840 incident as the catalyst to pass "a more stringent law declaring all Negro-white marriages to be null and void (illegitimating children, incidentally) and defining the offense as a felony," including fines and imprisonment. See Monahan, "Marriage across Racial Lines in Indiana," 633.

16. Thornbrough, *Since Emancipation*, 2. Black men were given the right to vote only in 1881—despite the Fifteenth Amendment—and Black people were not allowed to serve in the state's militia until 1936. Jury duty and court testimony were granted in 1885. See Robbins, *African Heritage in Morgan County, Indiana*, 9.

17. Sdunzik, "Indiana," 292.

18. Crenshaw, *"Bury Me in a Free Land,"* 13; Andersen, *Negro Education in Tippecanoe County*, 8.

19. Madison, *The Indiana Way*, 107; Lyda, *The Negro in the History of Indiana*, 17.

20. Lyda, *The Negro in the History of Indiana*, 33. Since Indiana still governs under the 1851 Constitution, though amended over the years, it is important to note that Article XIII was declared invalid by the Indiana Supreme Court in 1866.

21. Anthrop, "Indiana Emigrants to Liberia," 9, 11.

22. Wright, "Slavery in the District Remarks," 1468.

23. Thornbrough, *Indiana in the Civil War Era*, 14.

24. Longworth, *Caught in the Middle*, 103.

25. The Knox County file in the Black History Project is unique in that it contains what seems to be a "slave register," listing the owner's name, slave name, and year recorded when they came to the county.

26. I make this assertion based on accounts, such as Lyda's *The Negro in the History of Indiana*, that describe strategies slave masters used to delude their slaves into signing what they believed to be emancipation papers but turned out to be new indentures,

often with a life-long agreement or a period of thirty-five years, which would expand beyond the 1850 census. See Lyda, *The Negro in the History of Indiana*, 12.

27. Rose, "Quakers, North Carolinians and Blacks in Indiana's Settlement Pattern," 36, 42.

28. The 1860 census is the first census recording data for all ninety-two Indiana counties, which is why it serves as a point of reference here, in addition to the fact that the numerical increase of the Black population comprised only 166, mainly due to the prohibition of Black people entering and settling in the state, manifested in the 1851 Constitution. The six counties with no Black residents were Benton, Blackford, Brown, Crawford, Newton, and Pulaski counties. But the Early Black Settlement research project, conducted by the Indiana Historical Society during the summer of 2014, identified sixty-one early Black settlements, including one unnamed one in Newton County, Indiana's youngest county (boundaries finalized in 1859).

29. Moore, "A Treasure Hunt. Black Rural Settlements in Indiana by 1870," 25.

30. Because it is the only Black rural community of the sixty-one identified in Indiana that still houses an active farming community today, the National Museum of African American History in Washington, D.C., celebrates its ongoing legacy. For more information, see my chapter "Indiana" in *A State-by-State History* (283–99).

31. Interesting scholarly treatment of Black farming communities in Indiana include Steven A. Vincent's *Southern Seed, Northern Soil* and Gary Alan Fine's "The Pinkston Settlement."

32. Cord, "Black Rural Settlements in Indiana before 1860," 104. Again, note the passive tone in the question tag "what" in reasons for the exodus.

33. Emma Lou Thornbrough appears to have been the first scholar to have noted the racial cleansing in Washington County. In her 1957-published *The Negro in Indiana before 1900*, she called it "an exodus of nearly all of the colored residents," as the result of growing intolerance toward Black residents and acts of intimidation and murder against them (225).

34. Preserving or reconstituting political authority was a prime reason for the expulsion of Black residents, as Guy Lancaster corroborates in his *Racial Cleansing in Arkansas, 1883–1924*, 12–14.

35. Jaspin, *Buried in the Bitter Waters*, 6, 29, 16. With only sixty-four Black residents in 2010 (0.2 percent), Washington County fulfills Jaspin's criteria of a "successful" racial cleansing. The other Indiana cleansing took place in Vermillion County in 1923, amid the first wave of the Great Migration, due to an alleged molestation of a white girl by a Black man. Vermillion's Black population dropped from 235 in the 1920 census to sixty-nine in 1930 (195). I will return to the racial cleansings in Washington and Vermillion counties in Chapter 3.

36. *Report and Testimony of the Select Committee of the United States Senate to Investigate the Causes of the Removal of the Negroes from the Southern States to the Northern States, Part III*, 166.

37. I will discuss the Kansas Exodus and the letters during the Great Migration, which use the term "loafer," in the next chapter.

38. On that note, I recommend reading Brent M. S. Campney's excellent work on racist violence in the Midwest, particularly *This is Not Dixie: Racist Violence in Kansas, 1861–1927* and his most recent book, *Hostile Heartland: Racism, Repression and Resistance in the Midwest*, particularly Chapter 3, in which he explores white Hoosier mob violence to prevent Black settlement in southern Indiana in the second half of the nineteenth century. Both Campney and I reject the notion of a hospitable Midwest by unearthing and expanding the definition of white supremacist practices prevalent in the region.

39. *The People*, Jan. 8, 1880, 1; Owen County Vertical File. Note the shift to passive voice in the last sentence, absolving white Hoosiers from the fact that they were the ones contemplating mob violence.

40. "The Negro Exodus into Indiana," *Indiana State Sentinel*, Aug. 18, 1880: Supplement. Similar perceptions of Black folk were noted by Lyda (see above).

41. Lipsitz, *The Possessive Investment in Whiteness*.

42. *The People*, Jan. 8, 1880, 1; Owen County Vertical File.

43. Historian Rayford W. Logan coined the phrase "nadir of race relations" to describe the deteriorating race relations in the period after Reconstruction, in which white America implemented a series of laws and practices disenfranchising Black America publicly, educationally, civically, and economically. He argued that "the last decade of the nineteenth century and the opening of the twentieth century marked the nadir of the Negro's status in American society," meaning nationwide acceptance had been at its lowest point, and racism at its highest. See Logan, *The Negro in American Life and Thought*, 52.

44. Wade, *Constituting Whiteness*, 158.

45. The 1890s witnessed an intensification of racial tensions, and lynching became an even more popular means to dissuade Black people from voting and enjoying other benefits of citizenship. With her 1892 *Southern Horrors* and 1895 *The Red Record*, Ida B. Wells-Barnett became the pioneer in recording the atrocities that Black folk experienced in the South at that time, uncovering lynching as a means of terror and economic repression. While most lynchings indeed took place on southern soil, scholars have explored such incidents nationwide, publishing state studies and regional (non-southern) analyses, such as George C. Wright's *Racial Violence in Kentucky*, Philip Dray's *At the Hands of Persons Unknown*, and Michael J. Pfeifer's *Rough Justice*. Brent M. S. Campney explores some of the nineteenth-century lynchings and racist violence against Black people in southern Indiana in his latest work, *Hostile Heartland*, particularly Chapter 3.

46. In *An Undergrowth of Folly*, Brian Butler goes even further, calling the legislation a failure when he discusses the Rockport lynching that took place in December 1900, where two Black men were lynched by a mob: "The mob riddled the two bodies with more than one hundred shots as the crowd cheered. Spencer County sheriffs took the third man to Boonville for his protection. But the next day a number of the mob followed and seized their third victim, hanging him, as well. The anti-lynching law seemed a failure, as no one was tried for these crimes." See Butler, *An Undergrowth*

of Folly, 169. I qualify the passing of the state law as "commendable" as the federal government failed to pass anti-lynching legislation throughout the twentieth century. The U.S. Senate officially and publicly apologized for that failure in 2005. After more than a century of Congress's failure to act, on February 26, 2020, the Emmett Till Antilynching Act was passed in the House of Representatives, making lynching a federal hate crime.

47. Wade, *Constituting Whiteness*, 10, 23, 156.

48. Clinton County's *Frankfort Morning Times* reported regularly in the Condensed State News section about White Caps activities across the state, including Morgan, Crawford, Perry, Harrison, and Hendricks counties in 1889 and 1890, occasionally describing them as a "public nuisance." In his work on racial cleansing in Arkansas, Guy Lancaster discusses whitecapping, or nightriding, as another act of vigilante violence to which white Arkansans turned to enforce their white spatial desires geographically. See *Racial Cleansing in Arkansas, 1883–1924*. In her dissertation on the White Caps in Harrison and Crawford counties, Indiana, Madeleine Noble connects the activities of the White Caps to the Ku Klux Klan, describing them as the "link between the first and second Ku Klux Klan" and arguing that white cappers blended the methods and tactics of the post–Civil War Klan with the mission of the 1920s Klan, with "the aim of defending the values of a declining rural America." See Noble, *The White Caps of Harrison and Crawford County, Indiana*, 10–11.

49. *Purdue Debris 1902*, 265; emphasis in original.

50. Pfeifer, *Lynching Beyond Dixie*, 286.

51. "Carlisle the Scene of a Fierce Race Riot," *Frankfort Morning Times*, Sept. 17, 1904, 2; emphasis added. The *Richmond Palladium* published an abridged, verbatim account of the article four days earlier. Ending with "Hammond was taken to the Sullivan jail for safe keeping," the paper did not disclose any of the lynch mob behavior of fellow white Hoosiers. See "Drove Negroes Out," *Richmond Daily Palladium*, Sept. 13, 1904, 7.

52. *The Freeman* [Indianapolis], June 14, 1902, 4, col. 2; June 21, 1902, 4, col. 4.

53. "Last Negro Leaves," *Indianapolis Recorder*, July 19, 1902, 1; "The Negro in Indiana," *Indianapolis News*, July 16, 1902, 4; "Negroes Driven Away. The Last One Leaves Decatur, Ind., Owing to Threats Made," *New York Times*, July 14, 1902, 1.

54. Chapter XVI, approved May 13, 1869, in *Laws of the State of Indiana*, 41.

55. Exhibit I, Wayne County file, Black History Project.

56. *Journal-Gazette* [Fort Wayne], June 27, 1982, 1LE; Steuben County BHP-VF; emphasis added.

57. Thornbrough, *Since Emancipation*, 25; emphasis added.

58. *Journal-Gazette* [Fort Wayne], June 27, 1982, 4LE; Steuben County BHP-VF.

59. "Every Day in Every Way," *Frankfort Morning Times*, June 7, 1925, 5; Heller, editor, *The 1979 History of Adams County, Indiana*, Adams County file, Black History Project.

60. The Indiana State Library probably holds the most extensive collection in this regard. According to their web entry, the Indiana Collection contains hundreds

of county histories in various formats, including microfiche, microfilm, and print ("ISL"). *The History of Hancock County, Indiana* (1882) and *The History of Delaware County, Indiana* (1881) seem to be rarities in the first wave of county histories. The former includes two men of color in its "Biographies and Sketches" section (Hancock County BHP-VF), one originally from the South, another from Boone County, Indiana; the latter discusses its first Black residents within its chapter on the African Methodist Episcopal Church; see Helm, *History of Delaware County*, 157. The information provided is sparse, but it is there.

61. Gilbert, *History of the City of Evansville and Vanderburg County, Indiana*, 179.

62. Rile Kelley, "Early 'Colored' Settlers of Union County," 15.

63. Ibid.

64. Heller, *The 1979 History of Adams County, Indiana*, 77.

65. Ibid.

66. Heller, *The 1979 History of Adams County, Indiana*, 78–79, emphasis in original.

67. Ibid., 79–80.

68. Ibid., 77, 80. I will discuss sundown towns further in Chapter 4.

Chapter 2. Crossroads of Desires

1. Trice Thompson, "Frankfort, Ind.," *Indianapolis Recorder*, Jan. 26, 1929, 7.

2. Seminal texts include Allan Spear's exploration of Chicago's Black neighborhoods in *Black Chicago: The Making of a Negro Ghetto, 1890–1920* and Gilbert Osofsky's investigation of Black New York in *Harlem: The Making of a Ghetto*. Both scholars note that the Great Migration's prospects of voting rights and political representation caused a major shift in the political landscape (Spear, *Black Chicago*, 7; Osofsky, *Harlem*, 177). St. Clair Drake and Horace R. Cayton's *Black Metropolis*, perhaps the greatest work of urban sociology in the United States, portrays the lives and opportunities of the Black community in Chicago within the rigid walls of residential segregation as well as job ceilings, which prevented social and economic uplift.

3. Southern Black migrants left the census-defined South and relocated across the nation—the North, the Midwest, and the West. Frequently, migrants and scholars alike refer to the destinations as "north or west." For simplicity, I will use "North" and "northern" to refer to all locations outside of the census-defined South.

4. Painter, *Exodusters*, 260.

5. Painter, *Exodusters*, 68.

6. I adopted the term from the *Chicago Defender* coverage of the Great Migration in 1917. For the first five months in 1917, while reporting on the migration of southern Black folk to the North, the *Chicago Defender* kept announcing May 15, 1917, as the specific date for the "Great Northern Drive," during which thousands and thousands more Black people were departing their southern homes (e.g., "Northern Drive to Start," *Chicago Defender*, Feb. 10, 1917, 3).

7. I use pseudonyms for all my interlocutors to protect their privacy, even though some participants gave me permission to use their real names. I conducted the in-

terview with William in the fall of 2015. This conversation constitutes the only one with a participant in the Great Migration; all other interlocutors were residents in midwestern small towns.

8. Great projects that include interviews on migrants' experiences in the urban North include Goin' North, a digital archive that captures the migration experience to Philadelphia, resulting from two university courses taught by Janneken Smucker and Charles Hardy; Isabel Wilkerson's *The Warmth of Other Suns*; and Timuel D. Black Jr.'s two-volume compilation *Bridges of Memory*, which provides accounts of migrant experiences establishing a new life in Chicago.

9. I build the evidence for rural desires on Scott's "Letters of Negro Migrants of 1916–1918" (henceforth "Letters") and "Additional Letters of Negro Migrants of 1916–1918" (henceforth "Additional Letters"). In total, Scott's publications hold 310 letters. All but ten letters are dated in 1917 (seven are dated in 1916, three in 1918). The analysis is based on 296 letters. As my focus is on the *anticipated* final destinations of the letter writers, I am excluding the last fourteen letters of "Additional Letters" from the analysis, as they were written by migrants who had already relocated—nine in cities, five in smaller towns in the Northeast and Midwest.

10. Scott, "Letters of Negro Migrants of 1916–1918," 290.

11. For example, see "Letters," 315; "Deridder, LA, April 18, 1917," "Letters," 330; Henri, *Black Migration*, x.

12. I coded the letters based on geographic indication—"north," "city," and "small town." References to "north" include "north," "eny where above the Mason Dixon line," "northern part of this country," and "up there" when the context clarified that the writer of the letter was referring to the dichotomy between South and North. Any city names, such as Chicago, Detroit, Cleveland, and Philadelphia, qualified as "city" references, as well as phrases like "in your city." "Small cities near Chicago," "small size town," "small town," and recurring farming references and offers to work on northern farms were marked as "small town." At times, letters expressed references in more than one category, and those were coded accordingly. Many of the letters contain grammatical errors and lack punctuation. I will quote directly from Scott's compilations without indicating "[*sic*]" after every mistake, to foster readability.

13. For example, James Grossman defines the Great Migration as "the first mass movement of black southerners to northern cities, during and immediately after World War I," *Land of Hope*, 3. For early migration works, see, for example, Frazier, *The Negro Family in Chicago*, and Drake and Cayton, *Black Metropolis*.

14. McCammack, *Landscapes of Hope*, 4. Other scholars such as Luther Adams in *Way Up North in Louisville* and Bernadette Pruitt in *The Other Great Migration* complemented and thus reinterpreted the Great Migration narrative by emphasizing that not all southern Black migrants left; some chose to remain in the South by relocating to southern urban centers such as Louisville and Houston, respectively.

15. "Atlanta, Ga., April 30, 1917," "Additional Letters," 430.

16. "Letters," 292, 293, 294, emphasis in original; "Additional Letters," 429.

17. For example, "Greenwood, Miss., Apr. 22nd, 17," "Letters," 311–12.

18. "Winina, Miss., Mar the 19 1917," "Letters," 312; "Houston, Tex., April 29, 1917," "Additional Letters," 428.

19. "Letters," 295.

20. "Letters," 303.

21. "Letters," 337, 331; "Additional Letters," 436.

22. "New Orleans, LA., April 23, 1917," "Letters," 294.

23. For example, see "Letters," 294; "New Orleans, La., 5-5-17," "Letters," 295; "Pensacola, Fla., May 7, 1917," "Additional Letters," 431; "Hamlet, N. C., May 29, 1917," "Letters," 310; "New Orleans, La., 5/5×17," "Additional Letters," 433; "New Orleans, April 22, 1917," "Letters," 307.

24. Grossman, *Land of Hope*, 8.

25. Dickerman, "A Plan for the Southern Migrant," 217.

26. For example, "Pensacola, Fla., 4-2-17," "Letters," 331; "Mobile, Ala., May 15, 1917," "Letters," 328.

27. "Sherman, Ga., Nov. 28, 1916," "Letters," 338–39; "Additional Letters," 451–52; emphasis added.

28. "Deo Volente, Miss., April 30, 1917," "Additional Letters," 435–36.

29. "Crescent, Okla., April 30, 1917," "Additional Letters," 434–35.

30. Dickerman, "A Plan for the Southern Migrant," 218.

31. "Letters," 309; emphasis in original.

32. "Letters," 298.

33. Topeka was one of the major destinations during the Kansas Exodus, resulting in a 400-percent increase in its Black population, making up 23.6 percent of its total population in 1880. In the next three decades, Topeka's total population almost tripled, while the Black population grew by only 20 percent. The proportional drop in population might have resulted in a loss of social and economic capital among the Black populace and could explain increased tensions between Black and white people, the latter of which was expressed in the letter.

34. Cox, Thomas. *Blacks in Topeka Kansas*, 166–71. Rampant racism and segregation caused Black people to build parallel institutions, such as clubs and unions. Concerted efforts defeated the extension of school segregation from elementary to high school in the early years of the twentieth century, and the expansion of segregated schooling options from cities over 15,000 to cities over 2,000 in 1917. However, many Kansan schools remained segregated until the 1950s. Scholars frequently note that a wave of discrimination swept across Kansas at the beginning of the twentieth century. For example, see Cox, *Blacks in Topeka Kansas*, 167, and Campney, *This is Not Dixie*, 157.

35. Grossman, *Land of Hope*, 128.

36. Topeka's Black population actually dropped between 1910 and 1920, for the second decade in a row, which could serve as further indication of exacerbating race relations at the time and that many Black residents, like the letter writer, decided to relocate to another, slightly more promising, environment within or beyond the Midwest.

37. "Port Arthur, Texas, 5/5th/17," "Letters," 327; "New Orleans, LA., 5/20/17," "Additional Letters," 442; "Mobile, Ala., Jan. 8, 1917," "Additional Letters," 444.

38. Haynes, "Migration of Negroes into Northern Cities," and "Negroes Move North." Born in the South, Haynes moved to the Northeast for graduate school. A sociologist by training, Haynes was the co-founder and first executive director of the National Urban League and dedicated his career to the betterment of urban Black communities, which began to sprawl under his tenure.

39. Walton, "Negroes in Terror Fleeing the South," M-4; emphasis added.

40. Ibid.; Walton, "Cotton Fields Lie Weed Choked as Negro Stampedes"; Walton, "Negro Migrants Say Southerners Force Them Out."

41. "New Orleans, La., April 22, 1917," "Letters," 330–31; "Brook Haven, Miss., 4/24/1917," "Letters," 300.

42. Suffice it to say that the *Chicago Defender* did not exclude small northern hamlets in its coverage and therefore did not foster the urban-only narrative of the Great Migration. Other featured articles on small towns over the years include: "Small Towns in Illinois Are Growing Fast," June 27, 1925, A1; "Fine Chance to Rise in Small Towns," July 31, 1926, 8; "Former Show Folks Settle in Small Town," Aug. 24, 1929, 7; Kelly Miller, "The Race Out West," Sept. 10, 1927, A1; Farm in the North," Apr. 2, 1932, 14.

43. "The Farming Situation," *Chicago Defender*, Feb. 2, 1924, 11.

44. "Small Towns in Illinois Are Growing Fast," *Chicago Defender*, June 27, 1925, A1.

45. "The Hoosier State," *Chicago Defender*, Feb. 24, 1917, 9.

46. Not much has been written about the Terre Haute Civic League, but the *Indianapolis Recorder* regularly reported on its activities, including speaker and meeting announcements. Dr. Dennis Anderson Bethea, himself a southern migrant from South Carolina to Terre Haute, presided over the league for many years. Upon arrival in Terre Haute in 1907, Bethea opened a medical practice, serving a "large clientel [*sic*] of white as well as colored patients" ("A Sketch of Dr D. A. Bethea's Life of Terre Haute," *Indianapolis Recorder*, May 22, 1909, 2). Before coming to Terre Haute, Bethea studied medicine in Chicago. While pursuing his medical degree, he found time to compile and publish *Colored People's Blue Book and Business Directory*, which celebrated achievements of Black Chicagoans. For further references on the Civic League, see also the *Indianapolis Recorder* news columns "News from Round About—Terre Haute," Oct. 16, 1915, 6; Oct. 23, 1915, 6; Apr. 29, 1916, 6; and William H. Wiggins Jr.'s Chapter 5 "The Politics of Protest" of his book *O Freedom!: African American Emancipation Celebration*.

47. "The Hoosier State," *Chicago Defender*, Feb. 17, 1917, 7; and Feb. 24, 1917, 9.

48. The *Green Book* is named after Victor Hugo Green, who compiled the Black traveler's guide from 1936 to 1966.

49. *A Stronger Kinship*, 6.

50. Almost three-fourths, or 118 of 159 sampled articles, included explicit migration references. I conducted a thorough search of the *Readers' Guide to Periodical*

Literature from 1900 to 1970 with the following keywords: "Negro," "Migration," "Immigration," "Ku Klux Klan," "Middle West," and "Indiana." The search resulted in a total of 1,213 articles for the seven decades. Based on the titles, I separated thirty-two Indiana-related articles and thirty-nine Indiana Ku Klux Klan–related articles (general KKK-related articles were kept within the decennial counts). The *Readers' Guide* is known to index mainstream periodicals in the country, "300 of the most popular and important periodicals published in the United States and Canada," according to its publisher ("Readers' Guide"). Yet it is also known to largely overlook the Black canon of newspapers and periodicals in its indexing practices. But it is precisely this selectivity in its inclusion criteria that renders my analysis of the national coverage of the Great Migration valuable. This is how the mainstream media covered and interpreted the historical phenomenon over seven decades. The national press provided social commentary written by academics, ministers, writers, statisticians, and Black spokespeople, to name but a few. My discussion is based on a close reading of 159 articles from a plethora of national newspapers and journals from 1900 until 1970, including *Survey*, *Literary Digest*, and *U.S. News and World Report*. My focus was particularly on the first wave of the Great Migration (1915 to 1930), as these articles coincide with the migration letters. For the remaining four decades, I sampled a minimum of ten articles (random selection).

51. Lipsitz, *How Racism Takes Place*; sociologist James Loewen describes sundown towns as *invisible* "until a black wayfarer appears and the townspeople do something about it" (193). Sundown towns will be discussed further in the next two chapters.

52. Adams, "A Question to Democracy," 524–25.

53. "And This Is Civilization," *Chicago Defender*, Aug. 1, 1925, 22.

54. "And This Is Civilization," *Chicago Defender*, Sept. 7, 1929, A2.

55. Ibid. To answer the question, they did not—at least not in the near future, hence the need for publications like the *Green Book*. Marcus Anthony Hunter and Zandria F. Robinson fittingly describe the *Green Book* as a "crowd-sourced account of safe places to eat, sleep, and picnic during Jim Crow, evidences that we are now learning more about the process and strategy it took to make a life, to make a place to be free, in an anti-Black country." See Hunter and Robinson, *Chocolate Cities*, 79.

56. Urban race riots constitute the only well-known example that made northern white violence visible. As a detailed discussion of the race riots in the early twentieth century is beyond the scope of this book, see, for example, Roberta Senechal's *The Sociogenesis of a Race Riot*, Cameron McWhirter's *Red Summer*, and Walter Rucker and James N. Upton's edited two-volume *Encyclopedia of American Race Riots*.

57. Leonard and Washington, "Welcoming Southern Negroes," 332.

58. Hartt, "When the Negro Comes North," 322–23.

59. "All Negroes Driven from Indiana Town," S5.

60. Schuyler, "Jim Crow in the North," 663.

61. Ibid., 666.

62. Ibid., 667, 669.

63. Leonard, “Jim Crow, Northern Style,” 82; Paton “The Negro in the North,” 70.

64. “Race Trouble in the North: When a Negro Family Moved into a White Community,” 29–32. It definitely echoes Anna-Lisa Cox’s observation about the “odd Midwestern racism” that does not require any Black presence to ban Black people from public facilities or communities altogether (*A Stronger Kinship*, 6).

65. “South in the North,” 85.

66. Ibid. This point inspired my sub-heading for this section, “White Supremacy by Home Address.”

67. Alsop and Quayle, “What Northerners Really Think of Negroes,” 17.

68. Ibid., 19, 21.

69. McKittrick, *Demonic Grounds*, xiii.

70. “Negro Transient Taken in Custody by U.S. Marshal,” *Frankfort Morning Times*, Mar. 13, 1942, 1.

71. “Trespasser Detained,” *Frankfort Morning Times*, Mar. 31, 1942, 8. The placement of this brief snippet is worth noting, too. It follows “Racial Unrest is Stirred by New Housings,” an article about the racial friction in Detroit, written by Frank Kenesson. Until recently, Kenesson had been a staff member of the *Morning Times*, but not until he joined the Detroit staff of the Associated Press did we read anything about the ongoing Great Migration in the *Morning Times*. Kenesson noted that race troubles were nothing new in Detroit, “But it was not until the great migration of southern and foreign labor in 1917–21 to Detroit’s mammoth motor industries that racial problems became acute.” He later explained the cause for the unrest this time around—the fact that housing authorities planned a housing development project for Black people too close to white neighborhoods, causing much resentment among the white residents. Yet again, housing was the number-one factor for visibly executed white animosity toward Black newcomers.

72. “Negro Transient Hurt in Jump from Boxcar,” *Frankfort Morning Times*, June 8, 1949, 1; “Negro Transients Find Trouble Still Dog Their Trail,” *Frankfort Morning Times*, Sept. 17, 1949, 1; “Transient Negroes Are Fined, Given Freedom,” *Frankfort Morning Times*, Sept. 20, 1949, 1; emphasis added.

73. Price, “Problem of Race Relations Not Confined to South; Discrimination in North, Too,” *Frankfort Morning Times*, May 11, 1956, 2; emphasis added. Price noted the enforcement of all-white communities in 1956, right at the peak of sundown town policies, as sundown town expert James Loewen’s findings reveal, “Between 1947 and 1967, more towns were established on a whites-only basis than ever before. Almost every suburb that sprang up or expanded after World War II was whites-only.” See Loewen, *Sundown Towns*, 127. Without having a term for it back then, Price already raised awareness of this problem while it was peaking.

Chapter 3. Erasing Histories

1. Carroll County Historian, March 9, 1988, Black History Project, Carroll County file. Carroll County was founded in 1828, so the statement refers to 160 years of county

history that allegedly does not contain any Black experiences. Census records alone challenge the veracity of the claim the Carroll County historian made, as the 1980 census, for example, lists seventeen Black residents in the county.

2. Claybaugh, *History of Clinton County, Indiana*, 290.

3. Ibid., 179.

4. The 1870 census lists the following four Black individuals in Sugarcreek Township, Clinton County, Indiana: C., Mary, Jane, and John Cambridge, all natives of Kentucky, and they are listed as "mulatto." Their ages range between twenty-eight and thirty-four. Both men are listed as farmers, both women as housewives. In 1880, both brothers have their own residences in Sugar Creek Township. Jane lives with C. P. Cambridge and is listed as his sister. John lives with his sister Minerva and her daughter Anna. They have also adopted thirteen-year-old John Snider. All of their marital statuses are listed as single. The birthplace of their respective parents is indicated as Maryland.

5. "Colored Boys Given Sendoff by Friends," *Frankfort Morning Times*, Aug. 24, 1918, 1.

6. The draft registration card for John Williams identifies him as a native of Homer, Louisiana, where he was buried in 1952, so he eventually returned home after the war. He came to Frankfort during the 1910s and was employed as a laborer for the railroad before being drafted in Clinton County. There is no local record of him after the sendoff to war, leading me to believe that he returned to Louisiana, where he eventually died.

7. "Concert of Negro Spirituals," Sept. 30, 1931, 2; "Colored Folk Planning Big Time Sunday," July 12, 1932, 1; "Colored Notes," Feb. 23, 1935, 6.

8. Mills, *The Racial Contract*, 19; emphasis in original.

9. After multiple inquiries over the course of two years, Steuben, Newton, Wells, Jay, Madison, Putnam, Switzerland, Lawrence, Martin, and Delaware counties remained unresponsive. These respective folders in the Black History Project remain empty, as county officials to this day never returned any kind of communication to the IHS.

10. Trouillot, *Silencing the Past*, 53.

11. "Black History of Thorntown," BHP, Boone County file.

12. BHP, Warren County file, Oct. 2, 1987; BHP, Whitley County file, Nov. 12, 1987; BHP, Scott County file, Oct. 26, 1987.

13. In her seminal work on the African American experience in Indiana, *The Negro in Indiana*, Emma Lou Thornbrough notes that Scottsburg and Lexington, Scott County, barred Black folk (226). James H. Madison elaborates on her observation, noting that "some small towns and rural areas, particularly in southern Indiana, developed reputations for special hostility and intimidation, causing black folk residing there to leave and discouraging potential newcomers. Washington County's anti-black reputation helped account for a decline there from 187 in 1860 to 3 in 1880, while towns such as Leavenworth, Aurora, and Scottsburg effectively barred black residents. Restaurants, hotels, theaters, and barber shops often refused service to blacks. By the late nineteenth century such discrimination was apparently on the rise

not only in southern Indiana but in northern parts of the state as well, a reflection of the Jim Crowism blossoming in the former Confederate states," see Madison, *The Indiana Way*, 170–71.

14. Mills, *The Racial Contract*, 18.

15. The BHP archivist also reached out to the person in the county but was met with reluctance. This is rather surprising, as a newspaper article featured her and the history of the land, which has been owned by her family for the past 115 years (BHP, article included in Greene County file, Dec. 2, 1987). Being in a community that seems to not care much about the Black presence in their midst, this Black family is another testimony to Black Hoosier resilience.

16. BHP, Starke County file, Sept. 13, 1989.

17. BHP, LaGrange County file, Feb. 4, 1988.

18. BHP, Clark County file, July 13, 1989. For Thornbrough's discussion of Clark County, see *The Negro in Indiana*, 45–46, 226, 277–78.

19. BHP, Posey County file, Feb. 18, 1988; emphasis in original.

20. "All Negroes Driven from Indiana Town; White Miners at Blanford Act after an Assault on a Young Girl." *New York Times*, Jan. 21, 1923, S5.

21. Jaspin, *Buried in the Bitter Waters*, 193–95. Not only was Vermillion a stronghold of the KKK, but it also had four chapters of the National Horse Thief Detective Association by the time the cleansing occurred. Since the state government was entrenched with Klan members and granted the NHTDA "the same powers as the police," enough intimidating powers were at play that led to the enforced Black departure. In *Constituting Whiteness*, Erik Wade discusses in detail the alliance between the Indiana KKK and NHTDA: see 197–261. The KKK and NHTDA will be discussed further in the next chapter.

22. BHP, Vermillion County file, Feb. 8, 1988, and Feb. 24, 1988, respectively. Again, note the conventional wisdom of white Hoosiers that distance Black folk from the soil, as Vermillion's farming environment was not "conducive to blacks."

23. Kunnecke, "Washington County—Early Black Settlements by County."

24. Jaspin, *Buried in the Bitter Waters*, 7.

25. Heller, *The 1979 History of Adams County, Indiana*, 77–80.

26. Mills, *The Racial Contract*, 19; emphasis in original.

27. "Hanna's History" and "Hanna's Mission," *Hanna Community Center*, https://www.hannacntr.org.

28. Rehmer, "Brotherhood Week," 2.

29. "Report Re University Policy Concerning Listing of Off-Campus Housing Facilities," *Board of Trustees Minutes*, 516; "Report Re Letter from Purdue Friends of S.N.C.C. and Petitions Concerning University Policy on Non-Segregation," *Board of Trustees Minutes*, 962. The university policy statement solely states that "All Purdue University student services, programs, student employment, and housing in University-operated facilities under the legal control of The Trustees of Purdue University shall be maintained on a non-discriminatory basis at all times." Regarding private off-campus arrangements, the statement says that "the State of Indiana has not given

The Trustees of Purdue University any legal power or authority to control in any manner whatsoever the rental of private housing accommodations for students and/or employees. Property owners who provide housing accommodations for rent are themselves fully subject to all civil laws applicable and the enforcement of these laws is vested in the duly constituted civil authority and cannot impose compliance with the laws on the part of individuals not under the direct jurisdiction of the University. However, Purdue University will not knowingly recommend private rental accommodations whose owner are not in full compliance with all the laws applicable to such private enterprise." See "Adoption of Purdue University Policy Statement Re Discrimination," *Board of Trustees Minutes*, 383.

30. Oberlander, "Blacks Say Beering Insensitive," A1–2.

31. Barone, "Little Church Reveals Story from Frankfort's Past," *Frankfort Morning Times*, Feb. 20, 1978, 1.

32. George Lipsitz makes this argument in his seminal text *How Racism Takes Place.*

33. The *Frankfort Morning Times* caught itself omitting race-related incidents when covering racially induced scandals. Regarding the pool debate in Clinton County, see "Frankfort Violating Law by Not Letting All in Pool, Says Minister," July 22, 1954, 1–2, and "Public Hearing on Pool Segregation Issue Canceled; Pool is Open to All," July 24, 1954, 1–2. Regarding the pool debate in Marion, Evansville, and Muncie, see, for example, "No-Damages Given in Pool Case," Aug. 1, 1954, 1, and "Racial Friction Breaks Out Over Swimming Pools," June 13, 1956, 1.

Chapter 4. Silencing Memories

1. "Klansmen Conduct Funeral of Member," *Frankfort Evening News*, Sept. 17, 1923, 1; "Parker Funeral Will Be Held Next Monday," *Frankfort Evening News*, Sept. 20, 1923, 1; "Local Klansmen Joined Gathering at Flora, Ind.," *Frankfort Evening News*, Sept. 22, 1923, 1; "Klansmen Will Gather in Colfax for Meeting," *Frankfort Evening News*, Sept. 25, 1923, 1.

2. I sampled seventeen articles on Indiana, published between 1908 and 1968.

3. Jackson, "This Is My America"; Wilson, "Indiana"; Riis and Waldron, "Fortunate City."

4. Moore, "A Klan Kingdom Collapses"; Merritt, "Klan and Anti-Klan in Indiana"; Frost, "The Klan Shows Its Hand in Indiana"; Johnson, "The Ku-Kluxer"; Davis, "Have Faith in Indiana."

5. This thought is based on my personal experience that as soon as I presented my research publicly, people inquired about the role of the Ku Klux Klan, directly or indirectly drawing the conclusion that Indiana's KKK past is the cause of all racism and explains the absence of people of color in the state. As established throughout this book, this is far from being an accurate or comprehensive representation of Indiana's racist attitudes, as those preceded the forming of KKK chapters across the state and persisted way beyond their heyday.

6. BHP, Clay County file, Oct. 8, 1987; BHP, Boone County file, Nov. 2, 1987.

7. BHP, Hamilton County file. Noblesville was forced to deal more explicitly with its Klan history after 1995, upon the discovery of hundreds of Klan documents and membership lists. Fortunately, the contractor who found the documents in a trunk decided against "burning history" and donated the documents to the historical society. However, Noblesville citizens still prefer to be remembered for bringing down Grand Dragon D. C. Stephenson in his trial in 1925, rather than for supporting and fostering the Klan throughout the 1920s. In his article "'You Can't Burn History': Getting Right with the Klan in Noblesville, Indiana," history professor Allen Safianow recounts accounts and survey data from local residents about the Klan. His findings show that residents frequently perceived the Klan more like a fraternal organization than a hate group. See page 152.

8. St. Joseph Vertical File, BHP-VF.

9. "South Bend Negroes Get Warning Letter," *Frankfort Evening News*, Sept. 12, 1923, 1.

10. "Rebuilt Klan is Planned for Hoosier State," *Frankfort Morning Times*, Feb. 16, 1940, 1.

11. See, for example, "KKK Slates Rally in Ind. This Weekend," *Frankfort Morning Times*, Nov. 4, 1965; "Indiana Klan to Parade Saturday in Full Regalia, *Frankfort Morning Times*, July 22, 1967; "KKK Holds Fiery Rally," *Frankfort Morning Times*, Sept. 1, 1970; Oberlander, "Blacks Say Beering Insensitive"; Bangert, "Bangert: Strategy Last Time KKK Came to Lafayette."

12. Carden, "Museum Tells Indiana's History Using 200 Objects."

13. It is beyond the scope of this work to discuss both the history of lynchings and the production of such cultural artifacts extensively. For excellent discussions in this regard, see, for example, James Allen et al.'s *Without Sanctuary*; Amy Wood's *Lynching and Spectacle*; and Rasul A. Mowatt's "Lynching as Leisure."

14. The Sterilization Bill was displayed in a frame, about 8" by 11," regular paper size.

15. "About the Indiana State Museum," *Indiana State Museum and Historic Sites*, 2019.

16. Mills, *The Racial Contract*, 18.

17. Along the same lines of emphasizing the organization's innocuous nature, the *Complete Directory of Bartholomew County, Indiana, 1903–1904* lists NHTDA chapters in the county under "fraternities," naming all members of the various chapters across the county: see pages 52–53. My impression of their more fraternal understanding of the group is also echoed in Allen Safianow's "'You Can't Burn History,'" see page 152.

18. Wade, *Constituting Whiteness*, 22–23.

19. Specifically, Section 4171 of Article 3. Detectives of Acts 1907 stated: "That such constables shall have power to pursue and arrest horse thieves and all other criminals against the laws of the state of Indiana, and to serve all papers relating to the same, and to follow and pursue such criminals in and through any part of the

state of Indiana; and in the absence of warrant shall have power to arrest and hold in custody without warrant and for such time as may be necessary to procure a warrant." See Burns, *Burns' Annotated Indiana Statutes*, 324. The passage spells out that the powers of detective associations exceeded the arrest of horse thieves, including arrest and custody of "all other criminals."

20. Bentley, "The Ku Klux Klan in Indiana," 24.

21. Wade, *Constituting Whiteness*, 214. See in particular Wade's Chapter 5, pages 194–263. At a different point, Wade outlines the extent to which their missions and activities coincided, stating "the Klan gladly endorsed and participated in the activities the NHTDA pursued such as the desire to prohibit the wholesale and trafficking of liquor and intimate relations in parked cars. The two organizations saw themselves as key proponents of law and order in Indiana. However, the NHTDA and the Klan's mission was also tied together in racial terms since both were invested in protecting the rights of whites as opposed to other racial or ethnic groups. Law and order was, therefore, neither color-blind nor neutral" (213). Wade also notes that the two organizations should not be conflated; although leadership and cross-sectional appeal of their initiatives and missions bled over somewhat, some Catholic Hoosiers who were part of the NHTDA would have never been invited to become members of the KKK.

22. At least among my interlocutors. I share other acknowledgments further below.

23. In 2010, the *Frankfort Times* reported on a local history event during which the Clinton County historian recalled that "at least one business owner was forced to leave town" during the Klan era in Clinton County, confirming Tom's recollection. See Martha O'Brien, "Historian Shares Memories of County's Past," Feb. 5, 2010, A1, A8. Whereas it is beyond the scope of this chapter to explore Tom's recollection at great length, the history of the Rainbow Division is worth knowing. Unlike most divisions, which were formed in a single state, it stretched like a rainbow across the continental United States. It was seriously diminished by casualties during the war, which makes Tom's recollection of the community's treatment of a Rainbow Division veteran even more gut-wrenching.

24. "Male Help Wanted," *Indianapolis News*, Mar. 29, 1919, 18; Oct. 8, 1919, 22; Oct. 9, 1919, 26.

25. Like the lynching postcards discussed above, these KKK postcards certainly served to illustrate and manifest white superiority and supremacy, especially since many northern hamlets had postmen of color. Frankfort itself had Nat Powell, a Black mail carrier—a point of pride for the Black community and note of mention in the Frankfort portrait published in the *Indianapolis Recorder*, Feb. 25, 1911, 3 (see epigraph in Chapter 2). The *Frankfort Morning Times* reminisced about local postal employees from its past via photograph, featuring R. N. Powell among them as early as 1897. See Sept. 22, 1957, 1.

26. Some reference desk staff members in the Indiana Historical Society also attested to the exclusionary and hostile nature of Indiana towns by referencing Indiana's KKK past. When I was working on the BHP folder for Madison County, which did

not contain much information in general and was lacking a survey response, the staff member, a native of the state, simply noted that she was not "surprised because the KKK was active in Madison County." She continued the thought, expressing her surprise that the Tipton County folder was not empty, as it was another "KKK hotspot" and a place that "even after the Civil Rights Movement, if you saw a person of color, you would definitely not see them after dark" (personal conversation with author, Oct. 6, 2017). Her remark here invokes sundown town laws, which were unwritten and unspoken but commonly known rules that people of color should be out of town by the time the sun sets, hence "sundown" towns.

27. Thornbrough, *The Negro in Indiana*, 224, 46–47, 225–27, 186–87, 209–10.

28. BHP, Allen County file, Oct. 5, 1987. This statement is slightly ambiguous from a historical standpoint. It is unclear if the survey respondent alludes to the Black Codes, which became law in Indiana in 1831 and thus during the prime era of the Underground Railroad network establishment, or if he alludes to those ordinances that were commonly enforced during the time sundown policies spread widely in the state, between 1890 and 1970. Regardless, it proves Allen County's animosity toward Black residents in the past.

29. BHP, Boone County file, Nov. 2, 1987.

30. Heller, *The 1979 History of Adams County, Indiana*, 77.

31. One other newspaper article, enclosed in the Perry County file, alludes to the sundown phenomenon, though the writer does not use the term explicitly. In "Racial Barriers Nonexistent in Old TC Schools," Indiana Journalism Hall of Famer Edward W. Schergens writes, "I can remember many other black families living in Tell City. They were all educated just like the white children and we all lived here together as though we had the same color and were of the same race. There was never any difference shown. Cannelton had much the same situation. *However, in Troy, for many years, a black person was not allowed in town after dark*" (BHP, Perry County file, Aug. 7, 1989; emphasis added).

32. Price, "Problem of Race Relations Not Confined to South," 2; Heller, *The 1979 History of Adams County, Indiana*, 77; emphasis added.

33. BHP, Rush County file, Jan. 29, 1988.

34. For example, during his research on Goshen's sundown past, Goshen native Dan Shenk came across restrictive property covenants that limited ownership and occupancy of the real estate to "No person other than a person of the Caucasian race." See Shenk, "Portrait of a 'Sundown Town.'"

35. Other subtle mechanisms could be a siren on water towers at the edges of many Indiana small towns. In *Sundown Towns*, James Loewen recounts his discovery that Villa Grove, Illinois, installed a siren on its water tower that rang each evening at 6 p.m. to signal to African Americans that it is time to leave town. More obvious mechanisms included a sign at the city limits that spelled out the warning to African Americans that their kind is not desired. See Loewen, *Sundown Towns*, 64, 3. However, it is difficult to find residents today who would admit to such signs ever existing in their towns. None of the surveys admitted to it, and neither did any

interlocutors in my interviews. I wonder if these signs are as rare and highly desirable in the community as the KKK and NHTDA collectibles.

36. "Negro Woman Likes Fine Treatment at Hospital Here," *Frankfort Morning Times*, Jan. 31, 1970, 4. The paper falsely printed her last name as Mazey. Whereas it might have been a simple typo, it again illustrates the indifference and negligence toward the Black community in Frankfort. The death of her son in his mid-twenties in 1947 was also not noteworthy. Neither was the accident with a passenger elevator that killed Maxey's husband, George Floyd Maxey, in 1921 at the age of 20. He died the month his son was born. In other words, the daily hardship, experiences, and names of Black residents do not matter in the community, manifesting further the sense of *non*belonging.

37. In light of declining membership, the Bethel A. M. E. Church held various financial drives in the community from the 1940s through the 1960s, as the *Morning Times* reported sporadically. Maxey's remark sheds a different light on the fact that all these drives were successful even when membership was as small as four (as was the case in the late 1960s). After all, an open Black church might prevent Black residents from attending white houses of worship. In this way, some white congregations might have actively contributed to the fact that they were all-white.

38. In 1930, she and her eight-year-old son Leonard lived with her parents, who owned a home in town. By 1940, her mother had passed and she was living with her son and her father in a different home for rent. Like the Parker family, the Kerseys formed part of Frankfort's Black community across multiple generations. The city directories list the family as early as 1887. Charles Kersey, Martha Maxey's brother and a war veteran, remained a lifelong resident of Frankfort and passed away in the summer of 2017. Joining the plight of other local Black service members, his service in the U.S. Marine Corps is not commemorated at Clinton County's War Memorial. Though I already conducted research in the community, I did not have the pleasure of crossing paths with him before his death.

39. However, based on experience and personal conversations with non-native residents in West Lafayette, some property owners and housing managements still discriminate against domestic people of color and international students in the twenty-first century.

40. The Black History Program archivist, a Black native of Indianapolis, was quoted in 2017 recalling one of these cautionary tales, "I remember someone saying, 'Any place that's got 'green' in it, don't go there—Greenwood, Greencastle, Greenfield.'" See Higgins, "'We Need to Acknowledge It': Martinsville Tries to Remake Its Racist Image." Regarding public acknowledgment and apology, Goshen, the county seat of Elkhart County, builds the only exception here, as it passed a resolution acknowledging the "racially exclusive past of Goshen, Indiana" in 2015; see Crothers, "Goshen City Council Approves Resolution Acknowledging 'Sundown Town' Past."

41. For example, when Frankfort experienced a cross-burning in late 1969, the incident failed to catch the attention of the *Frankfort Morning Times* staff. A concerned citizen in the community wrote a letter to the editor informing the people

responsible for the cross burning that "this is NOT 'Klan Kountry,'" which makes the failure to report the incident by the local daily newspaper noteworthy. See "This Isn't 'KKK Kountry,'" Nov. 26, 1969, 4.

42. Abram Smith, Thomas Shipp, and James Cameron were arrested the night before and charged with the murder of Claude Deeter and rape of Mary Ball (who later recanted her story). As the news about the alleged crime spread like wildfire, a mob gathered around the prison where the three accused were being held. When the sheriff refused to hand over his prisoners, the mob stormed the jail and took hold of the three Black teenagers. They brutalized and lynched Smith, 19, and Shipp, 18. A voice from the crowd proclaiming Cameron's innocence prevented the third lynching that night. The lynching has received much scholarly attention, most recently by Brent M. S. Campney in his *Hostile Heartland.* For further information on the incident, see James Cameron's memoir *A Time of Terror: A Survivor's Story* and James H. Madison's *A Lynching in the Heartland.* Journalist and Marion native Cynthia Carr investigated the lynching and the larger structures of racism and the KKK in *Our Town: A Heartland Lynching, a Haunted Town, and the Hidden History of White America.*

43. Robbins explained the drop in the Black population with the lack of employment opportunities: "In my genealogy study of selected families of color from Morgan County I found that many of their youths had migrated to nearby Indianapolis and/or other growing industrial cities [Terre Haute, Anderson, Richmond, Kokomo, and the Calumet region] seeking better employment opportunities and the security of living among a larger number of people socially and culturally like themselves" (email response to Elliot Jaspin, Aug. 25, 2002, BHP-VF, Morgan County file). A newsletter from the Morgan County History Society, dated Feb. 14–20, 1998, dedicated to the Black heritage in Morgan County, answers Jaspin's question slightly more directly: "Morgan County's black pioneers came here to find peace and prosperity. By the 1920s the climate in this, as in most other rural Indiana counties, was hostile and fearful, and our black communities left to find happiness elsewhere." To no surprise, it does not explicitly mention the "invisible empire" of the Ku Klux Klan as one of the potential reasons in the 1920s, but at least it acknowledges the anti-Black animosity experienced in the early twentieth century, rather than solely pursuing better job opportunities elsewhere (included in BHP, Morgan County file).

On a related note, the myth that Black people left Indiana towns and counties for better employment opportunity emerged in only three other counties. In a follow-up response, the Spencer County historian writes, "The black community is small because they have left the area for better positions in cities" (BHP, Spencer County file, Sept. 18, 1989). The Harrison County historian discloses that "Over the years, many of the Harrison County blacks have migrated to seek employment—many have gone to New Albany, Indianapolis, Anderson, Indiana and some went to Louisville, Kentucky" (BHP, Harrison County file, Oct. 14, 1987). Last, in 1994, the *Daily Greensburg News* ran a series on the Greensburg riot, in an attempt to correct the many inaccuracies that had surrounded the violent outbreak that took place in 1907 in Decatur County (and was central in Ray Stannard Baker's 1908 publication *Following the Color Line*). Columnist Pat Smith concludes the series by correcting the myth that all Black folk were driven out of town and explains that not only did African Americans continue to live in Greensburg after the riot, but that the "younger ones left for the same reason that so many young white people left back then. There were no jobs here then except those that paid little" (5; Decatur County BHP-VF). All these statements absolve the white communities of contributing to the absence of Black people in the counties—by placing agency with the Black residents themselves. They made the decision on their own and eventually turned their backs on these small towns, according to the data presented in the surveys.

44. Robbins, email response to Elliot Jaspin, Aug. 25, 2002, BHP-VF, Morgan County file.

45. Ibid.

46. Quoted in Rimer, "After Arrest, Town Shamed by '68 Killing Seeks Renewal."

47. Higgins, "'We Need to Acknowledge It': Martinsville Tries to Remake Its Racist Image"; Van der Dussen, "City Fights Racist Reputation," A7. Included in BHP, Morgan County file.

48. The idea that prejudice is natural builds one of the three pillars that anthropologist Jane H. Hill identifies as "the folk theory of race and racism." The other two ideas that complete her notions of folk racism are that race is biological and that racism is committed by white supremacists. See her excellent book *The Everyday Language of Racism*, an analysis of everyday language to attest to the pervasiveness and longevity of racism in U.S. society.

49. *The Freeman* [Indianapolis], June 21, 1902, 4, col. 4.

50. "Revived Ku Klux Klan Should Not Be Allowed to Exist in Hoosierland," *Frankfort Morning Times*, July 29, 1965, 4.

51. Both Jane H. Hill and Charles Mills identified evasion as powerful tools to perpetuate white dominance. See Hill, *The Everyday Language of White Racism*, and Charles Mills, *The Racial Contract*.

Chapter 5. When Black Folk Make the Record

1. "Obituaries—Franklin B. Jones," *The Kokomo Tribune*, July 22, 1999, 8.

2. Marilyn Tye, "AME Congregation Opens New Church," *The Kokomo Tribune*, Oct. 24, 1987, 3.

3. Although survey takers tended *not* to consult general historical documents such as the census and city directories, they did consult Negro registers, which signify public records specific to a former bygone era. However, question 11 of the survey specifically inquired about the existence of such documents: "Materials, such as deed books, tax records, Negro Registers and manumission records can reveal alot [*sic*] about history. Are you aware that any of these materials are available at your county courthouse or other locations?"

4. Counties in the Black History Project that acknowledged the existence of a

Negro register include Bartholomew, Crawford, Dearborn, Floyd, Harrison, Jackson, Jefferson, Knox, Montgomery, Morgan, Posey, Randolph, and Washington. Marion County was referenced in the Washington County file and is listed in Thornbrough's discussion of the registers; see Thornbrough, *The Negro in Indiana*, 70. Besides Bartholomew, Floyd, Harrison, Jackson, Jefferson, Knox, and Washington, Robbins discusses Franklin, Gibson, Hendricks, Martin, Ohio, Orange, and Switzerland in his 1994 compilation *Indiana Negro Registers, 1852–1865*. Furthermore, Jennings County's public library maintains what appears to be an online county history. The section "Anti-Slavery and African Americans in Jennings County" includes names of the local Negro register that was kept in the 1850s. That brings the total up to twenty-three counties in Indiana that are proven to have had these registers in the past (Map 8).

5. Thornbrough, *The Negro in Indiana*, 70.

6. As noted in Chapter 1, county personnel have the power to create and re-create the master narrative of their counties by determining what to remember and what to forget. Jacques Derrida discusses the connection between forgetting and remembering in archives, cautioning about the archive's power to incite "forgetfulness, amnesia, [and] the annihilation of memory." See Derrida, *Archive Fever*, 11.

7. Montgomery County's "Certificate of Registry" was in paragraph format but with the same scrutiny of detail. It also contains a newspaper notice, dated March 14, 1853, which called on "all negroes and mulattoes" to appear before the Circuit County clerk (BHP, Montgomery County file).

8. Chapter 74, *The Revised Statutes of the State of Indiana, Passed at the Thirty-Sixth Session of the General Assembly*, 375.

9. Mullin, *Flight and Rebellion*, 39–40.

10. Negro register records are included in the BHP's Jackson County and Harrison County files.

11. The act that enforced the Thirteenth Article of the 1851 Constitution, approved in 1852, was officially repealed by the Indiana Assembly on February 22, 1967; see Beecher, *The Statutes of the State of Indiana*, 360.

12. For the first twenty years, the *Frankfort Morning Times* was a weekly newspaper, and then it became a daily. Its motto since the beginning of the twentieth century has been to be the "Voice of the People." At times, it proclaimed to be "A Paper for the People." "Morning" was dropped in the seventies; thus, recent newspaper coverage will refer to the paper as *Frankfort Times*.

13. In 1931, the *Morning Times* reported on the death of Mrs. Elizabeth Harper, "one of the last of pioneer colored residents," during which we learn more about this "colored minister." She and her husband Rev. John W. Harper came to Frankfort in the early 1880s. Her husband is credited with being one of the founding members of a local church for Black folk ("Colored Woman Dies Thursday," *Frankfort Morning Times*, Oct. 16, 1931, 12). Further research revealed that he served in the Civil War in the Indiana 28th Regiment. John and Elizabeth were the parents of Ruth and Esther

Harper, who were the first Black graduates of Frankfort High School, depicted in the 1914 *Cauldron* ("John W.").

14. "Hounds Chase Negro," *Frankfort Morning Times*, Oct. 22, 1904, 1; "Negro Fugitive Captured after Desperate Struggle," *Frankfort Morning Times*, Oct. 29, 1904, 2.

15. DeVries, *Race and Kinship in a Midwestern Town*, 50.

16. Mills, *The Racial Contract*, 18.

17. "A Negro Girl Whose Heart Is on the Righ [*sic*] Side," *Frankfort Morning Times*, June 24, 1905, 8; "A Mysterious Negro," *Frankfort Morning Times*, Apr. 1, 1905, 1; "Colored Boy Arrest," *Frankfort Morning Times*, May 5, 1906, 2; "John Lewis A Negro Burglar is Convicted," *Frankfort Morning Times*, Nov. 9, 1907, 1, 4.

18. Nat Powell, the Black mail carrier featured in the photograph of the post office, might be the only exception here. But the photograph reminisced the good old days of the postal service of 1897, so he featured more or less accidentally; see *Frankfort Morning Times*, Sept. 22, 1957, 1.

19. *Frankfort Morning Times*, Oct. 4, 1927, 9.

20. *Frankfort Morning Times*, Apr. 15, 1928, 11. Cartoonist J. R. (James Robert) Williams was celebrated for his cartoons across the nation. His "Out Our Way" single-frame comics entertained millions of readers. He featured recurring small-town cowboy characters, including the Black character "Big Ick" who is featured in Figures 13 and 14. Although the *Morning Times* did not produce the comic, its staff decided which of the comic strips to reproduce. They selected many that featured Black people in stereotypical and ludicrous ways. Other demeaning caricatures can be found in various editions of the *Frankfort Morning Times*, for example, May 26, 1926, 11; Oct. 9, 1926, 11; and Feb. 26, 1927, 5.

21. "Colored Lad Eats Thirteen Watermelon in Six Days on Trip from South to Frankfort," *Frankfort Morning Times*, July 22, 1926, 1; "It's Melon Time in Georgia," *Frankfort Morning Times*, July 4, 1926, 1.

22. I referenced the lynching and the infamous photograph connected with it in previous chapters. Although it was based on false claims, the lynching in Marion constitutes "a tale of rape and revenge." See Chapter 1 for discussion of the photograph, which is said to have inspired Abel Meeropol to write the poem and song "Strange Fruit" and was included in the "Indiana in 200 Objects" exhibition. For further information on the incident, see Cameron's memoir *A Time of Terror*, Madison's *A Lynching in the Heartland*, and Carr's *Our Town*.

23. For example, the *Morning Times* wrote, "Prosecutor Hardin announced today that he would demand the death penalty for Cameron when the grand jury convenes, since, he declared, this youth had a hand in the affair as well as the others." In an attempt to assure the local Black community that this lynching was an aberration, he is quoted as having said he "did not believe the violence was a demonstration against the negro race, but that it was aimed against the individuals and the charges involved" and that the lynching "might have occurred even had the two men been

properly tried and sentenced to death." See "State Troops Are Sent to Marion," *Frankfort Morning Times*, Aug. 9, 1930, 1–2. Though Hardin was in charge of investigating the mob violence, he defended the Marion community before even beginning his investigation. Unsurprisingly, none of the mob members were ever convicted of the crime.

24. "Marion Negro Convicted of Manslaughter," *Frankfort Morning Times*, July 8, 1931, 8. Cameron was paroled in 1935 and pardoned by the State of Indiana in 1993—more than six decades later.

25. Emphasis added. Other coverage also referred to local Black youth as "colored man," such as "Colored Man Is Injured," referring to an eighteen-year-old boy who was hit by a truck while riding his bicycle. See *Frankfort Morning Times*, Nov. 25, 1933, 2.

26. Thirty years later, the arrest of two seventeen-year-old Black boys and their subsequent handling as adults in Anderson, Indiana, in 1962 stirred protest from the Black community, as the *Morning Times* reported, probably inadvertently revealing some of the larger fears and prejudices present among white Hoosiers in Indiana. The protest's alleged leader revealed that one of the boys arrested was singled out by the police officer "from a large group because he knew Newson had been dating a white girl." See "Arrests Stir Negro Pickets at Anderson," *Frankfort Morning Times*, Aug. 14, 1962, 2. Unfortunately, the *Morning Times* did not follow up on what happened to the teenagers, but it is noteworthy that this particular quote was printed. Dating across race constitutes one example where people of color were no longer invisible and definitely caught the attention of local white residents, as Walter, Tom, and the Anderson police officer corroborate.

27. Mills, *The Racial Contract*, 19.

28. "Two White Men Held in Negro Boy's Murder," *Frankfort Morning Times*, Sept. 1, 1955, 1.

29. This very seed of doubt about the state of Till's body later became one of the key arguments for the defense, eventually resulting in an all-white jury acquitting the murderers.

30. "Five Negroes Jailed; Police Halt Trouble," *Frankfort Morning Times*, Aug. 10, 1947, 1; "Negroes Fined in Assault Case," *Frankfort Morning Times*, Aug. 12, 1947, 1.

31. "Two Danville, Ill. Colored Men Are Arrested and Jailed," *Frankfort Morning Times*, Nov. 1, 1919, 1; "Colored Chef Leaves Frankfort in Hurry," *Frankfort Morning Times*, Dec. 13, 1919, 1; "Three Negroes Get Long Terms," *Frankfort Morning Times*, Aug. 9, 1930, 1.

32. "Negro Transient Taken in Custody by U.S. Marshal," *Frankfort Morning Times*, Mar. 13, 1942, 1; "Trespasser Detained," *Frankfort Morning Times*, Mar. 31, 1942, 8; "Negro Transient Hurt in Jump from Boxcar," *Frankfort Morning Times*, June 8, 1949, 1; "Negro Transients Find Trouble Still Dog Their Trail," *Frankfort Morning Times*, Sept. 17, 1949, 1; "Transient Negroes Are Fined, Given Freedom," *Frankfort Morning Times*, Sept. 20, 1949, 1.

33. Zick, "Constitutional Displacement," 549. Timothy Zick's "purified territories" result in George Lipsitz's "'pure' and homogeneous spaces" idealized by the white spatial imaginary; see Lipsitz, *How Racism Takes Place*, 29. When the power was given to community members to create such territories in Indiana in the past, we ended up with vigilante organizations like the White Caps. Zick notes that trespassing laws were strictly enforced against undocumented immigrants in the twenty-first century. He also connects these recent efforts to past endeavors "of early state exclusions of paupers, vagabonds and other unwelcome persons." He elaborates on the territorial displacement, noting: "These state and local laws are efforts to address problems purportedly related to illegal immigration, including higher crime rates and lower property values. The apparent hope is that by controlling access to places like residences and workplaces, local territories will become illegal immigrant-free zones. The nature and character of these local reforms raise the concern, however, that all aliens in the community will feel unwelcome and will perhaps be forced to move elsewhere." See Zick, "Constitutional Displacement," 564–65. In a similar fashion, Frankfort's white community might have hoped that enforcing trespassing laws against southern Black migrants would result in a migrant-free zone, sending a message of unwelcome and leading migrants to relocate elsewhere.

34. "Color Lines Drawn in Neighborhood Rumpus," *Frankfort Morning Times*, July 27, 1934, 1.

35. Goings, *Mammy and Uncle Mose*, xix.

36. Goings, *Mammy and Uncle Mose*, 11; emphasis in original.

37. BHP, Howard County file, Nov. 12, 1987. It is unclear whether the derogatory name was ever cemented in the county books, but it was a widely common and popular term used in the community, as county-related materials still incorporate the name, e.g., photo descriptions on *Ancestry.com*: "West County Road 400 North and about 750 West Nigger Pike (Colored Pike) Kokomo Indiana" (with search terms "Evelyn Merrell" or "Orman Benjiman Merrell"); a cemetery location description: "it is on north side of road formerly popularly known as 'Nigger Pike' and in a farming-area formerly inhabited by numerous Negro families" and in testimonies of long-term white county residents in local newspaper coverage from the 1990s: "'Nigger' didn't mean much in those days,' he said, recalling the northwestern Howard County road that was once widely called Nigger Pike. 'I called it that. Everyone just called it that. Now, 'nigger' is terrible.'" See Turner, "Racism's Past Still Singes: Longtime Kokomoans Remember the Bad Old Days," 1; and Henderson, "Family Cemeteries, No. 18: Bassett Cemetery, near Kokomo, Indiana," *Scuffalong: Genealogy*, accessed Jan. 20, 2020.

38. *The News*, Aug. 14, 1989; included in Perry County file, BHP.

39. DeVries, *Race and Kinship in a Midwestern Town*, 54; emphasis added.

40. Roediger, *The Wages of Whiteness*, 117; emphasis in original.

41. "Kiddies to See Minstrel Show," *Frankfort Morning Times*, Apr. 7, 1935, 1–2; "Rotarians in Minstrel Roles Score a Big Hit," *Frankfort Morning Times*, Apr. 12, 1935,

1, 6; "Lions Minstrel Show is Ready for Opening," *Frankfort Morning Times*, Mar. 20, 1949, 1; "Lincoln Minstrel to Be Presented at Own Twp School," *Frankfort Morning Times*, Feb. 26, 1950, 3.

42. Jacobson, *The New Nativism*, 5.

43. Elkhart City Historian, BHP, Elkhart County file, Feb. 10, 1988; emphasis in original.

44. BHP, Daviess County file, Oct. 19, 1987.

45. Cohen, *Belonging: Identity and Social Organisation in British Rural Cultures*, 3, and *The Symbolic Construction of Community*, 109. Cohen discusses the concept of community assertiveness when encroaching on community boundaries, which reifies a sense of belonging, as "members find their identities as individuals through their occupancy of the community's social space: if outsiders trespass in that space, then its occupants' own sense of self is felt to be debased and defaced." He continues, "A frequent and glib description of what is feared may be lost is 'way of life'; part of what is meant is the sense of self." See Cohen, *Symbolic Construction*, 109.

46. BHP, Pike County file, Nov. 13, 1987; BHP, Floyd County file, Feb. 1, 1988.

47. Mills, *The Racial Contract*, 18.

48. Barone, "Little Church Reveals Story from Frankfort's Past," *Frankfort Morning Times*, Feb. 20, 1978, 1.

49. "State Troops Are Sent to Marion," *Frankfort Morning Times*, Aug. 9, 1930, 1; "Frankfort Man Tells of Beating," *Frankfort Morning Times*, Feb. 15, 1964, 1. I mentioned the Kerseys in the previous chapter when discussing Martha Maxey's letter to the editor in 1970, which was the first Black voice printed in the local paper. The Kerseys had been in Frankfort for multiple generations. Through Charles's grandfather Robert L. Kersey Sr.'s obituary from 1945, for example, we find out about segregation of social organizations in Frankfort, as he was active in local Black organizations.

50. Scholarship in this regard has become even more expansive in recent decades, including historical evidence, narratives, and landmarks in counties such as Allen, Floyd, Harrison, Washington, Lake, Porter, La Porte, St. Joseph, Wabash, Huntington, Grant, Elkhart, Hendricks, and Monroe. The earliest scholarly explorations include Julie S. Conklin's "The Underground Railroad in Indiana" from 1910 and Richard R. Wright Jr.'s "Negro Rural Communities in Indiana" from 1908. Wright actually draws the connection between early Black settlements in the counties and their respective involvement in the Underground Railroad network, as "Every one [of the Black settlements] was a station and did valiant work in helping the slaves to find Canada." This connection becomes significant when juxtaposed with the overall attitudes of white Hoosiers pre–Civil War. Conklin reminds us, "In fact, the sentiment of a large portion of the settlers was strongly against them. Even among those who disapproved of the slave system were many who opposed the methods used by those engaged in the work of the Underground Railroad, and looked upon them as no better than thieves; for, they maintained, it was worse to steal a negro than to steal a horse, for the reason that a negro was worth more than a horse." See Wright, "Negro Rural Communities in Indiana," 168, and Conklin, "The Underground Railroad in Indiana," 64–65.

51. Owen County Historian, BHP, Owen County file, Mar. 22, 1988.

52. BHP, Warrick County file, Oct. 5, 1987.

53. BHP, Tipton County file, Sept. 29, 1989.

54. BHP, Vermillion County file, Feb. 24, 1988.

55. Quoted in LaRoche, *Free Black Communities and the Underground Railroad: The Geography of Resistance*, 2.

56. Survey Response for City of La Porte, BHP, La Porte County file, Dec. 17, 1987.

57. Powell, *History of Cass County Indiana*, 320.

58. BHP, Ripley County file, Oct. 21, 1987.

Conclusion

1. Ted Evanoff and Tania E. Lopez, "Frankfort Rolls Up Its Welcome Mat," *Indianapolis Star*, Oct. 21, 2007, A1.

2. "Colored Chef Leaves Frankfort in Hurry," *Frankfort Morning Times*, Dec. 13, 1919, 1.

3. Indiana Historical Society staff member, personal conversation with author, Oct. 14, 2017. Over the years, staff members decided to make the files available to researchers who might be interested in the information found in the folders. IHS staff is planning to process the material as a collection and add it to the IHS Online Catalog. Currently, unless one specifically inquires about information regarding Black history in the state, one does not know about the treasure trove that lies hidden in the IHS's archives.

4. BHP, White County file, Oct. 7, 1987.

5. Brundage, *Where These Memories Grow*, 5. Brundage is also echoing Trouillot's point on the selective nature of making archives and Mills's observation of misunderstanding, misrepresenting, and evading matters related to race. See Trouillot, *Silencing the Past*, 53, and Mills, *The Racial Contract*, 19.

6. Brundage, *Where These Memories Grow*, 4.

7. BHP, Noble County file, Jan. 22, 1988; BHP, Ohio County file, Feb. 1, 1988.

8. As was the case with White County above, this statement is partially inaccurate, as census records indicate a minuscule number of residents—seven in 1890—which may constitute one Black family. The historical society, however, may not have held all the available census records.

9. BHP, Brown County file, Nov. 6, 1987; BHP, Blackford County file, Feb. 1988.

10. "County Historian Information," Black History Project, Folder 3.1, 8–9.

11. During a follow-up visit in March 2019, an IHS staff member qualified such responses as "pathetic," as the negligence clearly reflected that survey takers didn't care to "give much attention because they don't look like them." She also speculated about how the survey would be received nowadays and to what extent the provided information would change. Good question.

12. Jaspin, *Buried in the Bitter Waters*, 9.

13. Ibid., 10–11.

14. The two of the ten unresponsive counties that would increase the counties to eighty-one are Jay and Newton counties.

Bibliography

Archives and Digital Collections

Frankfort Public Library
Hoosier State Chronicles. Indiana's Digital Historic Newspaper Program
Indiana Historical Society
Indiana State Library
New York Public Library Digital Collections
Purdue University Digital Collections
Wabash College Digital Collections

Census, Government, and Legal Records

Ancestry.com. *1850 United States Federal Census*, Ancestry.com Operations, Inc., 2009.

Ancestry.com. *1870 United States Federal Census*, Ancestry.com Operations, Inc., 2009.

Ancestry.com and the Church of Jesus Christ of Latter-Day Saints. *1880 United States Federal Census*, Ancestry.com Operations, Inc., 2010.

Ancestry.com. *1900 United States Federal Census*, Ancestry.com Operations, Inc., 2004.

Ancestry.com. *1910 United States Federal Census*, Ancestry.com Operations, Inc., 2006.

Ancestry.com. *1920 United States Federal Census*, Ancestry.com Operations, Inc., 2010.

Ancestry.com. *1930 United States Federal Census*, Ancestry.com Operations, Inc., 2002.

Ancestry.com. *1940 United States Federal Census*, Ancestry.com Operations, Inc., 2012.

Ancestry.com. *Indiana, Birth Certificates, 1907–1940*, Ancestry.com Operations, Inc., 2016.

Ancestry.com. *Indiana, Federal Naturalization Records, 1892–1992*, Ancestry.com Operations, Inc., 2016.

Ancestry.com. *Indiana, Death Certificates, 1899–2011*, Ancestry.com Operations, Inc., 2015.

Ancestry.com. *U.S. City Directories, 1822–1995*, Ancestry.com Operations, Inc., 2011.

Ancestry.com. *U.S., Find a Grave Index, 1600s–Current*, Ancestry.com Operations, Inc., 2012.

Ancestry.com. *U.S., Social Security Applications and Claims Index, 1936–2007*, Ancestry.com Operations, Inc., 2015.

Ancestry.com. *U.S., Social Security Death Index, 1935–2014*, Ancestry.com Operations, Inc., 2014.

Ancestry.com. *U.S., World War I Draft Registration Cards, 1917–1918*, Ancestry.com Operations, Inc., 2005.

Ancestry.com. *U.S., World War II Draft Registration Cards, 1942*, Ancestry.com Operations, Inc., 2010.

Beecher, S. Clifford. *The Statutes of the State of Indiana: Containing the Revised Statutes of 1852, with the Amendments Thereto, and the Subsequent Legislation. With Notes and References to Judicial Decisions, Volume 3.* W. H. Bingham, 1870.

Burns, Harrison. *Burns' Annotated Indiana Statutes: Showing the General Statutes in Force January 1, 1908; Embracing the Revision of 1881 as Amended, and All Permanent, General and Public Acts of the General Assembly Passed Since the Adoption of That Revision; Containing Also the United States and Indiana Constitutions, All Completely Annotated.* The Bobbs-Merrill Company, 1908.

Constitution of the State of Indiana and the Address of the Constitutional Convention. Kent & Norman Printer, 1851.

Laws of the State of Indiana, Passed at the Special Session of the General Assembly. Acts, 66 vls. Alexander H. Conner, 1869.

Report and Testimony of the Select Committee of the United States Senate to Investigate the Causes of the Removal of the Negroes from the Southern States to the Northern States, Part III. 3 vols. 46th Congress, 2nd Session 693. Government Printing Office, 1880.

Revised Laws of Indiana, 1831. Douglas and Maguire, 1831.

The Revised Statutes of the State of Indiana Passed at the Twenty-Seventh Session of the General Assembly: Also, Sundry Acts, Ordinances and Public Documents Directed to Be Printed with the Said Statutes: To which are Prefixed the Constitutions of the United States and of the State of Indiana. J. Dowling and R. Cole, 1843. 1131 pp.

The Revised Statutes of the State of Indiana, Passed at the Thirty-Sixth Session of the General Assembly: Also, Sundry Acts, Ordinances, and Public Documents Directed to be Printed Along with the Said Statutes: To which are Prefixed the Constitution of the United States and of the State of Indiana: Printed and Published According to Law, Volume 1. J. P. Chapman, 1852.

United States Bureau of the Census. *Fifteenth Census of the United States: 1930. Population.* Government Printing Office, 1931.

United States Bureau of the Census. *Fourteenth Census of the United States: 1920. Population.* Government Printing Office, 1921.

United States Bureau of the Census. *Thirteenth Census of the United States: 1910. Population.* Government Printing Office, 1911.

United States Bureau of the Census. *Twelfth Census of the United States—1900. Population Part I.* United States Census Office, 1901.

Wright, Joseph. "Slavery in the District Remarks." *Congressional Globe. The Official Proceedings of Congress*, 1862, pp. 1467–70.

Newspapers

Chicago Defender

Frankfort Evening News

Frankfort (Morning) Times

Indianapolis *Freeman*

Indianapolis News

Indianapolis Recorder

Indianapolis Star

Journal and Courier

Kokomo Tribune

New York Times

Noblesville Ledger

Richmond Palladium

Books and Articles

"About the Indiana State Museum." *Indiana State Museum and Historic Sites*, 2019.

Adams, Faith. "A Question of Democracy." *The Nation*, vol. 111, no. 2888, 10 Nov. 1920, pp. 524–26.

Adams, Luther. *Way Up North in Louisville: African American Migration in the Urban South, 1930–1970*. University of North Carolina Press, 2010.

"Adoption of Purdue University Policy Statement Re Discrimination." *Board of Trustees Minutes, 1965 May 05*, vol. 22, May 1966, p. 383.

"All Negroes Driven from Indiana Town; White Miners at Blanford Act after an Assault on a Young Girl." *New York Times*, 21 Jan. 1923, p. S5.

Allen, James, et al., *Without Sanctuary: Lynching Photography in America*. Fourteenth edition, Twin Palms Publishers, 2020.

Alsop, Stewart, and Oliver Quayle. "What Northerners Really Think of Negroes." *Saturday Evening Post*, vol. 236, 1963, pp. 17–21.

Andersen, Ruth J. *Negro Education in Tippecanoe County, 1869–1886*. Purdue University, June 1964.

Anderson, Joseph Leslie, editor. *The Rural Midwest Since World War II*. NIU Press, 2014.

Arbuckle, Alex. "Hate on Parade: When the KKK Marched on Washington." *Mashable*. Accessed 16 Apr. 2019.

Baker, Ray Stannard. *Following the Color Line: An Account of Negro Citizenship in the American Democracy*. Doubleday, Page & Company, 1908.

Bangert, Dave. "Bangert: Strategy Last Time KKK Came to Lafayette." *Journal & Courier*, 21 Aug. 2017.

Bartholomew County Directory Co. *Complete Directory of Bartholomew County, Indiana, 1903–1904: Embracing Membership in All Associations, Clubs, Church Boards with Alphabetic Lists of the Patrons of Rural Free Delivery Routes Towns and the City of Columbus, Etc.: An Indexed Map*. Bartholomew County Directory Co., 1903.

Bebout, Lee. *Whiteness on the Border: Mapping the U.S. Racial Imagination in Brown and White*. New York University Press, 2016.

Bentley, Max. "The Ku Klux Klan in Indiana." *McClure's Magazine (1893–1926); New York*, vol. 57, no. 1, May 1924, pp. 22–33.

Bethune, Mary McLeod. "The Problem of the City Dweller." *Opportunity*, vol. 3, Feb. 1925, pp. 54–55.

Bigham, Darrel E. *We Ask Only a Fair Trial: A History of the Black Community of Evansville, Indiana*. Indiana University Press, 1987.

"Black and White Ratios for Eleven Decades." *The Nation*, vol. 73, Nov. 1901, pp. 391–92.

Black, Timuel D. *Bridges of Memory: Chicago's First Wave of Black Migration*. Northwestern University Press, 2005.

Blocker, Jack S. *A Little More Freedom: African Americans Enter the Urban Midwest, 1860–1930*. Ohio State University Press, 2008.

———. "Black Migration to Muncie, 1860–1930." *Indiana Magazine of History*, vol. 92, no. 4, Dec. 1996, pp. 297–320.

Bloom, Stephen G. *Postville: A Clash of Cultures in Heartland America*. Mariner Books, 2001.

Bonilla-Silva, Eduardo. "Feeling Race: Theorizing the Racial Economy of Emotions." *American Sociological Review*, vol. 84, no. 1, Feb. 2019, pp. 1–25. https://doi.org/10.1177/0003122418816958.

———. *Racism without Racists: Color-Blind Racism and the Persistence of Racial Inequality in America*. Third edition, Rowman & Littlefield, 2009.

———. "When Whites Flock Together: The Social Psychology of White Habitus." *Critical Sociology*, vol. 32, no. 2–3, Mar. 2006, pp. 229–53. https://doi.org/10.1163/156916306777835268.

Bourdieu, Pierre. "Habitus." *Habitus: A Sense of Place*, edited by Jean Hillier and Emma Rooksby. Second edition, Ashgate, 2005, pp. 43–52.

Brundage, W. Fitzhugh, editor. *Where These Memories Grow: History, Memory, and Southern Identity*. The University of North Carolina Press, 2000.

Bucholtz, Mary. "The Public Life of White Affects." *Journal of Sociolinguistics*, vol. 23, no. 5, 2019, pp. 485–504. https://doi.org/10.1111/josl.12392.

Butler, Brian. *An Undergrowth of Folly: Public Order, Race Anxiety, and the 1903 Evansville, Indiana Riot*. Garland Pub., 2000.

Cameron, James. *A Time of Terror: A Survivor's Story*. Black Classic Press, 1994.

Campney, Brent M. S. *Hostile Heartland: Racism, Repression, and Resistance in the Midwest*. University of Illinois Press, 2019.

———. *This Is Not Dixie: Racist Violence in Kansas, 1861–1927*. University of Illinois Press, 2015.

Carden, Dan. "Museum Tells Indiana's History Using 200 Objects." *Northwest Indiana Times*, 26 Apr. 2016.

Carr, Cynthia. *Our Town: A Heartland Lynching, a Haunted Town, and the Hidden History of White America*. First edition, Crown Publishers, 2006.

Cayton, Andrew R. L., et al., editors. *The American Midwest: An Interpretive Encyclopedia*. First edition, Indiana University Press, 2006.

Cayton, Andrew R. L., and Susan E. Gray, editors. *The American Midwest: Essays on Regional History*. Indiana University Press, 2001.

Claybaugh, Joseph. *History of Clinton County, Indiana: With Historical Sketches of Representative Citizens and Genealogical Records of Many of the Old Families*. A. W. Bowen & Company, 1913.

Cohen, Anthony Paul. *Belonging: Identity and Social Organisation in British Rural Cultures*. Manchester University Press, 1982.

———. *The Symbolic Construction of Community*. Routledge, 1985.

Conklin, Julia. "The Underground Railroad in Indiana." *The Indiana Quarterly Magazine of History*, vol. 6, no. 2, June 1910, pp. 63–74.

Cord, Xenia. "Black Rural Settlements in Indiana before 1860." *Indiana's African-American Heritage: Essays from Black History News & Notes*, edited by Wilma L. Gibbs, Indiana Historical Society, 1993, pp. 99–110.

Cox, Anna-Lisa. *A Stronger Kinship: One Town's Extraordinary Story of Hope and Faith*. Bison Books, 2007.

———. *The Bone and Sinew of the Land: America's Forgotten Black Pioneers and the Struggle for Equality*. Unabridged edition, Public Affairs Hachette Book Group, 2018.

———. "When Anti-Immigration Meant Keeping Out Black Pioneers." *New York Times*, 20 Sept. 2019, https://www.proquest.com/docview/2294178553/abstract/1C065D6136DD4C8EPQ/1.

Cox, Thomas C. *Blacks in Topeka Kansas, 1865–1915: A Social History*. Louisiana State University Press, 1999.

Crenshaw, Gwendolyn J. *"Bury Me in a Free Land": The Abolitionist Movement in Indiana, 1816–1865*. Indiana Historical Bureau, 1993.

Crothers, Julie. "Goshen City Council Approves Resolution Acknowledging 'Sundown Town' Past." *The Goshen News*, 17 Mar. 2015.

Curtis, Susan. *Colored Memories: A Biographer's Quest for the Elusive Lester A. Walton*. University of Missouri Press, 2008.

Davis, Elmer. "Have Faith in Indiana." *Harper's Monthly Magazine*, vol. 153, 1926, pp. 615–25.

Derrida, Jacques, and Eric Prenowitz. *Archive Fever: A Freudian Impression*. University of Chicago Press, 1996.

DeVries, James E. *Race and Kinship in a Midwestern Town: The Black Experience in Monroe, Michigan, 1900–1915*. University of Illinois Press, 1984.

Dickerman, George Sherwood. "A Plan for the Southern Migrant." *Crisis*, vol. 144, no. 5, Sept. 1917, pp. 217–18.

Dochuk, Darren. *From Bible Belt to Sunbelt: Plain-Folk Religion, Grassroots Politics, and the Rise of Evangelical Conservatism*. W. W. Norton & Company, 2012.

Drake, St. Clair, and Horace R. Cayton. *Black Metropolis: A Study of Negro Life in a Northern City*. Revised and enlarged edition, Harper & Row, 1962.

Dray, Philip. *At the Hands of Persons Unknown: The Lynching of Black America*. Random House Publishing Group, 2002.

Feagin, Joe R. *The White Racial Frame: Centuries of Racial Framing and Counter-Framing*. Second edition, Routledge, 2013.

Fine, Gary Alan. "The Pinkston Settlement: An Historical and Social Psychological Investigation of the Contact Hypothesis." *Phylon (1960–)*, vol. 40, no. 3, 1979, pp. 229–42. https://doi.org/10.2307/274565.

Frankenberg, Ruth. *White Women, Race Matters: The Social Construction of Whiteness*. Fifth edition, University of Minnesota Press, 1993.

Frazier, Edward Franklin. *The Negro Family in Chicago*. University of Chicago Press, 1932.

Frost, Stanley. "The Klan Shows Its Hand in Indiana." *Outlook*, vol. 137, no. 5, June 1924, pp. 187–90.

Gerstle, Gary. *American Crucible: Race and Nation in the Twentieth Century*. Princeton University Press, 2002.

Gilbert, Frank M. *History of the City of Evansville and Vanderburg County, Indiana*. Pioneer Pub. Co., 1910.

Gilliam, Frances V. Halsell. *A Time to Speak: A Brief History of the Afro-Americans of Bloomington, Indiana, 1865–1965*. Pinus Strobus Press, 1985.

Gittins, Diana. "Oral History, Reliability and Recollection." *The Recall Method in Social Surveys*, edited by Louis Moss and Harvey Goldstein, University of London Institute of Education; Distributed by NFER Pub. Co., 1979, pp. 82–97.

Glenn, Elizabeth, and Stewart Rafert. *The Native Americans*. Indiana Historical Society, 2009.

Goings, Kenneth W. *Mammy and Uncle Mose: Black Collectibles and American Stereotyping*. Indiana University Press, 1994.

Gregory, James N. "The Second Great Migration: A Historical Overview." *African American Urban History Since World War II*, edited by Kenneth L. Kusmer and Joe William Trotter, 2009, pp. 19–38.

———. *The Southern Diaspora: How the Great Migrations of Black and White Southerners Transformed America*. University of North Carolina Press, 2006.

Grossman, James R. *Land of Hope: Chicago, Black Southerners, and the Great Migration*. University of Chicago Press, 1991.

"Gunnar Myrdal, Analyst of Race Crisis, Dies." *The New York Times*, 18 May 1987.

"Hanna's History." *Hanna Community Center*. Accessed 12 Apr. 2019.

"Hanna's Mission." *Hanna Community Center*. Accessed 12 Apr. 2019.

Hartt, Rollin Lynde. “The New Negro. When He’s Hit, He Hits Back!” *The Independent*, Jan. 1921, pp. 59–60, 76.

———. “When the Negro Comes North: An Exodus and Its Causes.” *The World’s Work*, vol. 48, no. 1, 1924, pp. 83–90.

———. “When the Negro Comes North: Future Results of the Migration.” *The World’s Work*, vol. 48, no. 3, 1924, pp. 318–23.

———. “When the Negro Comes North: Where Will the Migration Stop?” *The World’s Work*, vol. 48, no. 2, 1924, pp. 184–90.

“Hate Map.” *Southern Poverty Law Center*, https://www.splcenter.org/hate-map. Accessed 12 May 2022.

Haynes, George Edmund. “Migration of Negroes into Northern Cities.” *Proceedings of the National Conference of Social Work*, vol. 44, 1917, pp. 494–97.

———. “Negroes Move North: II. Their Arrival in the North.” *Survey*, vol. 41, no. 4, Jan. 1919, pp. 455–61.

Heller, Dick D., editor. *The 1979 History of Adams County, Indiana*. Adams County Historical Society, Inc., 1980.

Helm, Thomas B. *History of Delaware County, Indiana: With Illustrations and Biographical Sketches of Some of Its Prominent Men and Pioneers*. Kingman Brothers, 1881.

Henderson, Lisa Y. “Family Cemeteries, No. 18: Bassett Cemetery, near Kokomo, Indiana.” *Scuffalong: Genealogy*, 31 Aug. 2016.

Henri, Florette. *Black Migration: Movement North, 1900–1920*. Anchor Press, 1975.

Hicks, Ronald E., et al., *Native American Cultures in Indiana: Proceedings of the First Minnetrista Council for Great Lakes Native American Studies*. Muncie, Ind.: Minnetrista Cultural Center: Ball State University, 1992. *Internet Archive*, http://archive.org/details/nativeamericancu00hick.

Higgins, Will. “‘We Need to Acknowledge It’: Martinsville Tries to Remake Its Racist Image.” *Indianapolis Star*, 2 Nov. 2017.

Hill, Jane H. *The Everyday Language of White Racism*. New edition, Wiley-Blackwell, 2008.

Hillier, Jean, and Emma Rooksby, editors. *Habitus: A Sense of Place*. Second edition, Routledge, 2005.

Hine, Darlene Clark. *When the Truth Is Told: A History of Black Women’s Culture and Community in Indiana, 1875–1950*. National Council of Negro Women, Indianapolis Section, 1981.

Hunter, Marcus Anthony, and Zandria Robinson. *Chocolate Cities: The Black Map of American Life*. University of California Press, 2018.

Hurt, R. Douglas. “Foreword.” *Rural Midwest Since World War II*, Northern Illinois University Press, 2013, pp. ix–xii.

“ISL: Indiana County Histories on Microfilm or Microfiche.” *In.Gov*. Accessed 10 Apr. 2019.

Jackson, Margaret Weymouth. “This Is My America—A State That Is One Proud

Family of Home-Town Folks." *The American Magazine*, vol. 115, Feb. 1933, pp. 38–39, 138–39.

Jacobson, Robin Dale. *New Nativism: Proposition 187 and the Debate over Immigration*. University of Minnesota Press, 2008.

Jaspin, Elliot. *Buried in the Bitter Waters: The Hidden History of Racial Cleansing in America*. Basic Books, 2008.

"John W. 'Alias—James Hopkins' Harper (1842–1907)." *Find a Grave*. Accessed 19 Apr. 2019.

Johnson, Gerald W. "The Ku-Kluxer." *The American Mercury*, vol. 1, Feb. 1924, pp. 207–11.

Julian, George Washington. *Speeches on Political Questions*. Hurd and Houghton, 1872.

Kunnecke, Martina Nichols. "Washington County—Early Black Settlements by County." *Early Black Settlements by County—Indiana Historical Society*, 27 Aug. 2014.

Lancaster, Guy. *Racial Cleansing in Arkansas, 1883–1924: Politics, Land, Labor, and Criminality*. Lexington Books, 2014.

LaRoche, Cheryl Janifer. *Free Black Communities and the Underground Railroad: The Geography of Resistance*. First edition, University of Illinois Press, 2013.

Lauck, Jon K. *The Lost Region: Toward a Revival of Midwestern History*. First edition, University of Iowa Press, 2013.

Lay, J. Celeste. *A Midwestern Mosaic: Immigration and Political Socialization in Rural America*. Temple University Press, 2012.

Lee Moore, Hana C. *Re-Examining the 'Heartland': Korean American Religious and Ethnic Identity Formation in the Midwest*. Purdue University, Dec. 2018.

Lefebvre, Henri. *The Production of Space*. First edition, Wiley-Blackwell, 1991.

Leitner, Helga. "Spaces of Encounters: Immigration, Race, Class, and the Politics of Belonging in Small-Town America." *Annals of the Association of American Geographers*, vol. 102, no. 4, July 2012, pp. 828–46. https://doi.org/10.1080/00045608.2011.601204.

Lemann, Nicholas. *The Promised Land: The Great Black Migration and How It Changed America*. Vintage, 1992.

Leonard, George B. "Jim Crow, Northern Style." *Look*, vol. 20, no. 13, June 1956, pp. 75–84.

Leonard, Oscar, and Forrester B. Washington. "Welcoming Southern Negroes: East St. Louis and Detroit—A Contrast." *Survey*, vol. 38, July 1917, pp. 331–35.

Leonardo, Zeus. *Race, Whiteness, and Education*. Taylor & Francis Group, 2009.

Lipsitz, George. *How Racism Takes Place*. Temple University Press, 2011.

———. *The Possessive Investment in Whiteness: How White People Profit from Identity Politics*. Twentieth anniversary edition, Temple University Press, 2018.

Loewen, James W. *Sundown Towns: A Hidden Dimension of American Racism*. The New Press, 2005.

Logan, Rayford Whittingham. *The Negro in American Life and Thought, The Nadir, 1877–1901*. The Dial Press Inc., 1954.

Longworth, Richard C. *Caught in the Middle: America's Heartland in the Age of Globalism*. Bloomsbury Publishing USA, 2010.

Lyda, John W. *The Negro in the History of Indiana*. Indiana Negro History Society, 1953.

Madison, James H. *A Lynching in the Heartland: Race and Memory in America*. First Palgrave Macmillan paperback edition, 2003.

———. *Hoosiers: A New History of Indiana*. Indiana University Press, 2014.

———. *The Indiana Way: A State History*. Reprint edition, Indiana University Press, 1990.

"Mapping Prejudice: Visualizing the Hidden Histories of Race and Privilege in the Built Environment." https://www.mappingprejudice.org. Accessed 12 May 2022.

Matias, Cheryl E. *Feeling White: Whiteness, Emotionality, and Education*. First edition, Sense Publishers, 2016.

McCammack, Brian. *Landscapes of Hope: Nature and the Great Migration in Chicago*. Harvard University Press, 2017.

McCann, Eugene J. "Race, Protest, and Public Space: Contextualizing Lefebvre in the U.S. City." *Antipode*, vol. 31, no. 2, 1999, pp. 163–84. https://doi.org/10.1111/1467-8330.00098.

McKittrick, Katherine. *Demonic Grounds: Black Women and the Cartographies of Struggle*. University of Minnesota Press, 2006.

McWhirter, Cameron. *Red Summer: The Summer of 1919 and the Awakening of Black America*. First edition, Henry Holt & Co., 2011.

Merritt, Dixon. "Klan and Anti-Klan in Indiana." *Outlook*, vol. 144, Dec. 1926, pp. 465–70.

Millard, Ann V., and Jorge Chapa. *Apple Pie and Enchiladas: Latino Newcomers in the Rural Midwest*. University of Texas Press, 2004.

Mills, Charles W. *The Racial Contract*. First edition, Cornell University Press, 1999.

Monahan, Thomas P. "Marriage across Racial Lines in Indiana." *Journal of Marriage and Family*, vol. 35, no. 4, 1973, pp. 632–40. https://doi.org/10.2307/350876.

Moore, Samuel Taylor. "A Klan Kingdom Collapses." *The Independent*, vol. 113, no. 3888, Dec. 1924, pp. 473–75.

Moore, Wilma L. "A Treasure Hunt: Black Rural Settlements in Indiana by 1870." *Traces of Indiana & Midwestern History*, vol. 27, no. 1, Winter 2015, pp. 22–33.

Mowatt, Rasul A. "Lynching as Leisure: Broadening Notions of a Field." *American Behavioral Scientist*, vol. 56, no. 10, Oct. 2012, pp. 1361–87. https://doi.org/10.1177/0002764212454429.

Mullin, Gerald W. *Flight and Rebellion: Slave Resistance in Eighteenth-Century Virginia*. Oxford University Press, 1972.

Myrdal, Gunnar. *An American Dilemma: The Negro Problem and Modern Democracy*. Harper & Brothers Publishers, 1944.

Nelson, Lise. "Racialized Landscapes: Whiteness and the Struggle over Farmworker Housing in Woodburn, Oregon." *Cultural Geographies*, vol. 15, 2008, pp. 41–62. https://doi.org/10.1177/1474474007085782.

Nelson, Robert K., et al., "Mapping Inequality." *American Panorama*, https://dsl.richmond.edu/panorama/redlining. Accessed 12 May 2022.

Noble, Madeleine M. *The White Caps of Harrison and Crawford County, Indiana: A Study in the Violent Enforcement of Morality.* University of Michigan, 1973.

Oberlander, Susan. "Blacks Say Beering Insensitive." *Journal & Courier*, 17 Feb. 1987, pp. A1–2.

Olson, Joel. *The Abolition of White Democracy*. University of Minnesota Press, 2004.

Omi, Michael, and Howard Winant. *Racial Formation in the United States: From the 1960s to the 1990s*. Second edition, Routledge, 1994.

Osofsky, Gilbert. *Harlem: The Making of a Ghetto; Negro New York, 1890–1930*. Harper & Row, 1966.

Painter, Nell Irvin. *Exodusters: Black Migration to Kansas after Reconstruction*. Reprint edition, W. W. Norton & Company, 1992.

Paton, Alan. "The Negro in the North." *Collier's*, vol. 134, Oct. 1954, pp. 70–80.

Pérez, Raúl. "Racism without Hatred? Racist Humor and the Myth of 'Color-Blindness.'" *Sociological Perspectives*, vol. 60, no. 5, 2017, pp. 956–74.

Pfeifer, Michael J. *Lynching beyond Dixie: American Mob Violence Outside the South*. University of Illinois Press, 2013.

———. *Rough Justice: Lynching and American Society, 1874–1947*. University of Illinois Press, 2004.

Powell, Jehu Z. *History of Cass County Indiana: From Its Earliest Settlement to the Present Time: With Biographical Sketches and Reference to Biographies Previously Compiled*. Lewis Publishing Company, 1913.

Pruitt, Bernadette. *The Other Great Migration: The Movement of Rural African Americans to Houston, 1900–1941*. Texas A&M University Press, 2013.

Pulido, Laura. "Geographies of Race and Ethnicity 1: White Supremacy vs White Privilege in Environmental Racism Research." *Progress in Human Geography*, vol. 39, no. 6, Dec. 2015, pp. 809–17. https://doi.org/10.1177/0309132514563008.

Purdue University. Senior Class. *Debris*. 1902.

"Race Trouble in the North: When a Negro Family Moved into a White Community." *U.S. News & World Report*, vol. 45, Aug. 1957, pp. 29–32.

Rafert, Stewart. *The Miami Indians of Indiana: A Persistent People, 1654–1994*. Indiana Historical Society Press, 1996.

Razack, Sherene, editor. *Race, Space, and the Law: Unmapping a White Settler Society*. Between the Lines, 2002.

"Readers' Guide to Periodical Literature." *HW Wilson*. Accessed 5 Apr. 2019.

Rehmer, R. F. "Brotherhood Week." *Purdue Exponent*, 19 Feb. 1959, p. 2.

Reich, Steven A. *The Great Black Migration: A Historical Encyclopedia of the American Mosaic*. Greenwood, an Imprint of ABC-CLIO, LLC, 2014.

Reid, Debra A. "'The Whitest of Occupations'? African Americans in the Rural Midwest, 1940–2010." *Rural Midwest Since World War II*, edited by J. L. Anderson, Northern Illinois University Press, 2013, pp. 204–54.

"Report Re Letter from Purdue Friends of S.N.C.C. and Petitions Concerning University Policy on Non-Segregation." *Board of Trustees Minutes, 1966 Mar. 02*, vol. 22, Mar. 1966, p. 962.

"Report Re University Policy Concerning Listing of Off-Campus Housing Facilities." *Board of Trustees Minutes, 1965 June 04*, vol. 22, June 1965, p. 516.

Riis, Roger William, and Webb Waldron. "Fortunate City." *Survey Graphic*, Aug. 1945, pp. 339–41.

Rile Kelley, Elizabeth H. "Early 'Colored' Settlers of Union County." *Sesquicentennial Historical Record: Commemorating the 150th Anniversary of Union County, Indiana, 1821–1971*, edited by Sesquicentennial Historical Committee, Union County Sesquicentennial Committee, 1971, pp. 15–16.

Rimer, Sara. "After Arrest, Town Shamed by '68 Killing Seeks Renewal." *The New York Times*, 17 May 2002.

Robbins, Coy D. *African Heritage in Morgan County, Indiana*. Indiana African American Historical and Genealogical Society, 1991.

———. *Indiana Negro Registers, 1852–1865*. Heritage Books, 1994.

Roediger, David R. *The Wages of Whiteness: Race and the Making of the American Working Class*. New edition, Verso, 2007.

Rose, Gregory S. "Quakers, North Carolinians and Blacks in Indiana's Settlement Pattern." *Journal of Cultural Geography*, vol. 7, no. 1, Sept. 1986, pp. 35–48. https://doi.org/10.1080/08873638609478519.

Rucker, Walter, and James Nathanial Upton. *Encyclopedia of American Race Riots*. Greenwood, 2007.

Safianow, Allen. "'You Can't Burn History': Getting Right with the Klan in Noblesville, Indiana." *Indiana Magazine of History*, vol. 100, no. 2, June 2004, pp. 109–54.

Saunders, William Oscar. "Why Jim Crow Is Flying North." *Collier's*, vol. 72, Dec. 1923, pp. 15–17.

Schuyler, George. "Jim Crow in the North." *The American Mercury*, vol. 68, June 1949, pp. 663–70.

Scott, Emmett J. "Additional Letters of Negro Migrants of 1916–1918." *The Journal of Negro History*, vol. 4, no. 4, Oct. 1919, pp. 412–65. https://doi.org/10.2307/2713449.

———. "Letters of Negro Migrants of 1916–1918." *The Journal of Negro History*, vol. 4, no. 3, July 1919, pp. 290–340. https://doi.org/10.2307/2713780.

Sdunzik, Jennifer. "Indiana." *A State-by-State History of Race and Racism in the United States*, edited by Patricia Reid-Merritt, Greenwood, an Imprint of ABC-CLIO, LLC, 2018, pp. 283–99.

Sdunzik, Jennifer. *Mapping Whiteness: Uncovering the Legacy of All-White Towns in Indiana*. Purdue University, Aug. 2019.

"Segregated Seattle." *Seattle Civil Rights and Labor History Project*, https://depts.washington.edu/civilr/segregated.htm. Accessed 12 May 2022.

Senechal de la Roche, Roberta. *The Sociogenesis of a Race Riot: Springfield, Illinois, in 1908*. University of Illinois Press, 1990.

Shenk, Dan. "Portrait of a Sundown Town." *Mennonite World Review*, Jan. 2014.

Shortridge, James R. *The Middle West: Its Meaning in American Culture*. University Press of Kansas, 1989.

"South in the North." *U.S. News & World Report*, vol. 48, May 1960, pp. 82–85.

Spear, Allan H. *Black Chicago: The Making of a Negro Ghetto, 1890–1920*. University of Chicago Press, 1967.

Spickard, Paul. *Almost All Aliens: Immigration, Race, and Colonialism in American History and Identity*. Routledge, 2007.

"Stories from the First Great Migration to Philadelphia." *Goin' North*, https://www.goinnorth.org. Accessed 4 Apr. 2019.

Taylor, Robert M., and Connie A. McBirney, editors. *Peopling Indiana: The Ethnic Experience*. Indiana Historical Society, 1996.

Thornbrough, Emma Lou. *Indiana in the Civil War Era, 1850–1880, The History of Indiana Volume III*. Indiana Historical Bureau & Indiana Historical Society, 1965.

———. *Since Emancipation: A Short History of Indiana Negroes, 1863–1963*. Indiana Division American Negro Emancipation Centennial Authority, 1963.

———. *The Negro in Indiana: A Study of a Minority*. Indiana Historical Bureau, 1957.

Tolnay, Stewart E. "The African American 'Great Migration' and Beyond." *Annual Review of Sociology*, vol. 29, Dec. 2003, pp. 209–32.

Trouillot, Michel-Rolph. *Silencing the Past: Power and the Production of History*. Beacon Press, 1995.

Turner, Trisha. "Racism's Past Still Singes: Longtime Kokomoans Remember the Bad Old Days." *The Kokomo Tribune*, 15 June 1995, p. 1.

Van der Dussen, Kurt. "City Fights Racist Reputation." *Bloomington Herald-Times*, 7 Aug. 1989, p. A7.

Vega, Sujey. *Latino Heartland: Of Borders and Belonging in the Midwest*. New York University Press, 2015.

Vincent, Stephen A. *Southern Seed, Northern Soil: African-American Farm Communities in the Midwest, 1765–1900*. Indiana University Press, 1999.

Wade, Erik C. *Constituting Whiteness: The National Horse Thief Detective Association and Racial Mores in Indiana, 1850–1930*. Purdue University, 2011.

Walker, Lewis, and Benjamin C. Wilson. *Black Eden: The Idlewild Community*. First paperback edition, Michigan State University Press, 2007.

Walton, Lester A. "Cotton Fields Lie Weed Choked as Negro Stampedes." *New York World*, 12 Aug. 1923, p. M-8.

———. "Negro Migrants Say Southerners Force Them Out." *New York World*, 30 Sept. 1923, p. S-6.

———. "Negroes in Terror Fleeing the South; Whites Alarmed." *New York World*, 14 Jan. 1923, p. M-4.

Wells-Barnett, Ida B. *Southern Horrors: Lynch Law in All Its Phases*. New York Age Print, 1892.

———. *The Red Record: Tabulated Statistics and Alleged Causes of Lynching in the United States*. Donohue & Henneberry, 1895.

Wiegand, Shirley A., and Wayne A. Wiegand. *The Desegregation of Public Libraries in the Jim Crow South: Civil Rights and Local Activism*. Louisiana State University Press, 2018.

Wiggins, William H., and Frank and Virginia Williams Collection of Lincolniana (Mississippi State University Libraries). *O Freedom!: Afro-American Emancipation Celebrations*. First edition, University of Tennessee Press, 1987.

Wilkerson, Isabel. *The Warmth of Other Suns: The Epic Story of America's Great Migration*. First edition, Random House, 2010.

Wilson, William E. "Indiana." *Holiday*, vol. 8, Aug. 1950, pp. 27–34, 100–104.

Wood, Amy Louise. *Lynching and Spectacle: Witnessing Racial Violence in America, 1890–1940*. New edition, the University of North Carolina Press, 2011.

Wright, George C. *Racial Violence in Kentucky, 1865–1940: Lynchings, Mob Rule, and "Legal Lynchings."* Louisiana State University Press, 1990.

Wright Jr., Richard R. "Negro Rural Communities in Indiana." *Southern Workman*, vol. 37, Mar. 1908, pp. 158–72.

Zick, Timothy. "Constitutional Displacement." *Washington University Law Review*, vol. 86, no. 3, Jan. 2009, pp. 515–608.

Index

JENNIFER SDUNZIK is a postdoctoral research associate at the Evaluation and Learning Research Center at Purdue University.

The University of Illinois Press
is a founding member of the
Association of University Presses.

University of Illinois Press
1325 South Oak Street
Champaign, IL 61820-6903
www.press.uillinois.edu

FSC
www.fsc.org
MIX
Papier | Fördert
gute Waldnutzung
FSC® C083411

Zeitfracht Medien GmbH
Ferdinand-Jühlke-Straße 7
99095 Erfurt, Deutschland
produktsicherheit@kolibri360.de